know the faith

A Handbook for Orthodox Christians and Inquirers

REV. MICHAEL SHANBOUR

Ancient Faith Publications
Chesterton, Indiana

Know the Faith:
A Handbook for Orthodox Christians and Inquirers
Copyright © 2016 Michael Alan Shanbour

Published by:
  Ancient Faith Publishing
  A Division of Ancient Faith Ministries
  P.O. Box 748
  Chesterton, IN 46304

ISBN: 978-1-944967-01-7

Printed in the United States of America

Contents

Introduction

As the boundaries of "West" and "East" are increasingly blurred by immigration and modern technological advances in travel and communications, it becomes increasingly vital (and sometimes inescapable) for Orthodox Christians to enter into dialogue with Christians who have been formed by a radically different theological perspective and church ethos. The theological, philosophical, and cultural developments that occurred in the Christian West in the centuries following the Great Schism, combined with the West's alienation from the Orthodox East, resulted in the transformation of what can now be referred to distinctively as *Western* Christendom.

What began with innovations on two fundamental points of faith (the papacy and the addition of the *filioque* to the Nicene Creed) developed over the next few centuries into not only more doctrines alien to Orthodoxy, but a whole new theological mindset and approach. While the Eastern Church understands theology as the fruit of authentic prayer and purification of the heart, the scholastic theology that overtook Western Europe was centered in human logic and philosophical speculation.

Instead of theology borne of sanctification and union with God through the transformation of the *nous* (Rom. 12:2), the

7

"hidden person of the heart" (1 Pet. 3:4), human reason was exalted as the instrument for the acquisition of the knowledge of God. God could be firmly grasped with the mind, it was believed; for, as Thomas Aquinas (13th c.) believed, man's will was fallen but not his reason. Over time in the West, faith has increasingly become associated with information rather than spiritual formation and transformation.

The result is two widely divergent paradigms for approaching Christian faith. The eventual reaction of the Protestant Reformers to this new Western form of Christianity further exacerbated the confusion, since it dealt more with the symptoms than the real problem. For those who sought to reform the Western Church were themselves formed by it.[1] And try as they might to return to the authentic Tradition of the Church, their own tradition, along with the limits of their own well-intended logic or understanding of Scripture, ultimately prevented it.

Therefore, the problem we confront in dialogue with other Christians is greater than the sum of whatever innovative doctrines have been adopted by any given person or church group. The real predicament is that a non-Orthodox Christian comes to the table with a whole different theological method and paradigm. He or she comes, as it were, with a whole different language. Even more difficult is the fact that this language often uses a common vocabulary, yet with disparate nuances and meanings.

---

1   In this regard, it is significant that the followers of Martin Luther, in their
     dialogue with Jeremiah II, Patriarch of Constantinople, argued vehemently
     for the Roman Catholic position on the *filioque*. (See George Mastrantonis,
     Augsburg and Constantinople, Brookline, MA: Holy Cross Orthodox Press,
     1982.)

Pick a word: *sacrament, faith, grace, salvation, tradition*. In each case, the word is biblical and part of a common lexicon for all Christians; yet the same word may be loaded with theological presumptions that evoke very different understandings. For Orthodox Christians, these are not merely words but doors opening up to a whole experience pregnant with meaning— meaning that does not come from a systematic handbook of definitions but is conversant with the authentic Tradition and experience of the Church.

Keeping in mind the above, we must begin somewhere. And it is often only by beginning to discuss particular doctrinal points that we can bring someone to a more complete and orthodox understanding. Such an approach has biblical precedent. According to the Acts of the Apostles, when Aquila and Priscilla heard the preaching of Apollos, who knew only of the baptism of John, "they took him aside and explained to him the way of God more accurately" (18:26). And the Apostle Paul often "reasoned" with the Jews in the synagogues, seeking to persuade them from the Scriptures regarding the faith of Christ (Acts 17:2; 18:4, 19).

My main purpose in writing this book is to accurately present the Orthodox Christian Tradition and teaching in a way accessible to most Orthodox Christians and inquirers. In this way I hope to equip those in the Church with a good defense (1 Pet. 3:15) for the Faith that has been believed "everywhere, always, by all,"[2] by the one, holy, catholic, and apostolic Church, and to supply them with a worthy arsenal of evidence for Orthodox Christian teaching. Secondly, I hope to inform and persuade, in

---

2   St. Vincent of Lérins, *Commonitory*, ch. 2, http://www.newadvent.org/fathers/3506.htm

an introductory way, those exploring or approaching the Orthodox Church.

In an attempt to convey the message more vividly and to give
it flesh, as it were, I have used the scriptural account of the first
Gentile convert, Cornelius (Acts 10). Each chapter opens with
a brief, imagined synopsis, from Cornelius's own perspective,
of what he may have experienced as he began to encounter life
in the Church. Needless to say, I have expanded the story far
beyond the scriptural account, which ends suddenly with his
baptism. I have done so, not to scandalize any brother or sister,
but as a teaching aid. By adopting the historical, biblical character of the new convert, Cornelius, we are able to consider the
inevitable trajectory of his post-baptismal Christian experience,
using what we know of the Church's unchanging and apostolic
Tradition.

As part of the arsenal of evidence for Orthodox teaching, I
list scriptural quotes applicable to each topic toward the end of
each chapter. Those of us who speak regularly with Protestant
Christians are well aware that we will have little credibility with
them unless we are prepared to bring Holy Scripture to bear in
support of our convictions. In some cases, those we meet will
be entirely unaware of the scriptural passages we present.[3] In
reality, many have a limited store of memorized verses they
have acquired to support their positions, which they often quote
without context or deep reflection.

I have also supplied readers with a modest supply of representative quotes from early Church Fathers as a support for the

---

3   As an example, a young but well-trained Seventh Day Adventist I encountered
     knew nothing of the "tradition" passages in St. Paul, i.e., 1 Cor. 11:2; 2 Thess.
     2:15; 3:6.

historical and traditional teaching.[4] Is it possible for a point of view to have weight if it cannot be found in the writings of the mainstream proponents of the very Church of God we claim to espouse? Are we to believe that radically new opinions arising in the fifteenth, eighteenth, or even twentieth century without any precedent in the past can be considered legitimate Christian teachings? The very notion is unscriptural and is contradicted by the apostle's own words: "Remember those who rule over you, who have spoken the word of God to you, *whose faith follow,* considering the outcome of their conduct" (emphasis added). For "Jesus Christ *is* the same yesterday, today, and forever" (Heb. 13:7–8).

In some cases I have also offered selections from the teachings of the Protestant Reformers, whose faith the contemporary Protestant Christian is in theory following. However, here we often find the Reformers following the traditional teaching of the Church as opposed to the prevalent beliefs or practices espoused by modern mainline Protestants and evangelicals. This is true particularly with regard to the Church's teaching on the Virgin Mary and, to some degree, the Eucharist and ecclesiology.

Although I have not made an exhaustive attempt to explain why Roman Catholics or Protestants think as they do and how they have come to believe this, in most chapters I have attempted to provide a working knowledge from which to understand their views and the history of their development. Those who believe Orthodoxy and Roman Catholicism are essentially the same may be very surprised as they read through this book.

---

4   For a more complete collection of relevant quotes from the Church Fathers, visit http://www.wenorthodox.com/the-church-fathers-on.

The topics addressed and the order of their appearance have been chosen carefully. We begin with the chapter on the Orthodox Christian understanding of the Church, since this is the basis for all else. The ancient creed of the Church does not proclaim faith in one Bible but "in one, holy, catholic, and apostolic church." Our faith is in God's Church, the Body of Jesus Christ, which is the source of grace, salvation, the Eucharist, and the various topics dealt with thereafter. It is of God's Church that Christ promised, "the gates of Hades shall not prevail against it" (Matt. 16:18).

The chapter on grace follows naturally from that on the Church, for the doctrine of grace is essential to the understanding of salvation and, in general, what it means to be human as created by God. Because it is such a part of the cultural atmosphere, the evangelical Protestant view often seeps unconsciously into the hearts and minds of Orthodox Christians in the Western world. But without a firm grasp of the Orthodox teaching on God's grace, our Christianity is reduced to legalism or a mere moral philosophy; for grace is the means by which we are energized by and united to God.

The remaining topics—salvation; justification by faith (alone); Tradition and Scripture; Eucharist and Christian worship; ordination and priesthood; confession and repentance; icons, veneration, and worship; intercession of the saints; veneration of the Virgin Mary—are essential to knowing the Faith, especially if we wish to relay the Orthodox Christian position to others.

As we prepare to meet the challenge of dialogue with the multiplicity of heterodox Christian believers around us, there are a few things to keep in mind. The first, perhaps obvious, is that we can rarely argue a person into Orthodox belief, or into belief in God, for that matter. In attempting to do so, we are almost certain to cause our own defeat by inflaming the passions of the one who has now become our opponent. The conversation is no longer about Orthodoxy's merit or truth but has become a battle to defend the ego, including our own. In this case (one the author is too familiar with), it is best to invoke a blessing and walk away.

If we are to have any real success, we must be confident, at peace internally, humble and dispassionate, truly caring for the soul of the person before us. Our motivation must be love, not personal victory. A real conversion is usually a process that is accompanied by the formation of a relationship, with time for trust and affection to be developed.

Secondly, we have to gauge our fellow's level of understanding and knowledge. Often we have only a few minutes or even seconds to do this. But however long we have, we must listen first, and listen again, before we speak. Most Orthodox Christians are acutely aware that many around us have little to no knowledge of the Church we love. This situation has improved in recent decades but is still far from acceptable.

As a mission priest living in an area never before graced by the visible presence of the Orthodox Church, I can testify that what one needs most is patience and persistence. One encounters questions such as: "Didn't Orthodoxy start in Oxford, England?" and "Were the Orthodox in Constantinople before it became Catholic?" These questions reveal the need for a great deal of unraveling and unlearning before much positive progress can be made.

Finally, we should always remember that every human person is made in the image of God and thus intrinsically has some spark of grace and inkling of the true God. I am often amazed by those who have never heard the Church's teaching yet nod knowingly as they hear it articulated for the first time. We might say some have Orthodox Christianity "written in their hearts" (Rom. 2:15) though they have had no formal encounter with the Church. They have somehow managed to grasp the wheat and leave the chaff of heterodox teaching to blow away in the wind of God's Spirit, even when the chaff has been engrained in them. For this we must stand in awe of our good, gracious, and merciful God, who reveals Himself to whom He will and to those who are willing to hear Him. "He who has ears to hear, let him hear!" (Matt. 11:15).

My prayer is that this book would inspire Orthodox Christians to share their faith with more clarity and confidence, and that non-Orthodox readers might be challenged to a new and deeper appreciation of the long-standing beliefs and practices of the Orthodox Church. I am grateful to God for the opportunity to be an evangelist for the Church that continually inspires me, challenges me, and even manages to change me now and then. To our Lord and Savior Jesus Christ be glory, thanksgiving, and worship, with the Father and the Holy Spirit. Amen.

CHAPTER 1

The Church

And He put all things under His feet, and gave Him to be head over all things to the church, which is His body, the fullness of Him who fills all in all. (Eph. 1:22–23)

By God's providence and divine revelation, the Apostle Peter has been sent to Caesarea to a devout and God-fearing Gentile, Cornelius, whose prayers and alms are well pleasing to the Lord (Acts 10). As Cornelius listens to the preaching of the eyewitness of Jesus' Resurrection, it seems to him as if a veil has been lifted from his eyes. Suddenly the truth he has longed for, even as a young pagan, and only glimpsed in shadows as he became acquainted with the faith of Judaism, has unfolded before him in the Person of Jesus, the "Christ of God" (Luke 9:20). All the messianic prophecies he has heard in the synagogue in Caesarea now come to life and fill his heart, accompanied by a yearning to be united to the Crucified One, who has overcome death and inaugurated the resurrection.

Cornelius and his family desire to worship the Lord Jesus Christ and to follow the apostles, who have been enlightened by God's Spirit to be the stewards of the tangible grace that has entered the world. God's Kingdom has truly descended to the Earth in power through Jesus, whose Resurrection opens all flesh to be energized by the same divine life that is in His own resurrected Body.

Cornelius now understands that if he wishes to step into this life of faith and be energized by the Holy Spirit, he needs to be grafted into the risen Body of Jesus. Through belief and baptism, the apostle teaches, Cornelius and his family will become members of the Church, "the fullness of Him who fills all in all" (Eph. 1:23). As Noah and his family were saved from the flood, Cornelius's own family is entering the spiritual ark to be saved from the flood of this sinful world (1 Pet. 3:20).

What will this Church be like? he wonders. How will he experience the grace of God and be nurtured in this new faith? What does it mean to follow those who follow Jesus, those who have "seen" and "handled" the Word of the Father (1 John 1:1)? How will this faith be imparted to him and to his children in the Church, and who will lead and support them as they seek to remain faithful servants of the true God?

These and other questions swirl gently in Cornelius's heart but cannot quell the indescribable peace and grace he now feels in the depth of his soul as he approaches the baptismal font. This font is to be the "womb" through which he is born from above to a new Mother, the "heavenly Jerusalem" (Heb. 12:22), God's Holy Church.

Introduction

Cornelius and his household believed in Jesus as the Christ and were baptized. But exactly what church were he and his family baptized into? What church did he join? Was it the Independent Congregational Church of Caesarea? Or perhaps Cornelius initiated his own Gentile denomination as distinct from Peter's particular Jewish flavor of Christianity. The answer we give about Cornelius's church affiliation will likely reveal our most basic assumptions about what it means to be the Church.

Unfortunately, the account of Cornelius's conversion ends abruptly without providing the rest of the story, as do other stories in the Book of Acts—for example, that of the Ethiopian eunuch (8:26–39). We can be left then with the impression that in the apostolic age, the Church was a loose affiliation of self-determining Christian congregations and individuals free to discern for themselves the implications of belief in Jesus as Messiah and Lord.

But absence of information does not make a positive argument. That the Apostle Luke did not think it necessary to include more detail most likely means no explanation was required, since all Christians of his time knew exactly how the story continued based on their own personal experience in the apostolic Church.

The main purpose of St. Luke's history in the Acts of the Apostles was to chronicle the highlights of the evangelical efforts of the apostles (primarily St. Paul, whom Luke accompanied) and the spread of the gospel throughout the known world. But we are not left bereft of evidence of the early Christians' common understanding of their Church identity and unity.

What may seem to some a bit fuzzy in Scripture comes into clearer focus in the writings of the successors to the apostles—for example, St. Ignatius, Bishop of Antioch, originally a disciple of the Apostle John. As Antioch was one of the most prominent local churches in the Roman Empire and boasted a founding presence of both Saints Peter and Paul, what Ignatius has to say on the issue of the Church should be as credible as the writings of anyone of his time. On his way to Rome to be martyred for

Christ, he writes the following to the local church of the Trallians in Asia Minor:

> Similarly all are to respect the deacons as Jesus Christ and the bishop as a copy of the Father and the presbyters as the council of God and the band of the apostles. For apart from these no group can be called a church.[1]

And to the Philadelphians, the bishop of Antioch expounds on the manner in which the various local Christian congregations maintain their unity as the Church:

> For as many as belong to God and Jesus Christ, these are with the bishop. And as many as repent and come to the unity of the church, these also will belong to God so that they may be living in accordance with Jesus Christ. "Do not be deceived, my brothers": if anyone follows a maker of a schism he "will not inherit the kingdom of God." Be eager, therefore, to use one Eucharist—for there is one flesh of our Lord Jesus Christ and one cup for union with his blood, one sanctuary [i.e., Church], as there is one bishop, together with the presbytery and the deacons my fellow slaves—so that, whatever you do, you do it in relation to God.[2]

Far from an unorganized, footloose band of believers, the Church St. Ignatius inherited from the apostles in AD 69 was a strictly ordered and unified communion of local congregations fully expected to share the same doctrine, worship, and practical Christian way of life. And, in fact, we see the same in the time of the apostles themselves, in the description of the first Christian congregation in Jerusalem: "And they continued steadfastly in

---

1   Jack N. Sparks, ed., *The Apostolic Fathers* (Minneapolis: Light and Life Publishing, 1978), p. 93.
2   *Op. cit.*, p. 105.

the apostles' doctrine and fellowship, in the breaking of *the*[3] bread, and in *the* prayers" (Acts 2:42).

Nor were St. Ignatius and the local church of Antioch a mere anomaly, an exception to the norm. Another bishop of the first century, St. Clement of Rome, is a witness to the same vision of church unity and order. In a letter he wrote to the church at Corinth to assist in dispelling a rebellion by a few against the local clergy, we get another glimpse into the communion of faith shared by all the churches throughout the world. We note from this passage that St. Clement understands it is the Lord Himself who is the source for the order and unity existing in the Church. Using vocabulary with Old Testament overtones he writes:

> Now then, since this is quite plain to us . . . we ought to do in order all those things the Master has ordered us to perform at the appointed times. He has commanded sacrifices and service to be performed, not in a careless and haphazard way but at the designated seasons and hours. He himself has determined where and through whom he wishes them performed. . . . Thus to the high priest [bishop] have been appointed his proper services, to the priests [or presbyters] their own place assigned, upon the Levites [deacons] their proper duties imposed; and the layman is bound by the rules for laymen. Each of us, brethren, in his own rank must please God in good conscience, not overstepping the fixed rules of his ministry, and with reverence.[4]

And so we return to our original question: What church did Cornelius join? For Orthodox Christians, the answer is neither

---

3   In most English translations of the New Testament, including the NKJV here quoted, the definite article ("the") is unfortunately omitted. The "breaking of the bread" refers to the celebration of the Eucharist, and "the prayers" are fixed liturgical prayers.

4   *Apostolic Fathers*, p. 40.

difficult nor nuanced. Cornelius and his whole household were brought into the fellowship and communion of the one Church that was founded by the apostles and united in a mutual faith. In joining this community, they adopted and subjected themselves to the pattern of doctrine, governance, worship, and ascetic discipline that was shared, practiced, and passed down in all the apostolic church communities.

It is this pattern or blueprint of Christian life, received from Jesus Christ and handed down by the apostles, that forms the criterion for what it means to be "church," an assembly of Christians in the communion of the apostles. The apostles received it from the Lord, who, in His last vital words to them before His Ascension, entrusted them to teach those who would come into their communion through baptism "to observe all things that I have commanded you" (Matt. 28:20). From the earliest times this pattern has been known as the apostolic Tradition, which is the living expression of the Apostolic Faith.

Consequently, for those who seek authentic unity with the apostolic faith, it is vital to firmly seize and maintain this Tradition. "Therefore, brethren, stand fast and hold the traditions which you were taught, whether by word or our epistle" (2 Thess. 2:15). And the converse is true. It is a fatal mistake to do anything that is "not according to the tradition" (2 Thess. 3:6) of the apostles.

This Tradition is not abstract or invisible; it is not a secret kept by a few religious elites. But rather, as St. Irenaeus, the greatest theologian of the second century and bishop of Lyons, wrote to the gnostics, who denied that Jesus truly came visibly in the flesh:

It is within the power of all, therefore, in every [apostolic] church, who may wish to see the truth, to contemplate clearly the tradition of the apostles manifested throughout the whole world.[5]

It would not have entered the mind of Cornelius to start his own "church" or reinvent it according to his preferences and tastes, since the Church is a living organism with an historical and visible Tradition that one must be joined to, adhere to, and abide in. To swim in the streams of the apostolic Tradition, one must be thrown into the actual source of that river of Tradition, where it is perceptibly expressed, lived, and experienced—the Apostolic Church of history.

Therefore, according to the apostolic pattern, membership in the Church is an organic and actual union with an identifiable and organic Body and communion of believers represented by a visible and valid bishop (who is also in doctrinal and eucharistic communion with the other apostolic bishops). And this is not accomplished by merely imitating the original, any more than a virtual computer image can be said to be a human being, though it be made to look and act like one.

The Church can never be reinvented or recreated; it has once and for all been established and built (Matt. 16:18) by the Lord. Thus new members of the Church must be grafted into it organically, as a new branch is grafted onto a vine (Rom. 11:17; John 15:5). One must be united to Christ "the Vine" (John 15:1) through the vineyard of the Church in order to be enlivened and nourished by the divine sap that flows from it.

We do not create the Church's Tradition; we are brought into

---

5   Irenaeus, *Against Heresies* 3:3 [AD 189].

it through union with the Church, into the one, already existing, authentic Tradition that was received by the apostles and guarded in the historical Church concretely by visible, local communities accountable to that Tradition.

In our Orthodox Christian understanding, a community either lives and acts within this Tradition or it does not. It is either formally in communion with the other apostolic communities that maintain this Tradition or it is not. This is not said with a triumphalist or judgmental attitude meant to exclude anyone, but in love, to ensure and preserve the integrity of what has been handed down. The Church is one, and its unity, according to the unanimous testimony of the early Church Fathers, is expressed by the living Tradition known and experienced in its bosom.

> As I said before, the Church, having received this preaching and this faith, although she is disseminated throughout the whole world, yet guarded it, as if she occupied but one house. She likewise believes these things just as if she had but one soul and one and the same heart; and harmoniously she proclaims them and teaches them and hands them down, as if she possessed but one mouth. For, while the languages of the world are diverse, nevertheless, the authority of the tradition is one and the same.[6]

What Makes a "Church"?

And so the question for those who come to believe in Jesus Christ today is really no different from the one set before Cornelius or the one in St. Irenaeus's time: "What church should I join?" The crucial difference in our time is that there no longer exists a consensus as to what it means to be a church, and

---

6   *Against Heresies* 1:10:2 [AD 189].

therefore to be within the communion of the Church. The original understanding of *church* as an organic communion of believers holding the Tradition of the apostles passed down and preserved within history has been superseded by other, more external or subjective criteria for what it means to be in the Church.

The following is an attempt to summarize, in a simple and straightforward way, the criteria used by various Christian bodies to describe what makes a church.

ACCORDING TO ROMAN CATHOLICISM

Membership in the Church is dependent on unity with the pope, who is understood to be the successor of St. Peter:

> After his resurrection our Savior handed her [the Church] over to Peter to be shepherded (John 21:17), commissioning him and the other apostles to propagate and govern her. . . . This church, constituted and organized in the world as a society, subsists in the [Roman] Catholic Church, which is governed by the successor of Peter and by the Bishops in communion with him.[7]

ACCORDING TO CLASSICAL (REFORMED) PROTESTANTISM

The Church is founded on a perceived "purity" of preaching and administration of sacraments,[8] wherever and within whatever Christian body they may be found.

The Reformer John Calvin summarizes this succinctly: "Wherever we see the Word of God purely preached and heard,

---

7   Vatican II. *The Dogmatic Constitution on the Church,* ch. 1.
8   This status of "sacrament" is usually limited to baptism and the Eucharist.

and the sacraments administered according to Christ's institution, there, it is not to be doubted, a church of God exists."[9]

ACCORDING TO EVANGELICAL PROTESTANTISM
The Church is founded upon the Bible[10] and the individual believer's faith. One evangelical has defined it in the following way: An "Evangelical church is a Protestant Christian group that believes in four principles: being 'born again' or conversionism, activism (sharing of the gospel), cruci-centrism (Jesus' death) and Biblicism (teaching the Bible)."[11]

In practice, if one has "accepted Jesus Christ as his personal Savior," he is a member of the church, regardless of church affiliation or lack thereof. In this case, the church is understood as invisible and unidentifiable.

ACCORDING TO ORTHODOX CHRISTIANITY
The Church is founded in God Himself, in the communion of the Father, Son, and Holy Spirit.[12] The Church is the created

---

9   John Calvin, *Institutes of the Christian Religion,* vol. 4, ch. 1, sect. 9:2.1023. The conundrum of this conception of church is in the question of who decides what is "pure."

10   In theory, sola scriptura (Scripture as the only authority in the church) is a principle shared by both classical and evangelical Protestants. The former, however, in practice rely on aspects of Church Tradition, whereas the latter claim to adhere to the principle in a more literal way.

11   Note that Christ's Resurrection is noticeably missing. http://www.ask.com/wiki/Evangelicalism. See also a similar definition at http://religion.ssrc.org/reforum/Bryant.pdf, quoting R. Balmer, *Encyclopedia of Evangelicalism* (Waco, TX: Baylor University Press, 2004).

12   "And the books and the apostles declare that the church is not of the present [only], but is from the beginning. For she was spiritual." (Second Clement, 7.521). "He said, 'It is the church.' And I said to him, 'Why, then, is she an old woman?' He replied, 'Because she was created first of all. On this account she is old. And the world was made for her sake.'" (*The Shepherd of Hermas,* Book I).

expression of the life of the Holy Trinity, which begins with the creation of the angels, continues in muted form after the Fall of Adam in the Old Testament Church, and is perfected through the Incarnation, death, and Resurrection of Jesus Christ, the God-Man, who is the only "Head" of the Church. A person or a community is part of the Church if he is grafted into the one Body of Christ through baptism and chrismation and is guided by the apostolic Tradition of the Church through communion with the brotherhood of faithful Orthodox bishops who guard and perpetuate this Holy Tradition. The boundaries of the Church are visible. One must not only be in historical succession from the apostles but must also hold the apostolic faith passed on by the apostles as expressed by the consensus of the saints in every age. St. Vincent of Lérins calls this the criterion of "universality, antiquity, [and] consent," or that which "has been believed everywhere, always, by all."[13]

Metropolitan Kallistos Ware expresses the Orthodox position in this way:

> What then holds the Church together? The Orthodox answer, the act of communion in the sacraments[14]. . . . Unity is not maintained from without by the authority of a Supreme Pontiff, but created within by the celebration of the Eucharist. The Church is not monarchical in structure, centered round a single hierarch; it is collegial, formed by the communion of many hierarchs with one another, and of each hierarch with the members of his flock. The act of communion therefore forms the criterion for membership of the Church. An individual ceases to be a member of the Church if he severs communion with his

---

13 *Commonitory*, ch. II.
14 In Orthodoxy, sacramental communion never exists apart from doctrinal unity.

bishop; a bishop ceases to be a member of the Church if he sev-
ers communion with his fellow bishops.[15]

The Church: What and Where?

Beginning with the Great Schism of 1054 and especially as a
result of the Protestant Reformation, usually dated 1517, a process of splintering was set in motion that has resulted in a proliferation of theological opinions leading to confusion, if not
chaos, on the question of the Church.

The result has been that the tragedy and travesty of denom-
inationalism (and later non-denominationalism) has been
accepted as the comfortable norm. Relativism—the idea that
one opinion is as valid as another—has become the prevailing
view in things religious. Differences in doctrine, worship, and
all aspects of church life are explained away as matters of personal preference, style, or taste.

For these and other reasons, in our age, more than in any
other, the crucial question for each and every Christian should
be, "What is the Church?" And another one that should immediately follow is, "Where is the Church?" Put another way, the
question for everyone who professes to be a follower of Jesus
Christ must be, "What is the Church, and where do I find it?"

WHAT IS THE CHURCH?

Before we can address where the Church is, we must comprehend what it is. According to the New Testament, Jesus equates
the Church directly with Himself (Matt. 16:18; Acts 9:4).
Therefore, if we find the Church, we have indeed found Christ in

---

15   Timothy Ware, *The Orthodox Church* (New York: Penguin, 1972), p. 250.

His fullness, inasmuch as He is the "head of the Church" (Eph. 5:23; Col. 1:18). The Apostle Paul also teaches that the Church is Christ's own Body (1 Cor. 12:27; Eph. 1:23; Col. 1:18). For Orthodox Christians this is not a mere metaphor but an organic, tangible, and even physical reality, for St. Paul emphasizes that members of the Church are "members of His body, of His flesh and of His bones" (Eph. 5:30).

Through this verse the apostle means to remind us of the creation of Eve. God put Adam to sleep and, taking a rib from his side, formed his bride, whom Adam recognized as "bone of my bones and flesh of my flesh" (see Gen. 2:21–24). Saints John Chrysostom, Gregory the Theologian, and other Church Fathers assert that as Eve was created from the side of the first Adam, the Church is born from the Body of the New Adam, Jesus Christ.

For as He "slept" in death on the Cross, the soldier pierced His side with a spear, and blood and water poured forth, anticipating the great Mysteries of Baptism and Eucharist that unite a believer to the Church. As Eve was created directly from the first man, Adam, the Church is created directly from the God-Man, Jesus Christ, and is therefore called His "Bride" (Rev. 21:9).

Through this marriage with the Church, Christ becomes the Father of a new race of people—"a royal priesthood, a holy nation" (1 Pet. 2:9). In the prophecy of Isaiah 9:6, it is Christ (not God the Father) who is called the "Everlasting Father," since by His Incarnation, death, and Resurrection, Jesus is the father of the new redeemed humanity.

In his Epistle to the Ephesians, the Apostle Paul equates the relationship of Christ and His Church with the relationship of husband and wife in the holy mystery of marriage. The implication then is that just as a married couple is "one flesh," so is Christ with His Church, His Body. Yes, this is a spiritual reality but not an immaterial one. It is expressed and manifested and lived out in a physical and material way, like the marriage of man and woman.

The spiritual unity of husband and wife is manifested visibly—they share the entirety of life together, live under a common roof, break bread together, and are exclusive in physical affection and in the conjugal act. All of these signs of union are physical and visible. Even today few would dispute that the boundaries of marriage are definable and clear, and that fidelity to one's spouse is foundational to maintaining the marital relationship.

The boundaries of the Church are also clear and require that her members share a common faith, doctrine, and way of life expressed by unity with a specific bishop (who holds the Orthodox Faith), under a common "household of faith" (Gal. 6:10), consummated by partaking of the one loaf and one cup (1 Cor. 10:16–17).

In Orthodoxy this criterion of unity, traditionally expressed as being "in communion," is not nebulous; it is tangible and verifiable. But it is also organic and personal. A husband who justifies his infidelity by suggesting that his lover is very similar to his wife will, I imagine, find little sympathy, especially from his wife. It will not suffice to point to common personality traits and physical features, since it is obvious these are two different women with two distinct and identifiable bodies.

Very few Christians would argue this point as it relates to

marriage. Yet today it is commonly believed that Christians of separate denominational bodies are free to participate together in the most intimate expression of unity in Christ—the Eucharist, or Holy Communion—yet without a real communion of faith.

For Orthodox Christians the Church is not primarily an institution or mere human organization like a corporation or club. It does not exist primarily to fulfill a worldly function such as social justice. The Church exists to bring men and women into communion with God through Christ, that they might become by grace what Christ is by nature.

The Church is not an organization but a living organism, divine and human, as it is truly Christ's glorified and resurrected Body. To be in true communion with the Church, then, is to have communion with Christ, and through Him with His Father and the Holy Spirit.

WHERE IS THE CHURCH?

Christ's Body, the Church, is tangible and visible. This should not surprise us. How many human bodies in this world are invisible? Even after the Resurrection, the Lord ate physical food, and Thomas could see and touch His physical body. At that moment the Body of Christ was in the upper room. The Church is also locatable, existing within the constraints of time and place, just as when Jesus lived on this Earth His human body was locatable geographically, whether in Nazareth in the manger or in Jerusalem on the Cross. As with Jesus' resurrected body, the fact that the Church is physical does not mean it is not also spiritual or mystical.

The Church, as a tangible Body, is historical; it exists in time and space. Since it has a history, it can be seen and identified throughout time. Having a history in time, the Church also has a lineage, a family tree. It is identified with concrete persons and events. Likewise, separations (i.e., schisms) from the Church have an origin and history. These also can be identified and distinguished within the continuum of the Church's history.

Orthodox Christians believe that the historical Church established by Christ continues in the Body of believers now commonly identified as the Orthodox or Eastern Orthodox Church. This conviction is based not on wishful thinking or "persuasive words of human wisdom" (1 Cor. 2:4) but on a verifiable historical and theological trail.

For the first one thousand years, the Christian Church existed as one main identifiable[16] Body throughout the known world, with a documented consensus of faith, until the Church of Rome, through its adoption of innovative teachings and unprecedented claims of authority, became increasingly estranged from the churches in the eastern portion of the Roman Empire. These differences multiplied and solidified in the centuries that preceded the Protestant Reformation, which began with Martin Luther in about 1517. The Reformation initiated a process of the proliferation of many separate bodies with disparate teachings, all claiming the title of *church* or even *the Church*. The communion of faith existing in the East remained as before through the

---

16 This is not to deny that there were schismatic and heretical groups throughout the first thousand years of church history. Yet there was a recognized and universal Christian Church throughout the known world, united in a consensus of Orthodox Christian tradition of faith, expressed by the unity of bishops, and visible in local congregations.

unity of faith shared among the patriarchates of Constantinople, Alexandria, Antioch, Jerusalem, and others.

The Eastern Orthodox Church, then, represents the continuation of the one, holy, catholic, and apostolic Church of history. This Church can be found on a worldwide or local level by identifying the bishops (and hence their congregations) who share the Orthodox Christian Tradition and are in communion with the bishops of the other Orthodox churches. The Orthodox Church is not a denomination serving an ethnic niche, nor is it one of many Christian communions that happens to have certain emphases, oddities, or decorative extras; rather, it is simply and merely the historical Christian Church.

In the last several centuries, under the influence of certain scholars, a theory was popularized among Protestants that the historical Church fell (apostatized) from the true gospel, either in the generation following the apostles or in the early fourth century, when the Emperor Constantine adopted Christianity. The suggestion is that the emperor inserted pagan ideas and practices into the life of the Christian Church. These supposed corruptions include liturgical worship and prayers, making the sign of the cross, incense, vestments, the priesthood and hierarchical order, the use of icons, and the practice of asking the departed saints to intercede on behalf of the living.

Few reputable scholars hold to this theory today, as there is ample evidence in early Christian writings and recent archeological findings that the practices in question are in continuity with the earliest Christian practice and have their source, not in paganism, but in the Judaism of Jesus' time and in apostolic practice. However, the apostasy theory is still commonly held among the majority of Protestant Christians, Mormons, and others.

The Church Is One

ONE APOSTOLIC TRADITION

The Orthodox Church, wherever it is scattered throughout the world, is united in faith. This faith is expressed by her common Tradition—her Scriptures, doctrine, liturgy, saints, iconography, and even architecture. This Tradition has been passed down, defended, and confirmed from generation to generation from the time of the apostles, whether "by word or our epistle" (2 Thess. 2:15). While every aspect of church Tradition, like church architecture, was not in full bloom at the time of the apostles, it was present in seed form with the promise that the Holy Spirit would guide the Church into all the truth (John 16:13).

Church Tradition is not an abstraction or an invisible idea; it is a visible and tangible "pattern" (2 Tim. 1:13) handed down and practiced in concrete, interconnected church communities. The apostolic design of doctrine, worship, and life is the pattern.[17] Each new generation of Orthodox Christians receives and maintains the original pattern, sometimes at a cost of great suffering. In this way the Church remains one—not on the basis of ideas but by following the divinely inspired, visible pattern that can be heard and seen and touched in the apostolic churches.

It was the gnostic heretical groups who claimed a secret and

---

17 The apostle writes in this way about the apostolic Tradition. He speaks of "the pattern of sound words" or teaching (2 Tim. 1:13) and "the pattern of good works" (Titus 2:7), and notes how Moses made the tabernacle (place of worship in the wilderness) "according to the pattern" shown to Him by God (Heb. 8:5).

invisible knowledge, whose "churches" were founded on ideas that could not be substantiated tangibly and were not in conformity with the apostolic pattern. Similarly, for today's evangelicals, long separated from any living connection with apostolic Tradition, the idea of Christ's Body seems to have become just that—an idea, an abstraction with no visible, historical basis. This conceptual "church" is understood to consist of many Christians from various denominational bodies with distinct and even contradictory beliefs and practices, with different origins, lineages, and histories. A picture of such a "bride" resembles more a distorted Picasso painting than the Bride of Christ portrayed in the Scriptures and the writings of the early Fathers.

The apostolic Tradition is not a grab bag of ideas but a whole way of normative faith and practice that brings one into union with Christ. As Clement of Alexandria affirms, "The tradition of the apostles was one."[18]

ONE APOSTOLIC CHURCH

When the Church of history composed the Nicene Creed[19] as a standard articulation of the faith of the apostles, she professed belief not only in one God the Father, one Son, and one Holy Spirit, but "in one holy, catholic, and apostolic church" and, consequently, "one baptism." In each case, the *one* of the Nicene Creed is not only quantitative (i.e., there is only one God and

---

18 *Stromata, A Dictionary of Early Christian Beliefs,* ed. David W. Bercot, Massachusetts: Hendrickson Publishers, Inc., 1998), *op. cit.,* Ante-Nicene Fathers, ed. Alexander Roberts & James Donaldson (Massachusetts: Hendrickson Publishing, Inc., 2004) vol. 2, p. 555.

19 The creed of the First Ecumenical Council in Nicea (AD 325) was formulated in response to the Arian heresy, using a current baptismal creed as a reliable starting point.

not two gods) but also qualitative (i.e., there is only one kind of God: the God who has revealed Himself as "Father," who has no origin, who eternally begets His Son, and from whom His Spirit eternally proceeds. He is a specific and unique divine Person with certain qualities, and there are no other persons who are God the Father).

As we recognize and confess one kind of God and one unique Christ, Jesus (the one is who perfect God and perfect Man, etc.), we also confess one kind of baptism—the baptism of the one apostolic Church. Other baptisms may be more or less similar in form to that of the Church, but they cannot properly be called the Church's baptism since they do not originate organically from within the bosom of the Church. Since the Church is one, her baptism (and all her sacraments) are also qualitatively one and unique. They are life-giving inasmuch as they spring from within the life-giving communion of the Apostolic Church. The sacraments (literally from the Greek, *mysteries*) of the Church are true sacraments because they flow from what Fr. Alexander Schmemann called "the Sacrament of sacraments," the Church.

Sacraments are not made valid simply because proper forms and correct formulas have been used, as essential as these are. The Holy Mysteries are real and filled with grace because they are actions of the grace-filled Apostolic Church. If the Church has at times accepted the baptism of those outside the Church, it does so as an exception, by *economia* (when the possibility and prerequisite conditions for using economia exist), but not as the rule or normative practice. Under these conditions the Church does not recognize or legitimize, but simply accepts a baptism performed outside the Church. If a genuine form is present,[20] the Church can then breathe life into it, as God breathed His Spirit into the lifeless, newly formed Adam. Again, St. Irenaeus, the second-century bishop of Lyons, helps to confirm this ancient, orthodox Christian understanding:

> For this gift of God has been entrusted to the Church. . . . And herein has been bestowed on us our means of communion with Christ, namely the Holy Spirit. . . . But they have no share in this Spirit who do not join in the activity of the Church. . . . For where the Church is, there is the Spirit of God; and where the Spirit of God is, there is the Church and every kind of grace.[21]

This principle is also affirmed by St. Ignatius of Antioch in relation to the Sacrament of the Eucharist: "Let no one deceive himself: unless a man is within the sanctuary [the one Church], he lacks the bread of God."[22]

From our confession of the Nicene Creed we understand that the Church is the very object of our faith, in the same way that God Himself is. This is true because the Church is Christ's very Body. As Christians we believe and trust not only in God, but in His Apostolic Church.

ONE APOSTOLIC SUCCESSION

One way the early Christians protected the integrity and unity of the Church is through the maintenance of apostolic

---

20 Thus, the Fathers of the Second Ecumenical Council determined that the Arians, Novatians, and others, whose baptismal service (but not their doctrine) was identical with that of the Church, could be received by chrismation whereas the Eunomian heretics, who baptized by single immersion, must be received by baptism. (7th Canon)

21 Henry Bettenson, ed. and trans., *The Early Christian Fathers* (Oxford: Oxford University Press, 1986), p. 83.

22 *Apostolic Fathers*, p. 79.

succession. St. Irenaeus confronted the heretics of his time by challenging them to show that their bishops had a lineage of ordination from the apostles, as did the Christian Church. He did this to demonstrate that they could not have a special secret apostolic knowledge unknown to the Church, as they claimed, and to expose that their innovative doctrines did not originate from the apostles.

True apostolic succession is not determined solely by whether a particular bishop was ordained by a previous bishop,[23] as is the primary emphasis in the Roman Catholic Church. It also must include the passing down of the true and full apostolic faith. To be in the Church is to be within the "apostles' doctrine" and their "fellowship" (i.e., communion) through "the breaking of *the* bread and *the* prayers" (Acts 2:42).[24] It is to be in living continuity with the faith and teaching of the apostles: "one Lord, one faith, one baptism" (Eph. 4:5).

ONE APOSTOLIC UNITY

In recent times various theories have been proposed to claim the existence of an abstract unity among various Christian bodies, despite a divergence of faith. By adding together various separated bodies, it is imagined, the fullness of the Church is found. Such theories are not acceptable to the mind of the Orthodox Church, which understands that the source of the Church's fullness is God Himself.

---

23 The early canons of the Church require at least three duly ordained bishops to consecrate a new bishop or, in cases of dire need, no fewer than two. This helps to ensure against ordinations by "renegade" bishops and attests to the conciliar nature of the Church.

24 "*The* breaking of the bread" is an idiom for the Eucharist, and "*the* prayers" indicates specific liturgical prayers. (See note 7.)

Schisms from the Church do not deplete the fullness of the Church, just as God's fullness is not diminished when His own creatures choose not to abide in Him. Our confession of "one holy, catholic, apostolic Church" means that the Church's fullness is dependent on God, the Holy Trinity, not on man. The Church is one because God is One. She is holy because God is Holy. She is complete (i.e., catholic) because He is catholic. Men can only be brought into communion with the one, holy, catholic, apostolic Church or be separated from her. This is and consistently has been the faith of the historic Orthodox Church.

This fullness is not a matter of human logic or mathematics. The fullness of the apostolic Church is not achieved by adding together every local congregation into some finally completed body. As the Apostle John testifies, "They went out from us, but they were not of us; for if they had been of us, they would have continued with us; but *they went out* that they might be made manifest, that none of them were of us" (1 John 2:19).

Unfortunately, the word *catholic* is usually translated as "universal." But the Greek word indicates fullness and completeness. St. Ignatius of Antioch, the first known to use the word, applies it to the local church: "Wherever the bishop appears, the whole congregation is to be present, just as wherever Jesus Christ is, there is the whole [catholic] Church."[25]

The faith of the Church is no less complete whether two or three hundred, or only "two or three are gathered together" (Matt. 18:20) with Christ in His Apostolic Church. Rather, the Church exists and is encountered, complete and whole, in each local Orthodox congregation throughout the world. This is the

---

25   Ignatius, *Epistle to the Smyrnaens* 7.2, in *Apostolic Fathers,* p. 113.

case because wherever a local apostolic church celebrates the Eucharist, there is the fullness of the Church, "the fullness of Him who fills all in all" (Eph. 1:23).

CLARIFICATIONS

When a Protestant hears the claims of the Orthodox, he or she may make two assumptions: (1) that we believe no one outside the Orthodox Church will be saved, and (2) that we believe all Orthodox Christians will be saved. Neither of these is correct. Although membership in the historical Church is the normative means of union with God, and it can be certain that the grace and life of Christ are found within her bosom, the Church does not make judgments about the salvation of any particular persons. The Orthodox Church follows the teaching of the Apostle Paul, who said, "For what *have* I *to do* with judging those also who are outside? . . . But those who are outside God judges" (1 Cor. 5:12–13).

Nor does the Church teach that all those who are baptized into the Orthodox Church will be saved, but rather "he who does the will of My Father in heaven" (Matt. 7:21). While it is our firm conviction that the Orthodox Church is the continuation of the one, holy, catholic, and apostolic Church of history, it does not follow that we believe all those who have been formally united to her will be saved. As there may be living and dead cells in a human body, there are also both living and dead members within Christ's Body.

Because we know the Church to be a tangible and identifiable communion of members sharing the same faith and way of life, we do not extend Holy Communion to non-Orthodox Christians. Our practice, which is simply a logical result of our understanding of what the Church is, may cause offense and hurt to those who do not understand the Orthodox view. Even the modern label attributed to our practice—"closed communion"—has a negative connotation, since to be "closed" implies lack of hospitality or narrow-mindedness and judgment. Yet few Christians would disapprove of "closed marriage" or, conversely, approve of "open marriage." So-called "open communion" did not exist even in Protestant churches until the twentieth century, and it only became widespread in the 1960s and '70s.

For Orthodox Christians, Holy Communion is directly connected to the communion of the Church. Historically, the sign of membership in a church was the reception of Holy Communion. To receive the Eucharist is to join and commit oneself to that church body and to embrace all that it teaches and practices. As a man cannot love two wives, he cannot join himself to two distinct church bodies. This might be called "spiritual adultery."

Holy Communion is communion not only with Christ, but also with the Church, with her living members, past, present, and future, and with the whole Tradition of faith that serves as the basis of their unity. The Church is community, "the Israel of God" (Gal. 6:16)—not "me, my opinion, and Jesus." Just as in the Old Covenant, when one desired to join the people of God (Israel), one was required to adopt the history, beliefs, practices, worship, and communal life of Israel, so it is in the New Covenant. Therefore "closed communion" is not a true description of the Orthodox practice. Communion is not "closed"; rather, it is open to all who are willing to embrace the faith of the Church. A better name for this apostolic practice is "monogamous communion."[26]

When we confess that the Church is an historical and visible reality, we should clarify that we also include in this the heavenly Church, consisting of Christians departed from this life. The "invisible church" doctrine of Protestantism began as a way to redefine the Church as having no visible boundaries. It espouses the idea that different people within different churches, which are known only to God, make up the real Church of Jesus Christ. This implies that we do not know where the Body of Christ is. If Orthodox Christians speak of an invisible Church, we mean something entirely different. We hold that the Church comprises the earthly and the heavenly Church. The heavenly aspect of the Church is usually invisible to our earthly eyes (although God from time to time makes it visible to some), yet it is one with the earthly Church. When Protestants speak of the invisible Church, they mean the entire Church is invisible.

THE HOLY SCRIPTURES ON THE CHURCH

Unity is expected in the Church

Rom. 12:16: Be of the same mind toward one another.

Rom. 15:6: . . . that you may with one mind *and* one mouth glorify the God and Father of our Lord Jesus Christ.

---

26 See http://www.wenorthodox.com/2015/05/monogamous-communion-a-defense-of-closed-communion-by-fr-michael-shanbour/ for a presentation that could be shared with others.

1 Cor. 1:10: Now I plead with you, brethren, by the name of our Lord Jesus Christ, that you all speak the same thing, and *that* there be no divisions among you, but *that* you be perfectly joined together in the same mind and in the same judgment.

1 Cor. 4:17: For this reason I have sent Timothy to you, who is my beloved and faithful son in the Lord, who will remind you of my ways in Christ, as I teach everywhere in every church.

2 Cor. 13:11: Become complete. Be of good comfort, be of one mind.

Eph. 4:5: . . . one Lord, one faith, one baptism.

Phil. 1:27: . . . that you stand fast in one spirit, with one mind striving together for the faith of the gospel.

Phil. 2:2: . . . fulfill my joy by being like-minded, having the same love, *being* of one accord, of one mind.

Phil. 3:16: Nevertheless, to *the degree* that we have already attained, let us walk by the same rule, let us be of the same mind.

Phil. 4:2: I implore Euodia and I implore Syntyche to be of the same mind in the Lord.

1 Pet. 3:8: Finally, all *of you be* of one mind.

The Church is the repository and fullness of truth

Eph. 1:22–23: And He put all *things* under His feet, and gave Him *to be* head over all *things* to the church, which is His body, the fullness of Him who fills all in all.

1 Tim. 3:15: *I write* so that you may know how you ought to conduct yourself in the house of God, which is the church of the living God, the pillar and ground of the truth.

Those who have become schismatic are separated from the apostolic Church

Acts 15:24: Since we have heard that some who went out from us have troubled you with words, unsettling your souls, saying, *"You must* be circumcised and keep the law"—to whom we gave no *such* commandment—

1 John 2:19: They went out from us, but they were not of us; for if they had been of us, they would have continued with us; but *they went out* that they might be made manifest, that none of them were of us.

The truth is revealed through the Church even to the angels

Eph. 3:10: . . . to the intent that now the manifold wisdom of God might be made known by the church to the principalities and powers in the heavenly places.

The Church is Christ's undivided Body

1 Cor. 12:27: Now you are the body of Christ, and members individually.

Eph. 3:6: . . . that the Gentiles should be fellow heirs, of the same body, and partakers of His promise in Christ through the gospel.

Eph. 4:4-6: *There is* one body and one Spirit, just as you were called in one hope of your calling; one Lord, one faith, one baptism; one God and Father of all, who *is* above all, and through all, and in you all.

Col. 1:24: I now rejoice in my sufferings for you, and fill up in my flesh what is lacking in the afflictions of Christ, for the sake of His body, which is the church.

Acts 9:4: Then he fell to the ground, and heard a voice saying to him, "Saul, Saul, why are you persecuting Me?"

THE CHURCH FATHERS ON THE CHURCH

St. Clement of Rome (c. AD 30–96)

The Apostles received the gospel for us from the Lord Jesus Christ: Jesus the Christ was sent from God. Thus Christ is from God, the Apostles from Christ: in both cases the process was orderly, and derived from the will of God. . . . They [the Apostles] preached in country and town, and appointed their first fruits, after testing them by the Spirit, to be bishops and deacons of those who were going to believe. And this was no novelty. . . . Our Apostles also knew, through our Lord Jesus Christ, that there would be strife on the question of the bishop's office. Therefore . . . they appointed the aforesaid persons and later made further provision that if they should fall asleep, other tested men should succeed to their ministry. (*First Epistle to the Corinthians* 42–43)

Tertullian (c. AD 155–c. AD 240)

The apostles, then, in like manner founded churches in every city, from which all the other churches—one after another—borrowed the tradition of the faith and the seeds of doctrine. And they are every day borrowing them, that they may become churches. Indeed, it is only on this account that they will be able to deem themselves apostolic—as being the offspring of apostolic churches. . . . Therefore the churches, although they are so many and so great, comprise but the one primitive church of the apostles—from which they all [spring].

We hold communion with the apostolic churches because our doctrine is in no respect different than theirs. This is our witness of truth. (*Prescription Against Heretics*, 3.252, 253 [AD 197])

St. Irenaeus of Lyons (c. early second century–AD 202)

By "knowledge of the truth" we mean: the teaching of the Apostles; the order of the Church as established from the earliest times throughout the world: the distinctive stamp of the Body of Christ, preserved through the Episcopal succession: for to the bishops the Apostles committed the care of the church which is in each place, which has come down to our own time, safeguarded without any written documents. (*Against Heresies* 4:33:8)

The catholic Church possesses one and the same faith throughout the whole world, as we have already said. (*Op. cit.* 1:10)

St. Cyprian of Carthage (c. AD 200–258)

The episcopate is one. . . . The Church is one. . . . So also the Church, flooded with the light of the Lord, extends her rays over all the globe: yet it is one light which is diffused everywhere and the unity of the body is not broken up. (*On the Unity of the Catholic Church*, 5)

This sacrament of unity [the Church], this bond of peace inseparable and indivisible, is indicated when in the Gospel the robe of the Lord Jesus Christ was not divided at all or rent, but they cast lots for the raiment . . . so the raiment was received whole and the robe was taken unspoilt and undivided. (*Op. cit.*, 7)

[A]nd the Church is made up of the people united to their priest, the flock cleaving to its shepherd. Hence you should know that the bishop is in the Church, and the Church in the bishop, and that if anyone is not with the bishop he is not in the Church . . . the Church is catholic and one, and may not be sundered or divided but should assuredly be kept together and united by the glue which is the mutual adherence of the priest. (Epistle lxvi. 7)

Some of our colleagues, by a curious presumption, are led to suppose that those who have been dipped [baptized] among the heretics ought not to be baptized when they join us; because, they say, there is "one baptism." Yes, but that one baptism is in the catholic Church. And if there is one Church, there can be no baptism outside it. . . . Our assertion is that those who come to us from heresy are baptized by us, not *re*-baptized. (Epistle lxxiv. 4–5)

CHAPTER 2

Grace

But Jesus said, "Somebody touched Me, for I perceived power going out from Me."(Luke 8:46)

As the Apostle Peter was preaching the good news of Jesus Christ to Cornelius and the relatives and friends he had gathered together, they received the gift of the Holy Spirit (Acts 10:44). Even as the apostle explained that the Word of God had become flesh to open all flesh to the life and power of God, these Gentile seekers were filled with divine grace through the descent of the Holy Spirit.

Now enlivened and energized by grace, Cornelius finds himself magnifying God in foreign languages, a tangible testimony to the presence of the Spirit. He feels reborn and filled with a new understanding that has enlightened and energized both his soul and body. He has been reborn by the divine energies of God, just as the Lord breathed His Spirit into the newly created Adam, making him a "living being" (Gen. 2:7). The life of grace lost by the first Adam is restored to mankind by the New Adam, Jesus Christ; for He came "that they may have life," and life "more abundantly" (John 10:10). This is the life God desired for Adam and his descendants from the beginning.

Cornelius realizes he has been enabled to know God in a way that transcends anything he has experienced before. His is not a knowledge of the intellect but of the heart and the understanding, for the grace of God has illumined his heart to "see God" (Matt. 5:8) as Moses met Him in the burning bush. This is not a temporary swell of emotion but a sober and profound encounter with God in the deepest place of his heart. He now understands the words of the psalmist, "Create in me a clean heart, O God, / And renew a steadfast spirit within me" (Ps. 51:10), and the prophecy of Ezekiel, "I will give you a new heart and put a new spirit within you; I will take the heart of stone out of your flesh and give you a heart of flesh." (Ezek. 36:26).

Cornelius and his family will now be called to nurture and increase this gift of grace that the Lord has bestowed upon them. For it is only by the acquisition of this grace that one truly becomes perfected as a son of God.

Introduction

The story of the first Gentile converts is unique in all the New Testament. This is the only instance in which the gift of the Holy Spirit is given *before* baptism. In all other cases, the Spirit is received after baptism through the laying on of hands by an apostle. This order remains to the present day in the Orthodox Church in the Sacrament of Chrismation that immediately follows baptism.

But in this one case, the Lord works in an exceptional way to drive home to the Jewish Christians that the grace of God indeed would be poured out on all the nations (i.e., Gentiles) by virtue of Christ's saving work. For since Christ had cleansed and renewed human nature by His Incarnation, overcome sin by His death, and glorified our nature through His Resurrection, the Holy Spirit could now dwell in those joined to Christ's Body.

As we shall see below, Orthodoxy teaches that this grace flows from *each* Person of the Holy Trinity, as each is divine, and grace is always imparted through the mutual activity of Father, Son, and Holy Spirit. The scriptures speak both of the "grace of God" (e.g., Luke 2:40) and the "grace of the Lord Jesus Christ" (e.g., Acts 15:11), as well as the "gift of the Holy Spirit" (Acts 2:38; 10:45). But as the economy of salvation unfolds, we see that grace is particularly associated with the Holy Spirit, whose ministry it is to make the Lordship of Jesus Christ and the glory of God known (see John 16:14; 1 Cor. 12:3). Again and again the prayers of the Orthodox Church speak of "the grace of the Holy Spirit."

Certainly the understanding of God's grace is at the heart of the gospel, for "grace and truth came through Jesus Christ" (John 1:17). And since salvation itself is a function of grace— "for by grace you have been saved" (Eph. 2:8)—we must have a firm grasp of what this grace is and how we participate in it. We should know that the way we view the meaning of grace is pivotal to our whole theological outlook on what was accomplished in Christ's death and Resurrection, the purpose and nature of the Church, and what it means to walk in the way of salvation and to live "in Christ."

Although the teaching on grace was essentially the same in both East and West prior to the Great Schism, differences did arise later—if not in dogmatic proclamation, in theological ethos and actual practice. It has been observed by writers like Vladimir Lossky that the adoption in the West of the *filioque* addition to the Nicene Creed—that is, that the Holy Spirit proceeds from the Father *and the Son*—caused a functional subordination of the Spirit that became apparent in the spiritual and liturgical life of the Roman Church. St. Augustine's popular formulation that the Holy Spirit is "the love between the Father and Son" may have also contributed to this tendency, depersonalizing the Holy Spirit and making Him a mere byproduct and afterthought of the other two Persons of the Holy Trinity.

This de-emphasis on the Person of the Holy Spirit was manifested liturgically in that the *epiklesis*,[1] the calling down of the Spirit upon the Holy Gifts, simply dropped out of the Roman Mass some time after the Schism, and certainly before the fourteenth century. Although this development cannot be directly traced back to the *filioque* addition, it is also notable that in the Roman Church, the Sacrament of Chrismation ("Confirmation" in the West), the seal of the gift of the Holy Spirit, has been separated from the Sacrament of Baptism. Thus an infant or child does not receive Chrismation (or Holy Communion) until he or she reaches "the age of reason."

This is not to say that the doctrine of the Holy Spirit was lost in Rome or that grace was not part of official church teaching. But it can be argued that this de-emphasis on the activity of the third Person of the Holy Trinity contributed to an institutionalism that, for all practical purposes, subordinated the role of the Spirit within the Roman confession. Certainly the Reformers saw it this way.

---

1   As the *Catholic Encyclopedia* states, "Epiklesis (Latin *invocatio*) is the name of a prayer that occurs in all Eastern liturgies (and originally in Western liturgies also) after the words of Institution, in which the celebrant prays that God may send down His Holy Spirit to change this bread and wine into the Body and Blood of His Son." (http://www.newadvent.org/cathen/05502a.htm.)

It is interesting that during this period, some in the West who claimed a very personal experience of God were considered suspect or even a threat by religious authorities. Whereas in the Orthodox Tradition mysticism refers to the union with God by grace that is to be pursued by *every* believer, in the West those who are called mystics are often viewed as a little off-kilter or outright unstable.[2]

In response to the theology of the Reformers, the Roman Catholic Church developed a rather detailed teaching on the workings of grace. However, while the Roman Church has tried meticulously to define *how* grace operates—the relationship between grace and the human will, various categories of grace and when and how they affect human persons—generally the West did not address the issue of *what grace is*.[3] In the Orthodox East, this question was definitively answered through the theological debate that arose between St. Gregory Palamas and Barlaam, sometimes called the hesychast or Palamite controversy. Let us look at that crucial theological debate, as it will help us better to appreciate the Church's teaching on grace.

The Palamite Controversy
SETTING THE STAGE
Even before the Great Schism, a new way of theologizing began to appear in the West, a method that focused on the speculative thought of the fallen human mind rather than on the revelation

2   Interestingly, the Orthodox Church even glorifies a category of saints called "fools for Christ" who, although clearly sanctified, either feign madness for the sake of humility or receive extraordinary grace despite a level of mental incapacity.
3   See James R. Payton, Jr., *Light from the Christian East: An Introduction to the Orthodox Tradition* (Downers Grove, IL: Intervarsity Press, 2007), p. 156.

of God and the experience of His saints. This new scholastic or academic method of theology exalted the intellect or reason of man over the experiential knowledge of the "pure in heart" who "see God" (Matt. 5:8) and are therefore able to confirm the authentic Tradition of the Church by their own personal experience. In a word, this method took theology out of the monasteries and the context of prayer and into the classroom. Scholasticism became the normative method for Western theologians by the twelfth century.

This was a clear departure from the ancient Christian understanding as summed up by the fourth-century ascetic, Evagrius of Pontus, when he said, "If you are a theologian, you will pray truly. And if you pray truly, you are a theologian."[4] In other words, theology was understood as the fruit and consequence of a holy life leading to direct union with God the Holy Trinity. Accordingly, a true theologian is one whose heart is purified of sinful passions and desires, whose mind has been refined through prayer, and whose noetic faculty (from the Greek *nous*, the "eye of the soul") has been illumined by God's grace, making him a vessel of the Holy Spirit.

Rather than producing theology from this spiritual perspective, the scholastic theologians sought to answer all questions related to the mystery of God through rational thinking, in the same way one learns about science or mathematics. The scholastic method attempted to use human logic and reasoning to resolve apparent contradictions. The method was marked by detailed analysis that produced positive theories about God and explored in minutiae any spiritual question that could be

---

4   *Philokalia*, Vol. 1, *One Hundred and Fifty Three Texts on Prayer*, trans. Palmer, Sherrard, Ware (London: Faber and Faber, 1990), p. 61.

conceived by the mind of man. Because of its methodology, the scholastic system produced *philosophy*, and not what Orthodox Christianity continues to define as theology.

Scholastic theologians adopted the philosophical categories and terminology of Aristotle in an attempt to comprehend theological questions such as how the bread and wine of the Holy Eucharist become the Body and Blood of Christ. The Aristotelian methodology produced conclusions that did not maintain the theological subtlety and paradox inherent in the mystery of salvation and grace. The rationalistic "slice and dice" approach to the mysteries of the Church was in contrast to the spirit of the Church Fathers, who, though they possessed great intellectual prowess, did not seek to unravel what has not been revealed.

BARLAAM OF CALABRIA

In the early fourteenth century, an intellectual from southern Italy, the land where scholasticism originated, came to Constantinople seeking to delve more deeply into the Hellenism of the ancient philosophers. Barlaam of Calabria, steeped in the spirit of the rationalism of his time, was welcomed into the intellectual circles and political classes of Constantinople and was given a teaching position at the university by the emperor. Intellectually he was a brilliant man with great knowledge in the sciences, astronomy, and mathematics, as well as being a student of the philosophy of humanism and theology.

Raised as an Orthodox Christian (southern Italy was at that time under the jurisdiction of Constantinople), Barlaam became a monk in Constantinople and even the abbot of the Monastery of Our Savior. He was also involved in the official theological dialogue sponsored by the emperor aimed at reunion with Rome. And although he wrote against the *filioque* addition to the Nicene Creed, the reasoning he used and his theology regarding the knowability of God, particularly of the Holy Spirit, set off alarms for the astute and refined spiritual mind of the Athonite monk Gregory Palamas. St. Gregory had a brief and unfruitful correspondence with Barlaam at this time.

But it was after an encounter with some poorly prepared monks who were attempting to practice the spiritual art of hesychasm, or unceasing prayer, that Barlaam began to make assertions that struck at the heart of the Orthodox Christian teaching on grace and how or whether one can know God. He began to write against the hesychasts' claim that it is possible to participate in God's grace and light in a real and objective way. He asserted that no human being can have a direct and unmediated communion with God, but we can know God only through rational means or through the created world.

ST. GREGORY PALAMAS AND
THE REFUTATION OF BARLAAM

Sensing the danger of Barlaam's teachings, St. Gregory Palamas began a rigorous defense of the traditional Christian understanding of God and the means of union with Him. Whereas Barlaam spoke only of God's essence and therefore proposed that God is transcendent and unknowable, St. Gregory elucidated that God is indeed unknowable in His essence or inner being, but is truly knowable and truly present by His grace, divine energies, and activities. St. Gregory referenced the "glory" of God seen by the Old Testament saints and prophets, the burning bush, and the light of transfiguration on Mount Tabor as epiphanies of God's divine grace, by which He shares His life with His creatures.

But Barlaam believed these were merely symbolic and created effects. Barlaamism then understands grace as *created*—not the sharing of God Himself but something created by Him to simulate His presence to human beings. In other words, grace is not God Himself but a created mediator between God and man. Illumination and knowledge of God is to be attained through a pursuit of reason and virtue, which perfects the rational nature of man. Confusing God's essence with His energies or grace, Barlaam argued that if God's grace could be seen or truly experienced, this would mean God's very essence is visible and knowable.

But St. Gregory demonstrated convincingly that while grace is not a participation in the transcendent and unknowable essence of God, it is a real experience of God through His divine energies. The divine energy or grace of God is not a created effect or substitute for God but a real partaking in His *uncreated* life and power. His creatures truly know and have union with Him by His grace, which is a real communication of the uncreated God.

This uncreated glory and grace of God was seen in the Old Testament as the cloud and pillar of fire in the wilderness (Ex. 13:21), beheld by the priests when the ark was brought into the tabernacle (1 Kin. 8:10) and upon the dedication of the Jerusalem temple (2 Chr. 7:1), witnessed by Moses in the burning bush (Ex. 3:2) and on Mount Sinai (Ex. 24:16), and seen by others on many occasions. In the New Testament the same uncreated divine grace of God, appearing as light, knocked Saul (St. Paul) off his horse, temporarily blinding him. The same divine energies were also seen by the three apostles on Mount Tabor emanating from the flesh of the God-Man, Jesus Christ.

Another event from the life of Moses is instructive for us in regard to God's essence and energies, His transcendence and His imminence or nearness, His unknowability and knowability. When Moses asked to see God's face, the Lord responded that no one can see His face and live. Yet after His negative response, the Lord agreed to let Moses see his "back side." According to the Holy Fathers of the Church, this story of God's revelation to Moses presents to us both the reality of God's essence, which cannot be known or seen by creatures, and His uncreated energies or glory, seen by the prophets, apostles, and saints in all ages.

Barlaam's teaching of created grace was rejected officially by a series of councils held in Constantinople. After a short time Barlaam returned to Calabria, where he joined himself to the Church of Rome, in which, at least at the time, the Palamite teaching was strongly opposed. St. Gregory's teachings were affirmed and embraced as reflecting the unchanging Tradition of the Church. The importance of these councils is shown in part by the fact that some Orthodox theologians consider them to have the status of ecumenical councils.

What Is Grace in the Orthodox Tradition?

The theological controversy that occurred in the fourteenth century helps to refine and further clarify the Orthodox Christian teaching on grace. It provides a good background for us to begin to comprehend the Church's teaching on this topic and to compare and contrast with the ideas and formulations of other Christian traditions. Since, as the Scriptures tell us, we are saved "by grace," it is imperative to have an accurate understanding of what grace is and is not and of how it is acquired.

GRACE IS NATURAL

After the Lord formed the first man, Adam, from the earth, we are told He then breathed into him the breath of life (Gen. 2:7). Sometimes this breath of life is misinterpreted to mean the creation of Adam's human soul. But the teaching of the Church is that Adam's soul was created by God from the dust of the earth concurrently with his body, just as the saints also teach that the soul of every subsequent human being is created at the time of his or her conception.

If the breath of life is not the soul, then what is it? St. Seraphim of Sarov addresses this issue directly in his famous conversation with Motovilov. He tells his friend and disciple that what God blew into Adam at the time of his creation is His life-giving Spirit, the Holy Spirit. This teaching harmonizes with the post-Resurrection account in the Gospel of John in which the Lord breathed into the faces of the apostles, saying, "Receive the Holy Spirit" (John 20:22). The word for "spirit" in both Hebrew and Greek can also mean "breath."

The Holy Spirit is not the soul itself but rather the life of the soul. The life of the body is the soul, but the life of the soul is the Holy Spirit. It was the very life of God that Jesus breathed into the apostles after His Resurrection. Without this grace and energy of the Holy Spirit, the soul is, spiritually speaking, dead. Therefore, in the Orthodox understanding, if one is to be an authentic and truly living human being, one must have the grace of God. And the more grace one has, the more truly human one becomes. In Orthodox anthropology (our understanding of man) we understand the indwelling of grace not as a supernatural phenomenon but as the most natural and normative condition of man.

This is particularly important because much of the theology of the West works from the assumption that grace is essentially foreign to human nature and certainly to fallen human nature. For instance, the Calvinist teaching on the total depravity of man, and likewise Luther's insistence that the image of God in man was completely destroyed after sin, are symptoms of this tendency. For all practical purposes man, in this view, is by nature a creature devoid of grace. Grace then becomes either an unnatural addition to human nature or a juridical release from condemnation independent of the condition of man's nature. And, in fact, Roman Catholic theology calls the holiness associated with the likeness of God *donum superadditum*, a superadded gift,[5] while many Protestants understand salvation by grace as a legal release from guilt.

Much of this tendency was inherited by the Reformers from Roman Catholicism and had its roots in the doctrine of original sin. In the West, following certain writings of St. Augustine, the understanding of Adam's sin, or "original sin," came to include not only the consequences of Adam's sin, but the *guilt* of Adam

---

5   The online *Dictionary of Philosophy* defines *donum superadditum*: "A theological term denoting a gratuitous gift of God superadded to the natural gifts which accompany human nature; hence a supernatural gift, like divine grace." (http://www.ditext.com/runes/d.html).

inherited by everyone born into the world. This condition of guilt, which was seen as a sentence of eternal damnation, makes one incapable of receiving God's grace. The "hereditary stain"[6] of original sin, it is taught, can only be washed away through baptism. Following this reasoning, the Roman Church deemphasized the Old Testament saints in their official liturgical calendar of commemorations. For how could the Old Testament righteous participate in grace before the saving work of Jesus Christ?

This same problem became the impetus for the modern doctrine of the Immaculate Conception of the Virgin Mary. In order to allow for her sanctification *before* the death and Resurrection of her Son, it was necessary, following the logic above, that she be exempted from "all stain of original sin . . . by a singular privilege and grace granted by God."[7]

By contrast, the Orthodox and early Church teaching is that the guilt of our first ancestors belongs to them alone. Those of us who come after them do not inherit their personal guilt. Rather, what we receive is a fallen, death-bound human nature, infected with the contagion of unnatural sinful passions, along with all the other consequences of the Fall.

Even in our fallen condition, however, grace is not something foreign to our nature. With the remnant of grace inherent to our nature and the image of God darkened but intact, a man may still choose to do good, to do God's will. The Old Testament righteous were not bereft of God's grace. The Holy Prophets and other Old Testament figures experienced the grace of the pre-incarnate Christ as He revealed Himself to them in manifold ways. The grace they experienced has no qualitative

6   *Catholic Encyclopedia* (http://www.newadvent.org/cathen/11312a.htm).
7   *Catholic Encyclopedia* (http://www.newadvent.org/cathen/07674d.htm).

difference from the grace that came after the Incarnation. Yet they could not be "made perfect" (Heb. 11:40), nor can anyone else, apart from the perfecting of human nature accomplished by Jesus' Incarnation, death, and Resurrection.

THE REVELATION OF THE UNCREATED GOD

In the Orthodox teaching, the grace of God is closely associated with the Person of the Holy Spirit, because it is the Spirit's ministry to take the grace of God that has been made accessible in Jesus Christ and pour it into the hearts of the faithful (Rom. 5:5). Grace is something that belongs equally to each Person of the Holy Trinity, but it is the Spirit who makes it manifest.

> "However, when He, the Spirit of truth, has come, He will guide you into all truth; for He will not speak on His own authority, but whatever He hears He will speak; and He will tell you things to come. He will glorify Me, for He will take of what is Mine and declare it to you. All things that the Father has are Mine. Therefore I said that He will take of Mine and declare it to you." (John 16:13–15)

This grace of God poured out to mankind through the Holy Spirit is not a mere theological idea, or even an effect produced in us by God; it is the very life of God, His power and energy, His self-revelation. Grace therefore is something real and concrete, although uncreated and immaterial—the energies and rays of divine life that flow from God to us. Grace imparts God Himself to His creatures and allows them to share and participate in His own uncreated and eternal life. However, as St. Gregory Palamas insisted, grace is not a participation in God's essence, because His essence cannot be experienced or comprehended by any creature, as the Scriptures (see John 1:18) and the Church Fathers[8] testify.

To use an earthly example: We all experience the power and energy of the sun. We truly experience and feel its warmth and light through the rays of energy that shine down upon us. These rays do not merely give us an impression of what the sun is; they are not a substitute for the sun; they do not present us with ideas about the sun; they do not merely illustrate what the sun is like; they are a real participation in the very energies of the sun itself. By our contact with the rays of the sun, we actually participate in the light and heat it produces. The sun's power interacts with our human cells, and real, organic changes occur in our human chemistry.

Similarly, the energy of the sun generates the natural process of photosynthesis in plant life. The sun's light interacts with carbon dioxide in the plant's cells, creating a chemical reaction that converts it into the necessary nourishment for the organism as well as releasing oxygen into the atmosphere.

Yet we cannot participate in or fully experience the *essence* of the sun. If we were to try to approach the scorching essence of the sun in an attempt to discover the inner source of its energies, we would be quickly overwhelmed and annihilated.

The same is true of God and His grace. His essence—how He exists in Himself—cannot be known or experienced by creatures, but He *is* known and experienced by His grace, the rays of

---

8   "It is by His energies that we can say we know our God; we do not assert that we can come near to the essence itself, for His energies descend to us, but His essence remains unapproachable." St. Basil the Great, quoted in Vladimir Lossky, *The Mystical Theology of the Eastern Church* (Crestwood, NY: St. Vladimir's Seminary Press, 1976), p. 72.

His divine energies and activities. As the created energies of the sun are real and provide us with a genuine and actual participation in the sun, so do the uncreated energies and grace of God give us a real experience of the uncreated God. And so, while we are capable of knowing God truly and intimately by His uncreated grace and self-revealing energies, yet He remains incomprehensible and unknowable in His essence.

The Orthodox Church teaches that a true and empirical knowledge of God comes when one directly experiences His uncreated grace in a pure heart, and not by the exercise of human logic or philosophical speculation, which is a product of the fallen human mind. True theologians, then, are those whose hearts have been purified of the sinful passions and are illumined by God's grace. In this way they receive God's self-revelation without distortion or imposition of their own ideas and imaginations. In the Orthodox mind, prayer and spiritual formation, not simply information, is the prerequisite to speaking about God. The fourth-century ascetic Evagrius succinctly summarizes the nature of theology when he says, "A theologian is one who truly prays; and one who prays truly is a theologian."[9]

Grace Confirmed in the Scriptures

That grace is a real and substantial thing given by God to His creation is verified by several important passages of Scripture. First, the Acts of the Apostles relate how many miraculous healings occurred through St. Paul, "so that even handkerchiefs or aprons were brought from his body to the sick, and the diseases left them and the evil spirits went out of them" (Acts 19:12).

---

9   *Philokalia*, Vol. 1, One Hundred and Fifty Three Texts on Prayer, 61.

Notice the passage is careful to specify that these personal items had been in contact with St. Paul's *body*. This is significant. If grace were a mere theological concept, there would be no organic connection between the apostle himself and the grace of God that worked the miracle. But since grace is indeed the real outpouring of God's divine energies, we can understand that the uncreated grace of God abiding in the holy apostle's body was literally transmitted to his garments by physical proximity.

Something similar is recorded in the life of St. Nectarios of Aegina. In 1920, after he reposed in a hospital in Athens, some medical staff began removing his clothes to clean his body, as was customary. In the process, they tossed his sweater onto the bed of the paralyzed man lying next to him. The man was instantly healed, got out of his bed, and began to walk. As in the example from the Book of Acts, the uncreated and immaterial grace of God abiding in the soul and body of St. Nectarios healed the sick, in this case through the means of a garment.

This understanding of grace is the basis for the Orthodox veneration of the relics (bodies) of the saints. The body, being the "temple of the Holy Spirit" (1 Cor. 6:19), participates in the holiness of the soul and becomes a vessel of divine grace. We see an example of this even in the Old Testament. Shortly after the Prophet Elisha's death, his grace-bearing relics raised a man from the dead.

> So it was, as they were burying a man, that suddenly they spied a band *of raiders*; and they put the man in the tomb of Elisha; and when the man was let down and touched the bones of Elisha, he revived and stood on his feet. (2 Kin. 13:21)

Perhaps the best example of grace as a tangible and organic reality is found in the earthly life of our Savior. As the Lord Jesus walked among a great crowd on his way to heal the daughter of Jairus, a woman afflicted with an issue of blood for many years, desperate but full of faith in the Lord, reached down behind Him to touch the fringe of His garment. She was immediately healed. But the important point for us is what happens next. Jesus, "immediately knowing in Himself that power had gone out of Him" (Mark 5:30), turned around and inquired who it was that had touched Him. The woman—known as St. Veronica according to tradition—revealed herself and what had happened when she touched, not Christ's body, but merely His clothing.

What then is this healing power that went out from the Lord that day? The Church teaches that it is the very same power that went forth from St. Paul and St. Nectarios in our examples above. The woman was healed by the uncreated and divine energies and grace of God. While Christ possesses this power infinitely by His very nature as God, His saints participate and share in it by grace.

GRACE AND WORKS

Since the time of the Protestant Reformation, there has been great confusion and controversy in Western Christendom regarding the issue of grace and/or works in relation to salvation. To this day it remains a polarizing issue among Protestants and Roman Catholics.

Of course, our view of works and salvation depends on our understanding of grace. If grace is merely a juridical release from the guilt of sin, man has no real function to perform in his own salvation, except perhaps to have faith, narrowly defined. And if grace is an alien and unnatural addition to an otherwise graceless being, then it can only create a façade of holiness or of union with the Holy.

But in Orthodox theology, grace is the very life-giving energies of God. It is the means by which God shares His divine life and light with His creation, and particularly with man, who is only truly human when he is permeated and penetrated by the grace of God. Grace is the natural condition of man, and only grace can make him fully human. The acquisition of this grace is the goal and purpose of the Christian life and of membership in the Church.

The Orthodox Church has never taught that man is saved by works. Rather, he is saved by grace. But works do ultimately have an impact on our salvation inasmuch as they either open or close us to God's grace. It is for this reason—and not merely because of some moral condemnation—that "the works of the flesh" (Gal. 5:19) are an obstacle to salvation. It is not because these sins represent the breaking of a moral law or because God becomes angry and desires to punish those who do them, but because they intrinsically darken and distort the soul's original created ability to receive the uncreated light and energy of God, that is, grace.

If we desire to feel the warmth of the sun, we must make the physical effort to walk outdoors and expose our skin to its rays, perhaps shedding some of our clothing. After being tanned by the sun's rays, we would claim not that our tan came about as the result of our own power, but rather that we desired it and put ourselves in a position to receive it.

And if there are clouds covering the sun, we do not say, "The sun is angry with me." The sun has not changed in any way, nor have the sun's rays ceased to shine. Rather, we acknowledge that the clouds are obstructing the sun's light and power, keeping it from having its natural impact.

The same is true in the spiritual life. If we desire to be in the presence of the spiritual Sun, we will adopt a way of life that naturally exposes us to the rays of God's grace. This is the way of love or of keeping the commandments of God—"If you love Me, keep My commandments" (John 14:15). It will not be *our* effort, our works, that save us, but the grace of God, which brings us into union and communion with Him.

When the Apostle Paul speaks of works in a derogatory or disparaging way, he is speaking contextually about the works of the law (Rom. 3:27–28; 9:32; Gal. 2:16; 3:2; 3:5; 3:10). But he always affirms good works, or fulfilling the "law of faith" (Rom. 3:27) and the "law of Christ" (Gal. 6:2). Good works are good because they place us in a position to receive God's saving energies and life. St. Seraphim of Sarov says that only good works done for Christ's sake attract this grace and are thus saving. And all of this is possible only because Jesus Christ overcame the law of sin in our human nature, trampled on the power of the devil and death, and opened our nature to divine grace.

Therefore, we never attribute salvation to our own works or power, or imagine that our works merit salvation. It is grace that saves us. However, we do the works to open ourselves to the possibility of receiving and keeping the gift of God's grace. St. Maximos the Confessor, one of the greatest theologians of the Church, tells us that grace actually resides in God's commandments.

The divine Logos of God the Father is mystically present in each of His commandments. . . . Thus, he who receives a divine commandment and carries it out receives the Logos of God who is in it. . . . In this way, he who receives a commandment and carries it out receives mystically the Holy Trinity.

Good works, living out the commandments of Jesus Christ, are a means to acquire the saving grace of God, for Jesus Christ Himself is revealed to us and shares Himself with us through the commandments.

On the other hand, sinfulness—works of darkness (whether manifested in thoughts, words, or deeds)—are clouds over the soul, inhibiting the rays of God's grace from shining into the heart, and out from the heart to the entire human person. As Clement of Alexandria affirms, "Into the impure soul, the grace of God finds no entrance."[10] Again, immorality is sinful because it blocks grace from penetrating the human soul, making a person less than human. The same is true of pride, envy, hatefulness, and all other sins.

THE FRUIT AND STAGES OF GRACE

The fruit of the acquisition of divine grace is not only good works and virtue but an actual union with God. First, grace works to purify the heart from all sinful passions and inclinations. Those who reach this spiritual state are called *dispassionate*. This does not mean that one is uncaring or disconnected, but that the energies of the soul have been directed away from anything evil and redirected toward God. The dispassionate person is not compelled by any sinful impulse. Rather, he is free

---

10 David W. Bercot, ed., *A Dictionary of Early Christian Beliefs* (Peabody, MA: Hendrickson Publishers, 2003), p. 577.

to love and to choose to love God and others without concern for self or for what others may think.

When the heart has been purified, grace then illumines the heart, giving discernment and spiritual understanding or knowledge. One who is illumined has spiritual vision and clarity and is able to recognize the true nature of created things and the presence of the uncreated. St. Paul refers generally to this spiritual condition when he writes of "the eyes of your understanding being enlightened; that you may know what is the hope of His calling, what are the riches of the glory of His inheritance in the saints" (Eph. 1:18).

Finally, grace works further upon the heart of the illumined to complete the union with God, so that "it is no longer I who live, but Christ lives in me" (Gal. 2:20). The Church Fathers use the term *theosis* or *deification* to describe this exalted spiritual state of union with God by grace. As the human nature of Jesus was fully infused and saturated by the divine energies flowing from His divine nature, so it is possible by grace for human beings to become vessels of divine grace.

The saints use the analogy of iron and fire, with iron representing human nature and fire, divine nature. When iron is placed in fire for some time it becomes red hot, having acquired the properties of fire. However, the iron has not become fire by nature but through continuous contact with the fire.

Similarly, one who by God's grace has been fully united with Him is permeated with His divine life in such a way that he exhibits spiritual gifts and fruits akin to God Himself. As the iron placed in the fire retains the properties of fire when removed, so the humanity of the spiritually perfect is united and mingled with the fire of divine life. He has become united with God in a permanent and abiding way and experiences His uncreated light as a continuous (and sometimes visual) reality. However, as the iron does not become fire itself, but participates and shares in the properties of fire, so human nature participates in God by grace, not by nature. Only the humanity of Christ received deification by nature as a result of its union with His divine nature.

These spiritual stages are not mutually exclusive or perfectly compartmentalized; there is progression (or digression) and overlap. The Church Fathers teach that God's grace is single; there are not different kinds of grace. However, grace works in each person according to his current spiritual condition.

The vast majority of Christians are still struggling for purification of the heart and should never imagine or measure ourselves as having reached great spiritual heights. Those who have attained great sanctity are always characterized by extreme humility.

Grace in Protestantism

The Protestant teaching on grace arose in reaction to the Roman Catholicism of the time, which lent itself, at least in practice, to the idea that salvation could be merited (or earned) by works. This current was given force by a teaching known as the "treasury of merits" or "treasury of the Church" proclaimed by Pope Clement IV (1291–1352). According to this teaching, the Church holds a treasury of superabundant merit (i.e., value, worth, grace) due to the work of Jesus Christ and the inexhaustible merits He has before God. The treasury also includes the prayers and good works of the Mother of God and the saints. The Church then dispenses these merits (or grace) to the faithful through the Sacraments and in return for acts of piety (which at one time included monetary gifts), thus making satisfaction (i.e., restitution, payment, or punishment) for sin. (Note: The issue of indulgences, the treasury of merits, etc., will be dealt with more fully in Chapter 3.)

The Protestant Reformers overreacted to this teaching by essentially claiming that man can do nothing to contribute to his salvation. Since they believed the image of God in man was completely destroyed after the Fall, they taught that man is incapable of doing any good; he can only sin. As John Calvin wrote, "his nature is so perverse that he cannot be moved, driven or led except to sin."[11] Over and against the idea of making satisfaction for sin through good works, they took the stand that man is saved by faith alone (*sola fide*) and by grace alone (*sola gratia*).

The typical Protestant view is that good works should be done out of gratitude for salvation but are not necessary for salvation and do not contribute to it. These works are encouraged only as a sign of fidelity to God but are not directly related to grace or salvation. Sanctification, or becoming holy, is generally understood to be independent of the issue of salvation. Sanctification has no direct relationship to grace.

The most common definition of grace provided by the Protestant tradition is, therefore, "the unmerited favor of God." In an attempt to eradicate any possibility of works contributing to the acquisition of salvation, Protestantism emphasizes that man is incapable of doing anything to attract God's grace. Grace is a

---

11   *Institutes*, 2:3.5.

free gift from God given when a person places his faith in Christ and is not dependent on any effort or tangible change in the one receiving it. Amazingly, in some forms of Calvinism, a person may receive this grace solely on the basis of his being elected by God—whether he wants it or not.[12]

In contrast to the Orthodox view of grace as a dynamic, transformative, life-giving interaction with God, here grace becomes a static, singular change of status from *not saved* to *saved*. In other words, before grace, God saw me as deserving of hell, but He now looks upon me with favor. He now views me as having the righteousness of His Son and is able to bestow forgiveness and salvation. A change has occurred in God but not in me.

In effect, the Protestant interpretation of "saved by grace" equates to a change in God's perspective. Grace is an idea about my eternal status rather than a reality of God sharing His very life and energies with me. God has saved me, but He has not touched me.

Imagine a young man who is madly in love with the girl next door. However, even from childhood she is not only unfavorable to his intentions, but she abhors everything about him. With time, however, her attitude changes, and she begins to see him in a new light, even taking a strong liking to him. The young man notices this obvious change, and the two begin spending a great deal of time together.

Finally the young man asks his beloved to marry him. She responds, "Most certainly, I will marry you, but I will not touch you."

Shocked, the young man says, "But don't you like me?"

---

12 This is usually referred to as the doctrine of "double predestination."

"Of course," says the young woman, "I like you very much, and I am disposed favorably toward you. Isn't that enough? We will be together for the rest of our lives; we just won't have physical contact."

"That is not what I had in mind!" protests the young man as he storms away with a broken heart.

The Protestant approach to grace has much in common with the story of the young man. For it teaches that when a person comes to faith in Christ, it is God's *attitude* that changes; He now views him favorably and no longer abhors him. As with the young woman, this favor does not include a real union, an exchange of life and energies. Grace removes the obstacle between God and man but still does not allow an organic communion to exist. In this way grace is essentially relegated to the world of ideas, and faith is reduced to mere mental belief rather than participation in the very life of Christ.[13] Salvation is merely a pardon of guilt rather than the means by which we become "partakers of the divine nature" (2 Pet. 1:4).

Grace in Roman Catholicism

While the understanding of grace in Roman Catholicism is much closer to that of Orthodoxy, there is still reason to be reticent about what exactly the Roman Church believes. At least from an Orthodox perspective, it is difficult at times to pin down what is meant by the Catholic teaching on grace. And, as was mentioned above, Western Christendom has rarely attempted to articulate what grace *is*. On the one hand, language is used

---

13   Therefore, when Orthodox Christians speak of being saved by grace, they mean something quite different. For the Orthodox, salvation is the acquisition of the very life of God, His grace.

that would suggest a similar teaching of uncreated grace as God's own life shared with man. On the other hand, the terms and definitions seem convoluted and confusing, often employing the philosophical language of Aristotle.

Roman Catholicism has identified various kinds of grace as defined according to the effect they have on the human being. *Actual* grace is said to be an external influence of grace used by God to nudge a person toward Himself. *Sanctifying* grace (also called *habitual* or *justifying* grace) is a permanent condition of grace in a man's soul, making him holy. *Gratuitous* grace is defined as grace that is given regardless of the moral behavior of the recipient. Surprisingly, the gifts of gratuitous grace can include prophecy, miracle-working, or the gift of tongues.[14] *Prevenient* grace is the means by which God brings a person to conversion. It precedes and leads one to justification. And even the phrase "created grace" has been used,[15] although it is purported merely to describe the fact that the target of God's grace (the human being) is created. Since a man receives grace beginning at some point in time, it is said, grace is called "created," since it begins within a human being at a moment in time.

Certain popular formulations also seem to miss the mark of the Orthodox teaching of grace as the uncreated energies of God Himself. For instance, it is often stressed in modern Catholic explanations of grace that one must make a distinction between the gift (grace) and the Giver (God). While in Orthodoxy we make a distinction between the essence of God and His energies, we understand both to be uncreated. The energies

---

14 http://www.catholicculture.org/culture/library/dictionary/index.cfm?id=33805.

15 By Thomas Aquinas, a Roman Catholic saint, and others.

(grace) are the very life of God Himself, not something distinct from God. As mentioned before, while in the West grace is typically termed "supernatural," Orthodoxy understands grace as the natural condition of human nature. The use of the word *supernatural* is misleading, since it implies that grace (and God Himself) is something unnatural to man and that the reception of grace makes one less than (or other than) human.

Since it is sometimes difficult to ascertain the clear Roman understanding of grace, perhaps it is best to allow the teaching as expressed in the *Catholic Encyclopedia* to speak for itself:

> Moreover, sanctifying grace as an active reality, and not a merely external relation, must be philosophically either substance or accident. Now, it is certainly not a substance which exists by itself, or apart from the soul, therefore it is a physical accident inhering in the soul, so that the soul becomes the subject in which grace inheres; but such an accident is in metaphysics called quality (*qualitas, poiotes*) therefore sanctifying grace may be philosophically termed a "permanent, supernatural quality of the soul."[16]

We can make several observations about this. First, the explanation of grace here is forced into the philosophical categories of Aristotle instead of being mined from Church Tradition as received from the experience and words of the saints and Church Fathers. It is a bit like hammering a square peg into a round hole. Strictly speaking, any system of human logic is inadequate to express God's self-revelation. This is because philosophy is ultimately a product of fallen human reasoning,[17] whereas

---

16 http://www.newadvent.org/cathen/06701a.htm. Main Heading: "Sanctifying Grace." Subheading: "The Nature of Sanctifying Grace."

17 It is worth noting that Thomas Aquinas, a saint and "doctor" of the Roman

authentic theology flows from a pure heart that encounters and knows God personally. Unfortunately, Aristotle's categories and definitions cannot convey the authentic experience of Abraham, Moses, the prophets, the apostles, and the saints who have come after them.

For example, in Aristotelian philosophy, *substance* (i.e., essence) means a primary mode of being, while an *accident* is defined as a secondary mode of being. Using Aristotelian terms, then, human nature itself belongs to the realm of substance. But whether a human being is male or female or has dark or light hair is *accidental* to nature. Accidents in this system include various attributes or qualities a particular human being might have.

Great difficulties arise for Orthodox Christians when these categories are applied to God's essence and grace as in the above explanation from the *Catholic Encyclopedia*. To begin with, in God there is no primary or secondary mode of being. The God of Abraham, Isaac, and Jacob does not exist according to a mode of being. God *is* Being. He *is* Existence. This is what He Himself revealed when He expressed His divine name to Moses on Mount Sinai: "I AM" (Ex. 3:14). God exists; or rather, He is Existence. And this existence is beyond anything we can imagine or describe as being or existence. God is beyond modes of being.

As God has existed from eternity, His divine and uncreated grace and energy have existed from all eternity; they are simply natural to His Being. Is it possible to have the sun without the energy of the sun? As the energy of the sun always emanates from the sun, so the energies of God emanate from Him from

---

Catholic Church whose philosophy depended heavily on Aristotle's, believed that while the will of man is fallen, his reasoning power is not.

all eternity. Yet the *Catholic Encyclopedia* teaches that God's grace is "not a substance which exists by itself."

Vladimir Lossky, summarizing the teaching of the saints, writes:

> The [divine] energy is not a divine function which exists *on account* of creatures, despite the fact that it is through His energies, which penetrate everything that exists, that God creates and operates. Even if creatures did not exist, God would none the less manifest Himself beyond His essence; just as the rays of the sun would shine out from the solar disk whether or not there were any beings capable of receiving their light.[18]

The Church Fathers make the distinction between God's essence and His energies in order to preserve the truth that God is both utterly incomprehensible and inexhaustible, yet self-revealing and truly knowable. God's essence refers to His inner existence, which no creature can fathom or comprehend or experience. Thus the Lord could say to Moses, "No man shall see Me, and live" (Ex. 33:20; see also John 1:18). The essence of God is incomprehensible and known only to the Persons of the Godhead. The Fathers insist that the only distinctions God has revealed about His inner existence are that God the Father is unbegotten, the Son is eternally begotten of the Father, and the Holy Spirit eternally proceeds from Him.

His grace or energies, on the other hand, make Him knowable yet inexhaustible. Grace refers to the natural overflowing of His life and love; it is the outward movement of His one Being that manifests His uncreated, eternal deity and power.

Essence and energy (grace) are not two modes of being. They

---

18   *The Mystical Theology of the Eastern Church*, p. 74.

are part and parcel of the one Being of God. God's essence and energies are not contradictory or opposite, but complementary and inseparable realities of the one God. While we make a distinction between the essence and energies of God, there is no disconnection, any more than a human person can exist without exuding the (created) energies natural to him.

According to our Orthodox teaching, God's grace is not accidental or secondary to His essence. For Aristotle, an accident has no necessary connection with the subject or essence of a thing. Therefore, whether a house is constructed of wood or stone, it is still a house. Wood and stone are accidental to the essence of the house and have no necessary connection with what makes it a house. But with God, there is no such disconnect. His divine grace, although not itself His essence, is necessarily connected to His essence. His grace is therefore a direct and genuine experience of God Himself. According to the teaching of the Holy Fathers, God "is wholly present in each ray of His divinity."[19]

In addition, grace is not a quality of the soul as Catholic teaching states, but the quality or qualities of God communicated to the soul. In Orthodox teaching, His energies are also called His attributes. Everything we know about God is from His energies or attributes. He is omniscient (all-knowing). He is immutable (unchanging). He is holy. He is just. He is kind. He is patient. He is merciful, and so forth. His attributes/grace/energies are eternal as He is eternal. There was never a time when the energies did not exist, for they naturally and eternally flow from His divine Being. They are not dependent on their relationship

19   *Mystical Theology,* p. 74.

to the human soul. When God's energies are distributed to His creatures, they are given according to His will, not out of some necessity of His essence.

Without this important distinction between essence and energies, God is found to be determined and imprisoned by His own essence. For instance, consider Thomas Aquinas, who confused the essence and energies of God and does not seem to have known of the distinction made by the Holy Fathers. He mistakenly ascribes the attribute of God's justice to His very essence. Therefore, he reasons that, since God is by essence just, He is unable to forgive sin until a just payment is made for sin on the Cross. Not understanding that justice is a divine energy or attribute of God freely communicated by Him according to His will, Aquinas imprisons God and His ability to act within the supposed restrictions of His own nature. Such a God does not act in freedom but by force and compulsively, according to His own necessary limitations. While God chose the means of the Cross to purge human nature of sin, it was not the *only* way He could do so. Nor was He lacking in forgiveness prior to the Cross due to an essential requirement of justice.

To say that grace does not exist apart from the soul is to make God's divine energies dependent on creation. If God's grace does not exist without a human soul, then how is it an objective divine and eternal reality? The Church Fathers teach that God's uncreated energies are part of His eternal Being. They exist independently of creation, just as He Himself exists independently of His creation. God's grace is not a product created to give an effect or impression to the soul. If grace is not a substance that exists by itself, then either God also does not exist by Himself, or grace is something created.

Also, if God's grace did not exist with Him eternally, then at some point in eternity God must have changed. Yet one of His divine attributes is immutability (He never changes). And if His divine grace did not exist with Him eternally, then grace cannot be uncreated. If grace came into existence at some moment apart from God, it must be a creation. And finally, if grace is a creation, it does not impart God Himself to us, and we are unable to truly know Him or participate in His divine life.

Next, if the human soul is the only subject (or primary mode of being) in relation to grace, God ceases to be a subject. But in reality God is *the* Subject whose uncreated power and energy overflow through love to His subjects. He is a personal God who wills to share His life personally with created human persons. God's divine energies are His *personal* energies, and they communicate His Person, His Godhead. One who shares in His grace shares the life of the Person, or more accurately, Persons, of the Holy Trinity.

Lastly, if grace is an accident in relation to the human soul, then by definition it is not essential to human nature. Is then God's divine energy or grace incidental to human nature as is, for instance, the color of one's hair or eyes? Not according to the Scriptures and the Church Fathers, which teach that the grace of the Holy Spirit constitutes the very definition of what it means to be a "living being" (Gen. 2:7). There is no real human life without God's grace, for it belongs properly and naturally to human nature. His divine grace, by which we truly know Him, cannot be a secondary mode of existence. It is part and parcel of His one mode of being, or rather the fact of His existence.

THE HOLY SCRIPTURES ON GRACE

God's grace as the experience of His power and presence

Luke 5:17: Now it happened on a certain day, as He was teaching, that there were Pharisees and teachers of the law sitting by, who had come out of every town of Galilee, Judea, and Jerusalem. And the power of the Lord was *present* to heal them.

Eph. 3:7: of which I became a minister according to the gift of the grace of God given to me by the effective working of His power.

Luke 8:42-46: But as He went, the multitudes thronged Him. Now a woman, having a flow of blood for twelve years, who had spent all her livelihood on physicians and could not be healed by any, came from behind and touched the border of His garment. And immediately her flow of blood stopped. And Jesus said, "Who touched Me?" When all denied it, Peter and those with him said, "Master, the multitudes throng and press You, and You say, 'Who touched Me?'" But Jesus said, "Somebody touched Me, for I perceived power going out from Me."

Matt. 14:35-36: And when the men of that place recognized Him, they sent out into all that surrounding region, brought to Him all who were sick, and begged Him that they might only touch the hem of His garment. And as many as touched *it* were made perfectly well.

Mark 6:56: Wherever He entered, into villages, cities, or the country, they laid the sick in the marketplaces, and begged Him that they might just touch the hem of His garment. And as many as touched Him were made well.

Rom. 1:20: For since the creation of the world His invisible *attributes* are clearly seen, being understood by the things that are made, *even* His eternal power and Godhead, so that they are without excuse.

Acts 19:11–12: Now God worked unusual miracles by the hands of Paul, so that even handkerchiefs or aprons were brought from his body to the sick, and the diseases left them and the evil spirits went out of them.

Synergy: Grace cooperates with man's will and effort

Matt. 7:7: Ask, and it will be given to you; seek, and you will find; knock, and it will be opened to you. [The Greek denotes continuous action: "Keep asking ... keep seeking ... keep knocking."]

1 Cor. 15:10: But by the grace of God I am what I am, and His grace toward me was not in vain; but I labored more abundantly than they all, yet not I, but the grace of God *which was* with me.

Phil. 2:12–13: Therefore, my beloved, as you have always obeyed, not as in my presence only, but now much more in my absence, work out your own salvation with fear and trembling; for it is God who works in you both to will and to do for *His* good pleasure.

James 2:17: Thus also faith by itself, if it does not have works, is dead.

James 2:18–22: But someone will say, "You have faith, and I have works." Show me your faith without your works, and I will show you my faith by my works. You believe that there is one God. You do well. Even the demons believe—and tremble! But do you want to know, O foolish man, that faith without works is dead? Was not Abraham our father justified by works when he offered Isaac his son on the altar? Do you see that faith was working together with his works, and by works faith was made perfect?

Rev. 3:20: Behold, I stand at the door and knock. If anyone hears My voice and opens the door, I will come in to him and dine with him, and he with Me.

THE CHURCH FATHERS ON GRACE

Clement of Alexandria (c. AD 150–c. 215)

Choice depended on the man as being free. But the gift [i.e. grace] depended on God as the Lord. And He gives to those who are willing, are exceedingly earnest, and who ask. In this manner, their salvation can become their own. For God does not compel. (*The Stromata*, Bercot, *op. cit.*, vol. 2, 593)

St. John Cassian (c. AD 360–435), commentary on 1 Cor. 15:10

When he says "I labored," he shows the effort of his own will; when he says yet not I, but the grace of God, he points out the value of the Divine protection; when he says with me, he affirms that grace cooperates with him when he is not idle or careless, but working and making an effort. (*Conferences* 13:13)[20]

In all these [scriptural quotations] there is a declaration both of the grace of God and the freedom of our will, because even of his own activity a man can be led to the quest of virtue, but always stands in need of the help of the Lord. (*Conferences* 13:9)[21]

For these two, that is, both grace and free will, seem indeed to be contrary to each other; but both are in harmony. And we conclude that, because of piety, we should accept both, lest taking on of these away from man, we appear to violate the Church's rule of faith. (*Conferences* 13:11)[22]

---

20   As quoted in Fr. Seraphim Rose, *The Place of Blessed Augustine in the Orthodox Church* (Platina, CA: St. Herman Press, 2007), p. 37.
21   *Ibid.*
22   *Ibid.*

St. Maximos the Confessor (c. AD 580–662)

The divine Logos of God the Father is mystically present in each of His commandments. . . . Thus, he who receives a divine commandment and carries it out receives the Logos of God who is in it; and he who receives the Logos through the commandments also receives through Him the Father who is by nature present in Him, and the Spirit who likewise is by nature in Him. "I tell you truly, he that receives whomever I send receives Me; and he that receives Me receives Him that sent Me" (John 13:20). In this way, he who receives a commandment and carries it out receives mystically the Holy Trinity. (*Second Century on Theology*, 71)

St. Seraphim of Sarov (AD 1754–1833)

Prayer, fasting, vigil and all other Christian activities, however good they may be in themselves, do not constitute the aim of our Christian life, although they serve as the indispensable means of reaching this end. The true aim of our Christian life consists in the acquisition of the Holy Spirit of God. As for fasts, and vigils, and prayer, and almsgiving, and every good deed done for Christ's sake, they are only means of acquiring the Holy Spirit of God. But mark, my son, only the good deed done for Christ's sake brings us the fruits of the Holy Spirit. All that is not done for Christ's sake, even though it be good, brings neither reward in the future life nor the grace of God in this.

That's it, your Godliness. In acquiring this Spirit of God consists the true aim of our Christian life, while prayer, vigil, fasting, almsgiving and other good works done for Christ's sake are merely means for acquiring the Spirit of God.

In the parable of the wise and foolish virgins, when the foolish ones lacked oil, it was said: "Go and buy in the market." But when they had bought, the door of the bride-chamber was already shut and they could not get in. . . . I think that what they were lacking was the grace of the All-Holy Spirit of God. These virgins practiced the virtues, but in their spiritual ignorance they supposed that the Christian life consisted merely in doing good works. By doing a good deed they thought they were doing the work of God, but they little cared whether they acquired thereby the grace of God's Spirit.

Of course, every good deed done for Christ's sake gives us the grace of the Holy Spirit.

And if we were never to sin after our Baptism, we should remain for ever saints of God, holy, blameless and free from all impurity of body and spirit. But the trouble is that we increase in stature, but do not increase in grace and in the knowledge of God as our Lord Jesus Christ increased; but on the contrary, we gradually become more and more depraved and lose the grace of the All-Holy Spirit of God and become sinful in various degrees. . . . Then through the virtues practiced for Christ's sake he will acquire the Holy Spirit Who acts within us and establishes in us the Kingdom of God.

The grace of the Holy Spirit is the light which enlightens man. The whole of Sacred Scripture speaks about this. . . . Thus the grace of the All-Holy Spirit of God appears in an ineffable light to all to whom God reveals its action. (*Conversation with Motovilov*)

CHAPTER 3

Salvation

For the message of the cross is foolishness to those who are perishing,
but to us who are being saved it is the power of God. (1 Cor. 1:18)

By grace and through faith, Cornelius and his family have now embarked upon the path of salvation. The eyes of their souls have been enlightened, and they understand that Jesus is "the way, the truth, and the life" (John 14:6), the "Alpha and the Omega" (Rev. 1:8; 22:13). He is indeed the "Savior of the world" (John 4:42), and "in Him dwells all the fullness of the Godhead bodily" (Col. 2:9).

Cornelius rejoices and ruminates on how this gift of God was imparted to him and his loved ones, even his dear children, "not by works" (Titus 3:5), but by grace through "water and the Spirit" (John 3:5). They have received forgiveness of their sins. They have "put on Christ" (Gal. 3:27) and have been joined to His Body. Cornelius, whose heart is now aflame with God's unspeakable love, is overwhelmed with God's presence and full of thanksgiving. He remembers the words of the psalmist—"How marvelous are Thy works, O Lord, and there is no word which is sufficient to hymn Thy wonders!" (Ps. 92:5).[1]

---

1   This psalm verse is proclaimed in the Orthodox baptismal service as part of

By being grafted into the glorified flesh of the resurrected Christ, who is both God and Man, Cornelius and his household have become "partakers of the divine nature" (2 Pet. 1:4). "This is salvation!" he spontaneously declares aloud to himself. "This is the purpose for which the Messiah Jesus, God's own Son, came down from heaven and was born of the Virgin—to enable us to share in God's own life and in His Kingdom. For God has united 'all things in Christ, both which are in heaven and which are on earth'" (Eph. 1:10).

The teaching of the Apostle Peter, who instructed and exhorted the newly baptized Gentile converts with many words after their baptism, still resounds in his ears: "And if you call on the Father, who without partiality judges according to each one's work, conduct yourselves throughout the time of your stay here in fear; knowing that you were not redeemed with corruptible things . . . but with the precious blood of Christ, as of a lamb without blemish and without spot" (1 Pet. 1:17–19).

Cornelius remembers the apostle's admonition that the grace he and his family have received this day is a seed, not a full-grown tree. They have begun the life of faith, Peter told them, but "the end of your faith" is "the salvation of *your* souls" (1 Pet. 1:9). They should not consider their salvation as something past and accomplished but as their "living hope through the resurrection of Jesus Christ from the dead" (1 Pet. 1:3).

The new convert realizes he is not "already perfected" (Phil. 3:12); he has not yet "come to the unity of the faith and of the knowledge of the Son of God, to a perfect man, to the measure of the stature of the fullness of Christ" (Eph. 4:13). Rather his call is to continue on the path of salvation: "Therefore gird up the loins of your mind, be sober, and rest *your* hope fully upon the grace that is to be brought to you at the revelation of Jesus Christ; as obedient children, not conforming yourselves to the

---

the blessing of the waters.

former lusts, as in your ignorance; but as He who called you is holy, you also be holy in all *your* conduct, because it is written, 'Be holy, for I am holy'" (1 Pet. 1:13–16).

Be on guard, the apostle told them, "because your adversary the devil walks about like a roaring lion, seeking whom he may devour" (1 Pet. 5:8). "Be even more diligent to make your call and election sure" (2 Pet. 1:10), he warned, for "God did not spare the angels who sinned" (2 Pet. 2:4). When the Lord comes again they should "be found by Him in peace, without spot and blameless" (2 Pet. 3:14).

Cornelius understands from all of this that salvation is not confined to the moment he believed but is a way of life and grace to maintain, nurture, and grow. He has not only "been saved" (Eph. 2:5) by God's mercy "through the washing of regeneration" (Titus 3:5); he is also "being saved" (1 Cor. 1:18; 2 Cor. 2:15) and must hold on to the "hope of salvation" (1 Thess. 5:8), lest he "neglect so great a salvation" (Heb. 2:3) and "drift away" (Heb. 2:1). He cannot only look backward but must "stand" in the present in the grace of salvation (Rom. 5:2; 1 Pet. 5:12), "work out [his] own salvation with fear and trembling" (Phil. 2:12), and "press toward the goal" to "lay hold" of this salvation (Phil. 3:14; 1 Tim. 6:12), now and always.

Before his departure from them, Peter counseled them not to turn back from the way of salvation. "For," he said, "it would have been better for them not to have known the way of righteousness, than having known it, to turn from the holy commandment delivered to them" (2 Pet. 2:20–21). Again, he exhorted them not to be "led away with the error of the wicked; but [to] grow in the grace and knowledge of our Lord and Savior Jesus Christ" (2 Pet. 3:17–18).

The apostle then repeated the words he heard from the lips of Jesus Christ Himself: "If you love Me, keep My commandments" (John 14:15). And so Cornelius encouraged his family to "commit their souls to Him in doing good, as to a faithful Creator" (1 Pet. 4:19). And in imitation of Noah and his family at the time of the flood (1 Pet. 3:20), they encouraged one another to remain in God's grace in His Holy Church, the ark of salvation.

Introduction

In the biblical account, an angel appears to Cornelius and proclaims exactly how he has found favor with God: "Your prayers and your alms have come up for a memorial before God" (Acts 10:4). It was his faithful prayer and love for the poor that placed Cornelius in a position to receive the visitation of God's grace. But this grace had still not come to dwell within him, for he was not yet regenerated in baptism.

God then led to him the Apostle Peter, who preached the good news of Jesus Christ and taught him the way of salvation. His entrance into the life of salvation began by water and the Spirit. He would then begin to participate in the life of grace and grow toward the "fullness of Christ" (Eph. 4:13) in the apostolic Church.

This is essentially no different from how one enters the Orthodox Church today. One who is seeking the true God, prompted ultimately by the Spirit, at some point encounters His apostolic Church. He hears the teaching of the gospel in its fullness and is made a catechumen (a "learner") by the Church. After a period of preparation in which he is taught the way of faith, he is baptized into Christ and receives the gift of the Holy Spirit through the Sacrament of Chrismation.[2]

---

2 The eighth canon of the Second Ecumenical Council (AD 381) summarizes the way pagans or heretics were received into the Church: "On the first day we make them Christians; on the second, catechumens; on the third, we exorcise them . . . and thus we instruct them and oblige them to spend time in the

But this is only the *beginning*. Salvation is not a legal or ritual removal of guilt that entitles one to go to heaven when he dies. It is not a stamped ticket to eternal life in exchange for a one-time confession of faith. Salvation is a real union with God, a participation in His divine and life-giving energies, through communion with the resurrected flesh of Jesus Christ and the indwelling of the Holy Spirit. This is why salvation requires repentance: because the heart must actually open up to the grace of God— and not just part of the heart, but the whole heart.

Salvation begins with the forgiveness of sins but must progress toward the actual remission of sins and to the healing of the passions, the source of these sins, if one is to abide within the reality of salvation. A man whose body is riddled with cancer and who is threatened with imminent death will not be comforted by news that his cancer is "forgiven." He will rejoice with great rejoicing, however, if he is told that his cancer is in remission. For then he knows that the death-bearing cancerous cells have receded, and life reigns in his body.

As another example, a wedding and a marriage certificate do not make a marriage, an actual communion of husband and wife. What is blessed by God and begun well must continually be lived out and realized within the arena of a daily struggle to actualize what St. Paul describes as marriage: an icon of Christ with His Bride, the Church (see Eph. 5:22–33).

According to the mind of the Church, salvation is the reorientation and healing of the human being. First it is the uncovering of the image of God and then a progression "from glory

---

Church, and to hear the Scriptures; and then we baptize them." (Metropolitan of Nafpaktos Hierotheos, *Entering the Orthodox Church,* trans. Marina Mary Robb (Yonkers, NY: Birth of the Theotokos Monastery, 2006), p. 20)

to glory" (2 Cor. 3:18), toward His likeness. For instance, in his *Questions to Thalassios*, St. Maximos the Confessor describes the process of salvation, or spiritual rebirth:

> The manner of birth from God within us is two-fold: the one bestows the grace of adoption, which is entirely present in potency in those who are born of God; the other introduces, wholly by active exertion, that grace which deliberately reorients the entire free choice of the one being born of God toward the God who gives birth. The first bears the grace, present in potency, through faith alone; but the second, beyond faith, also engenders in the knower the sublimely divine likeness of the One known.[3]

St. Maximos goes on to say that, although God gives the whole gift of grace at the outset to the one reborn, it cannot be actualized because the will has "not yet fully detached from its propensity to the flesh." In other words, one must voluntarily assent and conform to the life of grace, for God transforms us only to the extent that we have a "willing will."[4]

In order to actualize the grace of regeneration in baptism, great struggle is necessary to overcome the still imperfect and fallen will and desire. The Fathers teach us that our first effort must be in the practice of keeping Christ's commandments, for in this way we crucify the fleshly desires and receive God's grace. Because what we do either attracts or repels God's grace, it matters what we do in this life and to what extent we repent of those obstacles that obstruct our hearts from receiving His grace.

Salvation has a beginning. For some it is an obvious, dramatic

---

3   *On the Cosmic Mystery of Jesus Christ,* trans. Paul M. Blowers (Crestwood, NY: SVS Press, 2003), p. 103.

4   *Ibid.,* p. 104.

"road to Damascus" experience, but for others it is an almost imperceptible, slow-growing flame that has been burning with the help of the Church from infancy. It is not for us to say that we are "saved" in the sense that we have "already attained" salvation or are "already perfected" (Phil. 3:12). Even the great apostle Paul did not presume that. It is for us to abide in the way of salvation and strive toward "the measure of the stature of the fullness of Christ" (Eph. 4:13).

Far from being "guaranteed," salvation can never be taken for granted, since the moment we do so, we become presumptuous and stop striving for it. In Orthodoxy there is no "minimum requirement" of holiness or faith for salvation. This is because the goal is love for God and neighbor. There are no minimums when it comes to love. That would be the approach of a spiritual lawyer or accountant.

When a certain young man came to Jesus, he inquired about minimums: "Good Teacher, what good thing shall I do that I may have eternal life?" (Matt. 19:16). In response the Lord provided him with a maximal answer: "If you want to be perfect, go, sell what you have and give to the poor, and you will have treasure in heaven; and come, follow Me" (Matt. 19:21).

This does not mean we are to be constantly insecure and anxious about whether we are on the path of salvation. It is not, as it is sometimes presented, as if we Orthodox Christians have no clue whether or not we are striving to repent of our sinful habits and seeking to "be transformed by the renewing of [our] mind" (literally, the *nous*, or inner man, Rom. 12:2). Yet in humility we know we have much further to go along the path of salvation and, without God's grace, we are vulnerable to straying from the path.

This comes into sharper focus as we look to those who have gone before us, those we are instructed to "imitate" (1 Cor. 4:16; 11:1; Heb. 6:12) and "whose faith" we are to "follow, considering the outcome of *their* conduct" (Heb. 13:7). They are our examples, "because narrow *is* the gate and difficult *is* the way which leads to life, and there are few who find it" (Matt. 7:14). It is not only he who begins on the way, "but he who endures to the end [who] will be saved" (Matt. 10:22).

In the end, salvation means real union with God. Cornelius would not have known of atonement theories that seek to package God's redemptive work neatly into a juridical formula. Salvation for the early Church was about Christ's victory over the devil and death, the "last enemy" (1 Cor. 15:26). It was about the renewal of human nature in the Incarnation, the victory over sin on the Cross, and the ultimate goal—the deification of human nature in the Person of the resurrected Christ. Salvation is the good news that what Jesus is by nature, we also can become by grace.

The very word scripture uses to describe our personal assimilation of God's redemptive work—*salvation* (Greek, *soteria*)—signifies health, wholeness, safety, preservation, and deliverance from enemies. Ultimately, salvation is the condition of spiritual health and wholeness that comes by an organic union with God, through Jesus Christ and the Holy Spirit.

The Background
SALVATION: PURGATORY AND PROTEST

The Protestant Reformation largely hinged on the issue of salvation: whether one is saved by "grace alone," as the Reformers insisted, or also by works, Rome's position. But the context and catalyst for this debate was Rome's doctrine of purgatorial fire after death (purgatory) and the practice of granting indulgences as a means of escaping it. Protestants feared that salvation as a "free gift" (Rom. 5:18) from God had become entangled in a complicated and corrupt system of indulgences that seemed to promote a theology of salvation based on good works. When Martin Luther made a pilgrimage to the holy city of Rome, he was shocked and deeply pained by the blatant and egregious abuses taking place in his day.

The idea of indulgences originated in the West at earliest around the time of the Great Schism and bloomed under the influence of the scholastic theologians of the twelfth and thirteenth centuries. An indulgence was initially a way to relax or replace a penance (time away from Holy Communion) by requiring the penitent to fulfill certain extra good works, prayers, or pious donations. It was thus originally connected to the sacrament of repentance or penance. The most famous early use of the indulgence came at the hand of Pope Urban II when, in AD 1095, he offered complete remission of sins to those who had participated in the First Crusade (including those who had died in the effort). By AD 1195, Pope Gregory VIII introduced a new feature, offering a complete indulgence to those who contributed to the expenses of a crusade and even to those who found someone else to fight on their behalf.[5]

With time indulgences came to be separated from the sacrament of penance and took on a life of their own. It became fashionable to simply impose a donation as a replacement for acts of

5   Fr. Enrico dal Covolo, S.D.B., "The Historical Origin of Indulgences" (https://www.catholicculture.org/culture/library/view.cfm?recnum=1054)

repentance, and these indulgences were often not associated at all with a confession of sin.[6]

By this time also, in the West, sin had become associated with guilt and penance with punishment. The underlying basis for this practice, then, became the release from punishment. More precisely, an indulgence was believed to remit the temporal punishment due for sin and thereby release one from time in purgatory after death.[7] By the time of the false union of the Council of Florence–Ferrara (1438–45), where the doctrines of purgatory and indulgences were formally adopted by Rome, St. Mark of Ephesus utterly rejected the innovation, calling it nothing less than heresy.[8]

According to the Catholic Catechism, and as defined by Pope Paul VI in his Apostolic Constitution, the current official teaching is as follows:

> An indulgence is the remission before God of the temporal punishment due to sins already forgiven as far as their guilt is concerned, which the follower of Christ with the proper dispositions and under certain determined conditions acquires through the intervention of the Church which, as minister of

---

6   *Ibid.*
7   The Roman Catholic Church still firmly believes and teaches the doctrines of indulgences and purgatory, although seeking to do away with various abuses of the past and deemphasizing them in post-Vatican II catechisms.
8   Other differences involved the nature of the eternal fire of hell and the condition of sinners before the final judgment. In the past the Roman Catholic Church has insisted that the fires of hell are literal, something rejected by the Orthodox. The Church of Rome teaches that those who die in mortal sin go to hell immediately after death. In contrast, the Orthodox have always held that before the final judgment neither the righteous nor the sinners experience the final state of heaven and hell but rather a foretaste of one or the other.

the Redemption, authoritatively dispenses and applies the treasury of the satisfaction won by Christ and the Saints.[9]

There are three important elements of this teaching that caused objection and consternation in the Reformers:

» purgatory
» indulgences
» the treasury of merits or satisfactions.

Let's define these so we can understand the lens through which the West came to view salvation.

Purgatory is defined as a place where the departed faithful go for purification from the temporal punishment due to sin, prior to entering heaven. It is distinguished from hell primarily in that those there do not despair of their ultimate salvation. Temporal punishment is an automatic consequence of all sin, a kind of residue in need of purification, that must be atoned for before entering heaven. It can be likened to a debt owed to God that must be paid in this life by the penitent. Temporal punishment remains even after guilt has been forgiven. According to the teaching, grave or mortal sins create a guilt that demands eternal punishment unless forgiven and absolved through confession (although temporal punishment remains). Smaller or venial sins demand only a temporal punishment that must be purified either on Earth, through works of repentance or indulgences, or after death, in purgatory.

An *indulgence* is a remission of temporal punishment granted by the Church for various penances—good works, acts of self-denial, or piety. Thus an indulgence removes the temporal

---

9   Liguori Publications and Libreria Editrice Vaticana, *Catechism of the Catholic Church* (Liguori, MO: Liguori Publications, 1994), p. 370.

punishment, either in total (a plenary indulgence) or in part (a partial indulgence), eliminating or lessening the time a person must spend in purgatory. Indulgences can be acquired for oneself or for a departed loved one.

The third component is the *treasury of satisfactions* or merits. It is a sort of spiritual bank account in which are deposited the infinite merits of Jesus Christ and the superabundant merits of the saints. The merits of Christ consist of the satisfaction He made for sin on the Cross, which is unlimited, whereas those of the saints consist of their good works and virtues over and above what was needed for their own salvation. This treasury belongs to the Church (of Rome) by virtue of the pope's role as successor to St. Peter and is dispensed by him and those he delegates in the form of indulgences for the benefit of the faithful.

At the time of the Reformation, it seems a whole indulgence industry had arisen, with the buying and selling of indulgences dispensed by the pope in the form of certificates. Sometimes clerics sold papal indulgences at inflated prices or sold forgeries for personal gain. Others collected donations, ostensibly for charity, in return for indulgences, but instead of passing the proceeds to the poor, they kept them for themselves.

The practice of indulgences and the idea of earning or buying and selling salvation led Martin Luther and others to embrace a new doctrine that rejected any human contribution to salvation. Over and against the Roman view, the Protestants embraced the teaching of salvation by grace alone.

GUILT AND PUNISHMENT

At first glance, the Roman Catholic and Protestant views seem to be at opposite ends of the spectrum. Yet a deeper look shows the two positions are based on a similar foundation. Both look at sin and forgiveness through a legal prism of crime and punishment. As former members of the Church of Rome, the Reformers also viewed the primary problem of sin as guilt. Guilt implies the need for payment or punishment (satisfaction). Salvation, then, is a matter of obtaining release from guilt and the inevitable punishment associated with it, assuming one makes satisfaction for sin.

For Rome, release from punishment for sin in this life is obtained by carrying out penances or, if one fails to make full satisfaction through penance, with indulgences. Salvation is obtained in this life or in the life to come (in purgatory) by being purged through punishment.

Protestants accepted the same premise of punishment and guilt. For them, however, the guilt associated with sin is purged by Christ's sacrifice (i.e., punishment) on the Cross when one comes to belief in Him through faith. Note that punishment for sin is still a prerequisite for forgiveness. The classical Protestant doctrine is that the required punishment was paid in full by Christ on our behalf, thereby releasing us from guilt ("saved by grace," Eph. 2:8) and transferring Christ's righteousness to us regardless of (or even despite) our personal sinfulness (the doctrine of justification by faith; see Chapter 4).

The Orthodox Approach to Salvation

The Orthodox Christian approach to salvation is in stark contrast to the Western approach. While there is some guilt associated with sins, guilt is not the real problem; nor is punishment the solution. Christ did not come to save us from guilt but from sin and death.

In Orthodoxy, sin is not understood as a crime necessitating punishment but as an illness in need of cure. Man sins because his nature has been corrupted and needs to be healed and renewed, brought into union with incorruption. It is death and the fear of death that has held man in bondage (Heb. 2:15), not guilt.[10] And death can only be overcome by Life, that is, Jesus Christ.

Jesus, the God-Man, became incarnate to restore human nature to the likeness of God; He was crucified to destroy the power of sin; and He was raised to fill our nature with divine grace, God's divine energies, giving us power to overcome death. As we saw in Chapter 2, we are indeed saved by grace. Salvation is the condition of being united to the Savior by grace, that is, by receiving the uncreated grace and energies of God. As we will see in the next chapter, *justification* is the condition

---

10   Following the teaching of St. John Chrysostom, Fr. John Romanides writes, "Through the power of death and the devil, sin that reigns in man gives rise to fear and anxiety and to the general instinct of self-preservation and survival. Thus, Satan manipulates man's fear and his desire for self-satisfaction, raising up sin in him, in other words, transgression against the divine will regarding unselfish love, and provoking man to stray from his original destiny. Since weakness is caused in the flesh by death, Satan moves man to countless passions and leads him to devious thoughts, actions, and selfish relations with God as well as with his fellow man. Sin reigns both in death and in the mortal body because 'the sting of death is sin.'" (*The Ancestral Sin*, Ridgewood, NJ: Zephyr Publishing, 2002, p. 162.)

of faith that opens us to God's uncreated grace and thus intro-
duces us to the life of salvation.

For the Orthodox, salvation is not a mere one-time event but
a whole way of life that places us within the rays of God's saving
grace. Salvation has a beginning, which includes a confession of
faith in Jesus Christ as God and Savior, followed by Christian
baptism and chrismation. But salvation is also a lifelong process by which we incorporate Christ's life as our own, so that we
might be found spiritually in the same place as the Apostle Paul,
who, toward the end of his life, said, "it is no longer I who live,
but Christ lives in me" (Gal. 2:20).

While personal faith is always essential, one is saved in cooperation with the action of the Church: "On the first day we make
them Christians; on the second catechumens; on the third, we
exorcise them . . . instruct them . . . and then we baptize them."[11]
As the Body of Christ, the Church extends God's grace to the
world through the Holy Spirit. The Church facilitates and pre-
pares the soil of the heart of one who desires salvation. She then
immerses that soul in the life of salvation in God's Church,
Christ's Body.

In baptism we are joined to Christ (Gal. 3:27); we personally participate in His death and Resurrection (Rom. 6:3–5)
and are therefore "born again" (or "born from above," John
3:3). However, just as a newborn baby must be nourished and
grow in strength and character, the newly baptized must grow
in faith and continue to walk in the light of salvation (Eph. 5:8;
1 John 1:7).

For Orthodox Christians, salvation is not just a ticket to

---

11   Canon Eight of the Second Ecumenical Council, as quoted in *Entering the
Orthodox Church*, p. 20.

heaven after death; it is participation in the life of God *now* in this life, as well as a never-ending and ever-increasing participation in the life to come. Salvation is not merely a mental or cognitive acceptance or belief in Christ; it is an organic reality of communion with God through Christ by the acquisition of God's Spirit (or "grace").

The Orthodox do not believe and have never believed that we are saved by works. We believe in accordance with the Scriptures that we are saved by grace through faith (Eph. 2:8). However, the Orthodox know grace to be the real presence, power, and energies of God, freely given by Him to those who in faith have opened themselves to Him by their free will. God's grace is not imposed on anyone.

Grace is not merely a juridical release from guilt but a real participation in the life of God Himself. This entrance of grace into the human fabric was made possible when Jesus Christ joined His divine nature with our human nature, trampled down death by His death, and raised our human nature, now glorified and filled with grace, to the life of the Trinity through His Resurrection, Ascension, and sitting at the right hand of God.

We are saved by grace—by acquiring and abiding in this grace. According to the teaching of the Scriptures, the early Church, and the Orthodox Church today, salvation is the consequence of acquiring grace, which brings us into union with God. The Protestant understanding tends to make salvation a mere idea or concept, whereas the Orthodox teach that salvation is a real participation in God Himself.

God's grace is available and active through a life of authentic repentance, which means bearing one's cross and embracing ascetical self-denial. Grace is nurtured and deepened through partaking in the sacramental life and especially the Holy Eucharist, through the Church's services of prayer, through the reading and hearing of the Scriptures, and by obedience to His commandments, which include good works (Eph. 2:10).

However, His grace is never given automatically, nor does the Church dispense it in some mechanistic way. It is always given freely as a gift according to God's personal will. We can never earn it, but we can place ourselves in a position to receive the gift more readily: "Behold I stand at the door and knock. If anyone hears My voice and opens the door, I will come in to him and dine with him, and he with Me" (Rev. 3:20). By revelation we know that He gives in accordance with our faith in Him and love for Him, which is also manifested in love for our neighbor.

Again we agree with evangelicals that we are saved by grace through faith. However, for the Orthodox, faith is not mere cognitive belief in Christ, but "*life in* Christ" (Rom. 8:2). We live within this faith through the life of the Church, which is Christ's Body (Rom. 7:4; 1 Cor. 12:27), and by appropriating the faith of Christ into our lives. Baptism and Eucharist are not "works" but acts of faith and blessings of God's grace bestowed freely upon us by God through His Church. No one is baptized by his own work; God baptizes.[12] The same is true for all the Sacraments of the Church—God feeds us with the Body and Blood of His Son, God ordains to the priesthood, God forgives in Confession, God heals in Holy Unction, and so forth.

---

12   In Orthodox Christian baptism the priest does not say "I baptize you" but "The servant of God is baptized." The formula is important, since it reveals the understanding that it is God who is acting and doing the baptizing.

The Eastern Orthodox Church has never taught that the image of God in man was obliterated through Adam's sin. The Church Fathers taught that the image was "darkened" and that the God-given powers of the soul became misdirected and distorted. The consequences of the Fall included that man was inclined to sin, but he is by no means incapable of good. Even in fallen man, sin is not a necessity.

Yet, after the Fall, man could not be saved through his own efforts, no matter how righteous, since "death reigned from Adam to Moses, even over those who had *not* sinned according to the likeness of the transgression of Adam" (Rom. 5:14). It was necessary that man's nature be regenerated by the Incarnation of Christ, that sin be overcome by His death, and that death itself be defeated and transformed by His glorious Resurrection. Our human nature needed to be healed and opened again to the deifying rays of His grace.

SALVATION IS SYNERGY

We also understand salvation to be synergistic—it requires participation by God and man. This is not a just a fifty–fifty proposition but requires one hundred percent from God and one hundred percent from man. God plays the primary part by making it possible for man to be saved through His work of redemption and by His unending love and mercy. And God continually seeks man's salvation, awaiting his return like the father in the parable of the prodigal son. But man has an essential part as well, the part of cooperation and incorporation, since God has given free will to His creatures. God does not predestine anyone to salvation or condemnation; rather, He "desires all men to be saved and to come to the knowledge of the truth" (1 Tim. 2:4).

The Church has characterized the process of salvation in various ways. One of the most common models of what salvation is has been expressed as a progression in three "stages":

» purification
» illumination, and
» sanctification (deification or theosis).

Purification of the heart, we are taught, is the first and most difficult stage of repentance whereby we seek to uproot every sinful passion from the heart so that the grace of God can do the work of transformation and healing. This is the very practical, daily effort to deny ourselves, to bear our cross while trusting in God, to keep Christ's commandments, and to conform our deeds, words, and thoughts to His will.

In his work, *Indication of the Way to the Kingdom of Heaven*, St. Innocent of Alaska provides a helpful description of self-denial: "To deny oneself means to give up one's bad habits; to root out of the heart all that ties us to the world; not to cherish bad thoughts or desires; to suppress every evil thought; not to desire to do anything out of self-love, but to do everything out of love for God."[13]

If God's grace is to penetrate and abide in the heart, the heart must be purified from evil desire. When a farmer seeks to plant a seed, he must first till or soften the soil. The same is true in the spiritual life. The saints warn about the dangers awaiting those who claim to understand the things of God but have not "been previously purified in soul and body, or at the very

13 Archbishop Lazar Puhalo, *Innokenty of Alaska: The Life of Saint Innocent of Alaska* (Dewdney, BC: Synaxis Press, 2000), p. 40.

least are being purified."[14] For they often become puffed up by pride rather than filled with grace. St. Maximos the Confessor famously teaches, "Theology without practice is a theology of demons."[15]

In Jesus' parable of the sower and the seed, the heart is the ground and the seed is God's word of grace. A heart that is purified is the "good ground" (Matt. 13:8) that receives and grows the seed of the word of God. Jesus praises those who "hear [receive] the word of God and keep it" (Luke 11:28).

The purification of the heart occurs by God's grace through our obedience to His commandments and our desire to "cast off the works of darkness" (Rom. 13:12) in order to be united to Christ. St. John the Baptist is certainly an example of one whose heart was purified of evil desire and free of fear. The disciples of Christ were being purified in the three years they accompanied Christ in His ministry. Purification of the heart is also the purpose and goal of the period of preparation for baptism, known as the catechumenate.

Without this purification from the influence of the sinful passions, the grace of God cannot fully illumine and sanctify the soul with its light and power. St. Macarius the Great (AD 300–390) provides us with a representative teaching:

> Unless the man who is under the influence of the passions will come to God, denying the world, and will believe with patience and hope . . . such a man will never experience true life . . . the enlightenment of the Spirit will never shine in that benighted

---

14 St. Gregory the Theologian, Or. 27.3, http://www.newadvent.org/fathers/310227.htm.
15 Virginia Fabella, Sergio Torres, ed., *Doing Theology in a Divided World* (Orbis Books 1985), p. 15.

soul . . . and so come to know God of a truth through God's power and the efficacy of grace.[16]

Those who have reached a state of comprehensive purification are also called "dispassionate," as they are no longer disturbed or swayed by passions.[17] In that state, they begin to discern the spiritual reality (essence) of created things and enjoy enduring communion with God.

A heart that is purified can then be illumined fully by God's grace. This condition of spiritual illumination is the second stage of the Christian life. To be purified and illumined means that the heart is able to know and to see the Truth. "Blessed *are* the pure in heart, / For they shall see God" (Matt. 5:8). The Church Fathers teach that Adam and Eve were created in the spiritual condition of illumination. Therefore, Adam knew the names of the animals and was able to discern that Eve was "bone of my bones and flesh of my flesh" (Gen. 2:23), though he was asleep when God formed her. When one is fully illumined by God's grace, he has continual converse with God and continual prayer in his heart.

The stage of spiritual "perfection" (Matt. 5:48; Eph. 4:13) is called deification or theosis. This is a spiritual condition of being thoroughly saturated and filled with the Holy Spirit in an abiding way. Such is the state of the saints, who have become vessels of divine grace, exhibiting various spiritual gifts and miraculous

---

16 *Fifty Spiritual Homilies,* Homily 24 trans. Prof. Ivan Michailovich Kontzevich (Willits, CA: Eastern Orthodox Books, 1974), 1976–7.

17 St. Mark the Ascetic: "He who hates the passions gets rid of their causes. But he who is attracted by their causes is attacked by the passions even though he does not wish it." (*Philokalia,* "On Those Who Think They are Made Righteous by Works: Two Hundred and Twenty-Six Texts," p. 135)

works, fulfilling the words of the Lord: "Most assuredly, I say to you, he who believes in Me, the works that I do he will do also; and greater *works* than these he will do, because I go to My Father" (John 14:12). On the Day of Pentecost, the apostles and disciples received this level of sanctification (Acts 2:1), having been prepared and purified by their time with the Lord.

GRACE OR WORKS?

Then what about works? Is there a connection between grace and works? Imagine someone confided to you the whereabouts of a buried treasure. First you secretly travel to the designated location, perhaps across the world. Next you use a pick and shovel to dig up the treasure chest. Finally you break the lock and at last open the chest full of gold and precious stones. Now you are rich! But are you rich from traveling? Or was it digging that made you wealthy? Of course not! You are now rich beyond your wildest dreams because you possess the treasure.

Grace is analogous to the treasure; obedience to God's commandments and good works are the traveling and the digging. The latter were a means to acquire the chest, but it is the treasure alone that makes one rich. This does not mean we demean the necessity of the work you put in. The traveling and the digging, with all the energy they required, put you in the position to receive that wealth. And fasting, prayer, humility, and sacrificial love open the heart to receive God's treasure of grace.

Yes, it is true that one may travel or dig for the sake of traveling and digging, without any desire for finding a treasure. And I may also pray and fast and do good works as ends in themselves or, worse, out of selfishness or pride, and not out of a desire to receive the great treasure of the grace of God. But we can't throw away our pick and shovel just because some people use them incorrectly. Who are we to judge, anyway?

Both the Lord and His apostles teach the necessity of good works and keeping the commandments of God: "If you love Me, keep My commandments" (John 14:15).[18] And these are not just nice spiritual decorations to go with an already obtained and completed salvation. Rather, it is in doing the commandments of Christ that we discover and possess His grace. The good works done in obedience to God and for the sake of Christ open us to and attract to us God's saving grace. They contribute to our salvation inasmuch as they fill us with the wealth and treasure of the Holy Spirit. As the great, Spirit-filled eighteenth-century Russian saint Seraphim of Sarov summarized so succinctly, "The true aim of our Christian life consists in the acquisition of the Holy Spirit of God."[19]

And if we read his teaching in context, we see that the means (or tools) of acquiring the Holy Spirit are "indispensable means":

> Prayer, fasting, vigil and all other Christian practices, however good they may be in themselves, do not constitute the aim of our Christian life, although they serve as the indispensable means of reaching this end. The true aim of our Christian life consists in the acquisition of the Holy Spirit of God. As for fasts, and vigils, and prayer, and almsgiving, and every good deed done for Christ's sake, they are only means of acquiring

18 The passages are too numerous to quote, but we refer to a few here: Matt. 5:16; Acts 9:36; Rom. 2:9–11; 1 Tim. 5:9–10.

19 Helen Kontzevitch, *St. Seraphim, Wonderworker of Sarov and His Spiritual Inheritance,* trans. St. Xenia Skete (Wildwood, CA: St. Xenia Skete, 2004), p. 117.

the Holy Spirit of God. Mark my words, only good deeds done for Christ's sake bring us the fruits of the Holy Spirit. All that is not done for Christ's sake, even though it be good, brings neither reward in the future life nor the grace of God in this life.[20]

CLARIFICATIONS

Like the Roman Catholics, the Orthodox also generally hold that no one can enter into the Kingdom of God on the last day without purification from sin, for nothing impure can enter the Kingdom of heaven (Rev. 21:27). We agree as well that sins can be forgiven after death if the departed was already repenting and striving to be purified during his lifetime, as implied by the Lord's words in Matt. 12:32, "but whoever speaks against the Holy Spirit, it will not be forgiven him, either in this age *or in the age to come*" (italics added). However, neither the Holy Scriptures nor the Church Fathers conceive of a place where sins are burned away after death by fire. Rather, purification of the soul after death can only occur through the prayers of the Church (especially those offered at the Eucharist), by acts of charity done as an offering for the departed, and ultimately only by the mercy and goodness of God. As regards punishment, there is either forgiveness or punishment, not both.[21]

In Orthodoxy, penances are also given, not due to some necessity for punishment of sin, but as a medicine to heal the soul: to correct sinful behavior, to purify the heart from pas-

---

20 *Ibid.*, pp. 116–7.
21 As stated by the Orthodox contingent at the Council of Florence in the fifteenth century.

sions, to encourage sincere repentance and healing in the penitent, and with the help of God's grace to produce "fruits worthy
of repentance" (Matt. 3:8). Therefore, the purpose of a penance
is exactly in line with the goal of the Christian life—to open the
heart to the grace of God.

In our day, many evangelicals may be unaware of the specific
Roman Catholic doctrines or abuses that shaped the Protestant
theology of salvation. While for Luther and Calvin the understanding of salvation included participation in the Sacraments
of Baptism and Eucharist along with a faith that actively obeys
the gospel commandments, for evangelicals today salvation has
generally come to mean the mere acceptance of Jesus as one's
personal Savior. Salvation tends to be reduced to the idea of
going to heaven after death. This salvation is typically unrelated
to and not dependent upon the Church or membership therein.
Salvation is no longer understood as being actualized in and
through the Church but is understood as something that occurs
through an individual (i.e., private) decision of faith. Generally
salvation is seen as a singular and static event with a specific
date and time. Once forgiveness is received, one is "saved," but it
is not always clear how one receives forgiveness for future sins.
Church sacraments and ongoing repentance and purification
of the heart by ascetical means are usually nonexistent or seen
as an afterthought and irrelevant to the perceived acquisition
of eternal salvation. For this reason, one may choose most any
church group, since the church is not directly involved in affect-
ing salvation except in a highly subjective way, inasmuch as it
supplements and encourages the believer's faith. The important
thing is one's personal relationship with Christ. This acceptance

of Christ as Savior is understood to cleanse one of his or her sins and to make one eligible for heaven. Protestant denominations hold varying views on the importance of holiness, living a Christian way of life, and whether one can lose one's salvation.

Among evangelicals there is a great fear of anything that smacks of salvation by works. While St. Paul declares that we are not saved by "works of the law," evangelicals do not usually make a distinction between works of the law and "good works," which St. Paul commands (e.g., Eph. 2:10; 1 Tim. 6:18; Titus 1:16). In the evangelical lexicon, "works" often means any effort or anything done to contribute to one's salvation. This idea has progressed to the point that baptism itself is often considered a "work" and is thus rejected by some as normative to salvation. Baptism is understood only as an outward sign and symbol of a real transformation that has already occurred inwardly. The ascetical disciplines (fasting, prayer rules, etc.) and liturgical practices (anointing with oil, confession with a priest, etc.) present in the Church from the beginning are also perceived as works-based. Because of this perspective, Orthodox Christians are typically lumped together with Roman Catholics as believing in salvation by works.

These attitudes were also nurtured by the Reformers' view of human nature. Both Luther and Calvin believed that the image of God in man was destroyed through Adam's fall into sin. They therefore hold that man can do nothing good and that it is impossible for him not to sin. This contributes to a tendency for Protestants to believe there is nothing we can do to contribute to our salvation. Of course this is not consistent with their own teaching, which insists that one do or not do certain things—for example, consistently read the Bible and spend time in prayer, not curse or get drunk, not smoke cigarettes, and so forth.

Some Protestants (mostly certain Baptists) believe in what has been termed "once saved, always saved." This is the idea that once one has accepted Jesus, one cannot lose salvation regardless of what sins one commits. However, many biblical passages attest to the teaching that one can fall away from salvation after initially embracing the Christian faith (e.g., Heb. 6:4–6).

Those who persist strictly in the tradition of John Calvin[22] believe in double predestination, the idea that before the foundation of the world God predestined some for heaven and others for hell. In this view, every person is equally unworthy of salvation, and therefore salvation is extended simply by God's decision to have mercy on some and not on others. This predetermined destiny cannot be changed by anything one does, good or bad. It hinges on the position that, due to the fall of Adam, each person's will is in bondage to evil, and man is therefore not even capable of making a decision to trust in God. Such a decision (unless instigated by grace) would fall into the category of a "work" and would not be salvation by grace. God must first free a person from his enslavement to sin in order that he may trust in God and thus find salvation. In other words, God must first call man to salvation before man can respond in any way toward God. Once a person is called, Calvinists believe, God's grace is irresistible; thus the one called cannot reject his calling. This system is highly developed and has what we might

---

22 Today, very few Protestants are strict Calvinists. Those who hold to the more extreme and complete teachings of Calvin are often referred to as "hyper-Calvinists." Calvin developed his teaching from the idea of St. Augustine that God predestines some for heaven.

call loopholes that attempt to maintain its consistency and inner logic. For example, someone who renounces Christ after having believed in Him is viewed as having never truly been called or predestined by God to salvation.

As mentioned above, the Protestant conception of salvation is influenced by developments in Roman Catholic theology after the Great Schism. These developments make salvation an issue of legal release from guilt or original sin rather than an organic union with God through Christ and the Holy Spirit. Specifically, a new view of the atonement was accepted in the West. This satisfaction theory says that man's sin against God is a crime that offends and dishonors Him and for which an equal satisfaction must be made (paid). However, since God is infinite, no mere man can make this satisfaction. Therefore, God sends His Son to become Man and to be crucified. In this way God's sense of justice is satisfied, and He can then forgive mankind through Christ. The Roman view (Anselm's satisfaction theory of atonement) was developed further by John Calvin, who stated punishment is required in order to make satisfaction. In this view, Christ is punished in our place on the Cross, thereby satisfying God's wrath (anger) toward mankind.

THE HOLY SCRIPTURES ON SALVATION

Salvation is a continuum and way of life

1 Cor. 1:18: For the message of the cross is foolishness to those who are perishing, but to us who are being saved it is the power of God.

2 Cor. 2:15: For we are to God the fragrance of Christ among those who are being saved and among those who are perishing.

Phil. 3:12: Not that I have already attained, or am already perfected.

1 Tim. 4:16: Take heed to yourself and to the doctrine. Continue in them, for in doing this you will save both yourself and those who hear you.

Words are not enough

Matt. 7:21: "Not everyone who says to me, 'Lord, Lord,' shall enter the kingdom of heaven, but he who does the will of My Father in heaven."

Titus 1:16: They profess to know God, but in works they deny *Him*, being abominable, disobedient, and disqualified for every good work.

Salvation can be lost

1 Cor. 15:1–2: Moreover, brethren, I declare to you the gospel which I preached to you, which also you received and in which you stand, by which also you are saved, if you hold fast that word which I preached to you—unless you believed in vain.

2 Pet. 2:20–22: For if, after they have escaped the pollutions of the world through the knowledge of the Lord and Savior Jesus Christ, they are again entangled in them and overcome, the latter end is worse for them than the beginning. For it would have been better for them not to have known the way of righteousness, than having known *it*, to turn from the holy commandment delivered to them. But it has happened to them according to the true proverb: "A dog returns to his own vomit," and, "a sow, having washed, to her wallowing in the mire."

1 Cor. 15:1: Moreover, brethren, I declare to you the gospel which I preached to you, which also you received and in which you stand, by which also you are saved, if you hold fast that word which I preached to you—unless you believed in vain.

Heb. 2:1–3: Therefore we must give the more earnest heed to the things we have heard, lest we drift away. For if the word spoken through angels proved steadfast, and every transgression and disobedience received a just reward, how shall we escape if we neglect so great a salvation, which at the first began to be spoken by the Lord, and was confirmed to us by those who heard *Him*.

Heb. 12:14–15: Pursue peace with all *people*, and holiness, without which no one will see the Lord: looking carefully lest anyone fall short of the grace of God.

Baptism saves

Mark 16:16: He who believes and is baptized will be saved; but he who does not believe will be condemned.

1 Pet. 3:21a: There is also an antitype which now saves us—baptism.

Titus 3:5: not by works of righteousness which we have done, but according to His mercy He saved us, through the washing of regeneration and renewing of the Holy Spirit.

Humility more important than certainty of one's salvation

1 Tim. 1:15: Christ Jesus came into the world to save sinners, of whom I am chief.

God judges according to our works

1 Cor. 3:8: Now he who plants and he who waters are one, and each one shall receive his own reward according to his own labor.

2 Cor. 5:10: For we must all appear before the judgment seat of Christ, that each one may receive the things *done* in the body, according to what he has done, whether good or bad.

Gal. 5:6: Faith working through love.

Importance of good works in the life of salvation

Matt. 7:15-20: Beware of false prophets, who come to you in sheep's clothing, but inwardly they are ravenous wolves. You will know them by their fruits. Do men gather grapes from thornbushes or figs from thistles? Even so, every good tree bears good fruit, but a bad tree bears bad fruit. A good tree cannot bear bad fruit, nor *can* a bad tree bear good fruit. Every tree that does not bear good fruit is cut down and thrown into the fire. Therefore by their fruits you will know them.

Matt. 16:27: "For the Son of man will come in the glory of His Father with His angels, and then he will reward each according to his works."

John 8:39: They answered and said to him, "Abraham is our father." Jesus said to them, "If you were Abraham's children, you would do the works of Abraham."

1 Tim. 6:18: *Let them* do good, that they be rich in good works, ready to give, willing to share.

2 Tim. 3:17: That the man of God may be complete, thoroughly equipped for every good work.

Titus 1:16: They profess to know God, but in works they deny *Him*, being abominable, disobedient, and disqualified for every good work.

Titus 2:7: In all things showing yourself *to be* a pattern of good works; in doctrine *showing* integrity, reverence, incorruptibility.

Titus 2:14: Who gave Himself for us, that He might redeem us from every lawless deed and purify for Himself *His* own special people, zealous for good works.

Titus 3:8: This is a faithful saying, and these things I want you to affirm constantly, that those who have believed in God should be careful to maintain good works. These things are good and profitable to men.

Titus 3:14: And let our *people* also learn to maintain good works, to *meet* urgent needs, that they may not be unfruitful.

Heb. 10:24: And let us consider one another in order to stir up love and good works.

James 2:17: Thus also faith by itself, if it does not have works, is dead.

James 2:18: But someone will say, "You have faith, and I have works." Show me your faith without your works, and I will show you my faith by my works.

James 2:20: But do you want to know, O foolish man, that faith without works is dead?

James 2:21: Was not Abraham our father justified by works when he offered Isaac his son on the altar?

James 2:22: Do you see that faith was working together with his works, and by works faith was made perfect?

James 2:24: You see then that a man is justified by works, and not by faith only.

James 3:13: Who *is* wise and understanding among you? Let him show by good conduct *that* his works *are done* in the meekness of wisdom.

1 Pet. 2:12: . . . having your conduct honorable among the Gentiles, that when they speak against you as evildoers, they may, by *your* good works which they observe, glorify God in the day of visitation.

For patristic quotations regarding salvation, see Chapter 4, "Justification by Faith."

QUESTIONS AND ANSWERS
ON SALVATION

Q: What about the thief crucified on the right side of the Lord? He did no good works, nor did he go through a process in order to be saved, but he was saved instantly by the Lord's grace.

A: It is true, the Lord always saves by grace, both in the case of the thief and in all other cases, even though a person lives to be 120 and lives a righteous life through faith. Although good works can bring God's grace to us, we are never saved *by* the works but by the Lord. There is no good work that can make us worthy of salvation; it is always a gift of God, and it is His gift alone to bestow. The thief on the right came to true faith in Jesus as God, and thus Christ was moved to bestow the gift of salvation upon him whose heart had now become capable of union with Him. If the thief had somehow survived crucifixion, he would have needed to be baptized into the Church and would have had to maintain the life of faith and repentance and continue walking on the path of salvation if he hoped to be saved. In this case, his works would be consistent with his faith and would make it possible for him to remain in God's grace and be saved.

Q: When asked directly how one is saved, the apostle answered, "If you confess with your mouth the Lord Jesus and believe in your heart that God has raised Him from the dead, you will be saved" (Rom. 10:9). Therefore, does not salvation require only heartfelt belief and confession of Jesus as the Lord?

A: Indeed, true faith requires belief in Jesus Christ as Savior and God and a sincere confession of faith in His death and Resurrection. But the question then is, what does that imply, and what does that faith demand from a person? In this case it was not the apostle's intention to give a lecture on the whole life of salvation, but to emphasize that salvation comes through faith in Christ and not by anyone or anything else. The criterion St. Paul mentions is a brief summary of how one came to be baptized and became a member of the Church, thus entering into the life of salvation, the life of grace. But salvation is not a matter of mere mental belief, for "even the demons believe" (James 2:19). Rather, faith that is unto salvation implies a whole way of life by which one lives within the grace of God. This life of grace is experienced in the Church, which is "the fullness of Him who fills all in all" (Eph. 1:23). And according to the Scriptures, it is not merely faith in Christ, but the faith *of* Christ. The Apostle Peter, when asked a similar question to the one above asked of St. Paul, answered, "Repent, and let every one of you be baptized in the name of Jesus Christ for the remission of sins; and you shall receive the gift of the Holy Spirit" (Acts 2:38). Those who were baptized were then joined to the community of faith and the way of the life of grace in the Church.

Q: But aren't we saved by our faith? Wasn't Martin Luther right when he focused on faith instead of works regarding salvation?

A: According to the Scriptures, we are saved neither by works nor by faith but always by grace, by God's mercy. As the Apostle Paul writes to Titus (3:5), "not by works of righteousness which we have done, *but according to His mercy He saved us*, through the washing of regeneration and renewing of the Holy Spirit" (emphasis added). We are not saved by our own faith; otherwise salvation would again be based on our doing. Rather, we are saved by God's doing when by His mercy He joins us to Himself by His grace. This alone makes us worthy of salvation. Yet faith must be present in order for grace to come. We are saved by grace *through* faith. Faith in the biblical sense is not only an individualistic belief in Christ but the adoption of the whole reality of the faith of Christ, which normally includes the Church's baptism. Baptism (like every sacrament) is not something *we do* but something *God does to us* through the Church. When we confess Christ and approach the Church for baptism, this is an act of faith as well as our personal entrance into Christ's faith. Therefore, the apostle teaches that we are saved by baptism through faith: "He saved us, through the washing of regeneration [baptism] and renewing of the Holy Spirit [gift of the Spirit, or chrismation]."

Q: But isn't it essential that we say salvation comes by faith *alone* so that we are not led to believe we are saved by works?

A: The Bible never uses the words "faith alone" except to say that we are *not* saved by faith alone. In the Epistle of James (2:24) we read, "You see then that a man is justified by works, and not by faith only." There is no other record in the Scriptures that suggests we are saved by faith *alone*.

CHAPTER 4

Justification by Faith

Therefore we conclude that a man is justified by faith apart from the deeds of the law. (Rom. 3:28)

Coming out of the waters of baptism, Cornelius and his family hear these words from the Apostle Peter: "You are washed, you are sanctified, you are justified" (see 1 Cor. 6:11).[1] In this way the apostle affirms that through belief and baptism their hearts have been reoriented to receive the divine grace that is in Jesus Christ through the Holy Spirit.

This repositioning or reordering has occurred by "divine power" (2 Pet. 1:3), not by a simple declaration or contractual arrangement. It is something that has truly happened and is happening in them. They have become "new creations" (2 Cor. 5:17; Gal. 6:15), "partakers of the divine nature" (2 Pet. 1:4). The fallen humanity they inherited from Adam, the "old man," has been regenerated and renewed by being joined to the resurrected humanity of Christ, the New Adam.

Cornelius remembers the holy Peter expounding on the meaning of their baptism: They are now washed, he taught, inasmuch as they have died to sin with Christ, "having escaped

---

1   From the Orthodox baptismal service.

the corruption *that is* in the world through lust" (2 Pet. 1:4); they are sanctified also, "in sanctification of the Spirit" (1 Pet. 1:2), "begotten again to a living hope through the resurrection of Jesus Christ from the dead, to an inheritance incorruptible and undefiled" (1 Pet. 1:3-4); and they are justified by the faith of Jesus, "redeemed . . . with the precious blood of Christ" (1 Pet. 1:18-19), having their hearts opened to receive the life-giving rays of God's grace. Thus the newly baptized have been "justified freely by His grace through the redemption that is in Christ Jesus" (Rom. 3:24).

He reminded them that this life of faith that justifies is a whole way of living, a life of faith that opens them to "all things that *pertain* to life and godliness" (2 Pet. 1:3). It is manifested and nurtured by continually walking in the Spirit, putting to death all works of the flesh, and striving to acquire the fruits of the Spirit (Gal. 5:16-26). To faith must be added "virtue, to virtue knowledge, to knowledge self-control, to self-control perseverance, to perseverance godliness, to godliness brotherly kindness, and to brotherly kindness love" (2 Pet. 1:5-7).

Fulfilling the prescriptions of the law does not justify, but the way of faith is manifested in obedience to God's commandments. For "circumcision is nothing and uncircumcision is nothing, but keeping the commandments of God *is what matters*" (1 Cor. 7:19).

Cornelius reflects that he and his fellow Gentiles, "who are called Uncircumcision" (Eph. 2:11), have received a "circumcision of the heart" (Rom. 2:29), a "circumcision made without hands, by putting off the body of the sins of the flesh, by the circumcision of Christ, buried with Him in baptism" (Col. 2:11-12). They have been justified by faith, not by their own power, but by the faith and power of Jesus Christ.

Introduction

"Justified by faith" (Rom. 3:28, 5:1) is a phrase used by the Apostle Paul to express the radical contrast between the limited purpose and power of the Old Testament Law, which could not save man, and the saving work accomplished by God in the New Covenant. While the Law was good, it was only a "tutor" (Gal. 3:24–25), a guide to help man align himself morally with God and to prepare him for something greater (Gal. 3:23). The Law was *external* to man's being and could not transfigure him from the inside out; nor could it destroy the ultimate enemy, death, which resided as an invader within the human condition since the time of Adam's sin.

Yet the good news preached by St. Paul and the other apostles is that God re-created man from the inside out through the Incarnation of His Son, destroying the power of sin on the Cross and overcoming death on behalf of the whole human race by His glorious Resurrection. Christ has become the "New Adam," the father of a renewed humanity[2] that is joined to God and filled with His Spirit. Those who by faith are "baptized into Christ" and have "put on" (Gal. 3:27) the glorified humanity of the resurrected Christ are reborn in the image of the New Adam and thus become "sons of God" (Gal. 3:26). This rebirth is an organic, internal transformation expressed by the Old Testament prophets as the reception of a "new heart":

---

2   For this reason the Messiah (God's Son) is called "Everlasting Father" or "Father of the age to come," in Isaiah's prophecy: "For unto us a Child is born, / Unto us a Son is given; / And the government will be upon His shoulder. / And His name will be called Wonderful, Counselor, Mighty God, Everlasting Father, Prince of Peace" (Is. 9:6). Jesus is the "father" of a renewed human race.

"I will give you a new heart and put a new spirit within you; I will take the heart of stone out of your flesh and give you a heart of flesh" (Ezek. 36:26).

"I will put My law in their minds, and write it on their hearts" (Jer. 31:33).

St. Paul connects his discourse on justification by faith directly to baptism. For after admonishing the "foolish" Galatians that a man is not justified by works of the law (i.e., circumcision) but by faith, he reminds them of exactly *how* they were justified by faith.

> For you are all sons of God through faith in Christ Jesus. For as many of you as were baptized into Christ have put on Christ. (Gal. 3:27)

Through faith, baptism has bestowed upon them the new humanity of Christ, and so,

> There is neither Jew nor Greek, there is neither slave nor free, there is neither male nor female; for you are all one in Christ Jesus. And if you *are* Christ's, then you are Abraham's seed, and heirs according to the promise. (Gal. 3:28–29)

To this day, after baptism a new member of the Orthodox Church hears the words, "You are justified, you are illumined, you are sanctified, you are washed, in the name of the Father and of the Son and of the Holy Spirit."

St. Paul speaks of baptism as an act of faith.

> In Him you were also circumcised with the circumcision made without hands, by putting off the body of the sins of the flesh, by the circumcision of Christ, buried with Him in baptism, in

which you also were raised with *Him* through faith in the working of God, who raised Him from the dead. (Col. 2:11–12)

Far from a work of the law, baptism is the act of faith par excellence. For the candidate first publicly renounces the devil, confesses Christ as "King and God," recites the faith of the Church in the form of the Nicene Creed as his own personal confession, and then submits in faith to his own spiritual death and rebirth in baptism. His baptism is not his own work, but the work of God Himself at the hands of His ministers: "The servant of God, (*Name*), is baptized [not by the priest but by God] in the name of the Father and of the Son and of the Holy Spirit."

After laying out his rationale for justification by faith and not the works of the law in Romans 3—5, the apostle once again naturally reminds his hearers about the reality of their baptism.

Or do you not know that as many of us as were baptized into Christ Jesus were baptized into His death? Therefore we were buried with Him through baptism into death, that just as Christ was raised from the dead by the glory of the Father, even so we also should walk in newness of life. For if we have been united together in the likeness of His death, certainly we also shall be *in the likeness* of *His* resurrection. (Rom. 6:3–5)

In other words, the Christians in Rome were justified by faith through baptism, by which they died with Him and were raised with Him, being infused with the life of Christ's resurrected and undying humanity.[3] By His Crucifixion, Jesus destroyed the sin and death that had reigned in fallen human nature (Rom.

---

3   So vital to St. Paul's gospel was this preaching of the transforming power of Christ's Resurrection that the Athenians thought he spoke about two distinct deities, Jesus and the Resurrection (Acts 17:18).

5:14). In His Resurrection, Christ deified our human nature by joining it to His divine nature, filling it with His eternal power, grace, and energies.

Unlike the law, this was not an external bandage for the problem of sin and death, but a real, organic change to the human condition initiated within the humanity of the God-Man Himself, Jesus Christ. Therefore, the apostolic preaching is that we can only be reborn and partake of this new life through the faith of the Person of Jesus Christ, by which we are joined organically to God in His Body, the Church.

We are justified then, not by the Law of Moses, but by "the faith *of* Jesus Christ" (Rom. 3:22, 26; Gal. 2:16, 20). This phrase "the faith of Jesus Christ" is mistranslated in most English Bibles as "faith *in* Jesus Christ." Therefore justification results when one is opened to the faith of Jesus Christ—that is, to the whole way of life and grace that is in Him.

The apostle was compelled to clarify this point in his epistles repeatedly (especially to the Romans and Galatians) because of certain Jewish Christians who were teaching that salvation could be obtained through adherence to the law. Against such a teaching, which he understood nullified the good news of Christ's death and Resurrection, he emphasized both the impotence of the law to save fallen man and the reality that in Christ we are "justified by faith" (Rom. 3:28) and saved "by grace . . . through faith" (Eph. 2:8).

Of course, justification by faith is a thoroughly biblical teaching that the Orthodox Church has always affirmed. However, the way the Church understands St. Paul's teaching is in stark contrast to the classical Protestant view. The Orthodox Christian understanding of justification can be found in the liturgical prayers of the Church and the consensus of the Church Fathers from ancient times to the present.

Yet the Fathers never built a systematic theology around justification, nor did they treat it as something isolated from the whole context of the faith as it has been understood and lived out within the Church from earliest times. The historical Church has never known a teaching of "justification by faith *alone*," a sacred slogan of the Protestant Reformation. Indeed, the singular reference to the idea of "faith alone" is the negative one found in the Epistle of Saint James: "You see then that a man is justified by works, and *not by faith only*" (2:24).

The Protestant Doctrine of Justification by Faith Alone

Yet Martin Luther, whose express mission was to get back to the Scriptures,[4] was the first to espouse and define a doctrine of justification by faith alone. As he himself attests, "This one and firm rock, which we call the doctrine of justification, is the chief article of the whole Christian doctrine."[5]

The classical Protestant teaching can be summarized as follows. When a man comes to belief in Jesus Christ, God the Father imputes righteousness to him—that is, credits Christ's righteousness to him. He is declared by God innocent of sin

---

4   Luther's disdain for the Epistle of James is clearly revealed by the name he coined for it, "the epistle of straw." Luther's Works, vol. 35, *Word and Sacrament I* (Philadelphia: Fortress, 1960), p. 362.

5   Selected passages from Martin Luther, *Commentary on Galatians* (1538), trans. Herbert J. A. Bouman, "The Doctrine of Justification in the Lutheran Confessions," Concordia Theological Monthly 26 (November 1955) No. 11:801 (http://en.wikipedia.org/wiki/Sola_fide).

by virtue of Christ's redemptive work and is thus no longer subject to God's wrath or condemned to hell. In this interpretation of St. Paul, justification is simply God's pronouncement that a man is righteous by virtue of his faith in Christ's shed blood.

The Protestant doctrine does not speak of an internal change in man wrought through faith, but only a change in legal status, from guilty to innocent. In point of fact, it explicitly denies any real change:

> Justification is not something that occurs in man, nor is it a process. It refers to the legal, judicial and forensic declaration of God. "It is to declare forensically that the demands of the law as a condition of life are fully satisfied with regard to a person."[6]

This view does not acknowledge the value of man's repentance in relation to his new status. Rather, it refers only to God's declaration. But justification defined in this way is just as external and unrelated to man's true condition as was the Law of Moses. As another proponent defines it,

> Justification is the legal act where God declares the sinner to be innocent of his or her sins. *It is not that the sinner is now sinless,* but that he is "declared" sinless. This declaration of righteousness is being justified before God (emphasis added).[7]

But the doctrine of justification by faith alone directly contradicts the teaching of the early Church Fathers. For instance, St. Justin the Martyr, writing in AD 160, addresses the issue as if

---

6   Brian Schwertley, "Justification by Faith—Part I: Justification by Faith Alone" (http://www.graceonlinelibrary.org/doctrine-theology/justification/justification-by-faith-part-i-justification-by-faith-alone-by-brian-schwertley)

7   Matt Slick, from http://carm.org/verses-showing-justification-by-faith.

he were speaking not to a Jew but to the adherents of classical Protestant tradition.

> "Blessed *is* the man to whom the LORD does not impute sin" (Ps. 32(31):2). That is, having repented of his sins, he can receive remission of them from God. But this is not as you deceive yourselves, and some others who resemble you in this. For they say, that even though they remain sinners, the Lord will not impute sin to them, because they know God.[8]

Considering the above, it should go without saying that Protestants also believe a person's justification is not precipitated by any work or works. No deed or activity of man, even one motivated by faith or expressing faith, plays any role in the doctrine of justification by faith alone. Both the teaching that justification is a mere legal declaration and the idea that it excludes any effort by man are contrary to a true interpretation of Holy Scripture as understood by the early Church Fathers.

As is often the case, this teaching cannot be fully understood or refuted without digging deeper to find what lies underneath it. In fact, it is constructed upon other fundamental theological assumptions that are not in agreement with the Orthodox Christian Tradition. It will be helpful to mention some of these.

TOTAL DEPRAVITY OF MAN

The doctrine of justification by faith alone, as defined by most Protestants, is founded on the theological premise that man is totally depraved.[9] Martin Luther's most picturesque and pungent description of fallen man was nothing better than a "pile of

---

8   Justin the Martyr, *Dialogue with Trypho,* 1.270.
9   The adherents of John Wesley (Methodists) and others in the Arminian tradition are the exception to this rule.

dung." After Adam's sin there is nothing of God left within man that rightly belongs to his nature. As one commentator explains it, "The Doctrine of Total Depravity teaches that there was an *ontological* shift in the nature of humanity as a result of the Fall. According to this view, man is now, by nature, a sinner. In other words, sin is an essential part of what it means to be a human being."[10] As a radio preacher opined recently, "A sinner is not a sinner because he sins; he sins because he is a sinner."

Following this logic, fallen man can do nothing *but* sin, being in a condition without grace. As a sinful creature, he can seek neither God nor His righteousness. Both Martin Luther and John Calvin believed that the image of God in man was not only darkened and distorted, as the Church Fathers teach, but *destroyed* due to the Fall of Adam. The result is that it is impossible for man to cooperate with God for his salvation. As Luther himself is quoted as saying, "It is not in your power to turn to God. If you think that it is in your power to turn to God you have missed the whole Reformation and don't understand total depravity."[11]

With this non-biblical and non-patristic theological premise, the Reformers readily interpreted the biblical, patristic teaching of justification in an unprecedented and unorthodox way. Because Adam and Eve's Fall obliterated the ability of fallen human beings to pursue righteousness, justification (man being made righteous) becomes exclusively the work of God. Even the faith by which man is justified is a gift from God without any contribution from man, for faith is not the cause of justifi-

10 Matthan Brown, "Why I Don't Believe in Total Depravity," *The Christian Watershed* (blog), June 1, 2011 (http://thechristianwatershed. com/2011/06/01/why-i-don't-believe-in-total-depravity)

11 http://www.gospeloutreach.net/total_depravity.html.

cation. As John Calvin explains it, "We say that faith justifies not because it merits justification for us by its own worth, but because it is an instrument by which we freely obtain the righteousness of Christ."[12] Over and against Rome's emphasis on works, the Reformers' teaching stripped man's personal will of any contribution toward faith in God and the reception of His grace. "When a person believes in Jesus Christ, God the Father in the heavenly court declares that that person is righteous solely on the basis of Christ's full satisfaction for sin and perfect obedience to the law."[13]

If this is indeed the case, then anything man might do—even his seeking after God or righteousness—is of no consequence and cannot contribute to his justification. Justification is purely juridical, that is, a declaration of law that a man has become righteous inasmuch as God bestows upon him the righteousness of Christ. This pronouncement of righteousness takes away his previous guilt because Christ has satisfied the penalty due for sin on the Cross. As a grocery clerk once boasted to me about her newfound salvation, "When I believed in Jesus, it's like God put on Jesus-shaped glasses, so He no longer sees my sin; He sees the righteousness of Christ."

GRACELESS AND GUILT-RIDDEN
Another feature that lent support to the Reformation view of justification was one shared by both Protestants and Roman

---

12 Institutes 3,18, 8, cited from http://www.ccel.org/ccel/calvin/institutes.pdf, p. 667.
13 Schwertley, "Justification by Faith—Part I" (http://www.graceonlinelibrary. org/doctrine-theology/justification/justification-by-faith-part-i-justification-by-faith-alone-by-brian-schwertley)

Catholics—that grace is alien to man's nature, something external and foreign to humanity itself. If God's grace is not natural, it must be *super*natural. Then how is it that man is saved by grace? God must somehow override man's natural condition and impose or superimpose grace onto him in order to save him. This essentially makes God Himself foreign to human nature.

In this view, man is by nature a hopelessly graceless and guilt-ridden being whose salvation comes when God superimposes a legal pronouncement of justification. God essentially throws a blanket over the believer so that his sin can no longer be seen (by God, who sees all!). Such a view represents a radical departure from the content and spirit found in the teachings of the Church Fathers.

Using this frame of reference, various perspectives were formed in the West to explain how man could be saved. The Roman Catholic view focused on the washing away of original sin (i.e., the guilt of Adam) by baptism. In this way, both man's guilt and God's condemnation were eliminated. Freed of the guilt that previously condemned him, man could participate in a life of supernatural grace dispensed in the sacraments.

In the theology of John Calvin, man's gracelessness and inability to personally will and cooperate with grace was resolved by the doctrine of double predestination. In this view, God singularly and arbitrarily chooses who will or will not be saved. Each human being is predestined to heaven or hell even before God created the world. The human person and his will have no say in the matter.

Either way, we are saved from guilt, not from sin. And the removal of guilt becomes the point of concern for salvation.

Thus salvation is defined negatively in Protestantism: "To be saved means that God has delivered us (saved us) from His righteous wrathful judgment due us because of our sins against Him. It means that we will *not be judged* for our sins and be therefore sentenced to eternal damnation" (emphasis added).[14]

Neither is grace a positive gift of Godlikeness, of sharing in His life; it merely describes how God removes the guilt inherited from Adam and paints over fallen human nature with a coat of grace. In this paradigm there is no qualitative difference between the sheep and the goats at the Last Judgment (Matt. 25:31–46). Both are equally sinners. The sheep, however, will not be judged for their sins.

An Orthodox Response

The Reformers' doctrine of total depravity was simply not believed by *anyone* in the early Church; nor was justification by faith alone. Rather, the universal teaching was that the Fall distorted and darkened the image of God in man, covering over it but by no means destroying it. Man is still essentially good but in need of regeneration so that he may recover God's image, not by legal fiat but by an organic transformation through faith that unites him to God's Image, Jesus Christ.

The grace of God still works upon fallen man and can prompt him toward the good, because grace is his natural yearning. Since the early Christians believed this, they understood that even before baptism, man could cooperate or synergize with God. Because he is made in the image of God, the spark of grace is still in him. As in the case of all the righteous figures of the

---

14   Matt Slick, from: http://carm.org/verses-showing-justification-by-faith

Old Testament, fallen man can walk in the way of God's commandments. The holy men and women of old even participated in the grace of Jesus Christ in a limited way before His Incarnation (see 1 Cor. 10:4). What man could *not* do is regenerate his fallen human nature, nor overcome the consequences of the first parents' sin—corruption and death. Only God Incarnate can do that.

But mankind's Fall is not chiefly a matter of guilt. It cannot be resolved with a legal declaration of innocence. Christ did not come to save us from guilt but from sin and death. He came to overcome the inescapable corruption that had infiltrated the humanity of the old Adam. He, the New Adam, regenerated this death-bearing, corruption-ridden humanity by taking it upon Himself and filling it with His life-giving grace.

Those who by faith in Christ open themselves to this life-giving grace are justified. But this condition of justification grows and is perfected as one more fully enters into the reality of faith, through union with His resurrected Body (i.e., the Church) through baptism and the whole life of faith that causes one to be in Christ. This includes the personal, internal, and ascetic spiritual work of faith that is taken up by the baptized Christian in order to be fully freed from the passions so that "Christ is formed" (Gal. 4:19) in him.

The Law of Moses could not effect salvation precisely because it could not change the fallen human condition. The law could not extract the power of death from the humanity of the old Adam; it could not renew his nature. This could only be done organically, from within, in the flesh of Jesus Christ. This was St. Paul's point: that only the faith of Jesus Christ—

that is, receiving the effects of Christ's saving work organically into oneself—justifies a man, because it brings him into saving union with God.

So, in the Orthodox understanding, one is justified when by faith he places himself in the position of receiving Christ's saving grace. According to the Lord, the tax collector, not the Pharisee, was justified after praying in the temple. Why? Because the tax collector opened himself to God's grace and light through his contrition and humility. Abraham, by faith, was justified because he believed in God's word and acted upon it. By doing so he placed himself directly in the sunlight of God's grace and appropriated the righteousness and holiness of God. He did not appropriate a declaration or certificate of innocence, but the life-creating power of God. In the same way, by faith, St. Veronica received the grace of God when she touched the hem of the Lord's garment, for "power" went out from Christ's Body (Luke 8:46).

Although the Church Fathers did not seek to define justification, this seems to be how they understood it. The early Christians never taught that humans are incapable of doing good or overcoming sin in their lives. But they did teach that cooperation with God's grace was required in order to do so. They understood salvation as coming by God's grace, but man had to desire and seek that grace. As our Lord taught and commanded, "Seek, and you will find" (Matt. 7:7). If it is to be received, God's grace must be sought. Human cooperation is required. The Greek actually shows continuous action: "Keep seeking . . . keep knocking . . . keep asking." Typical of the way the early Church interpreted salvation and grace is the following passage from Clement of Alexandria:

A man by himself working and toiling at freedom from sinful desires achieves nothing. But if he plainly shows himself to be very eager and earnest about this, he attains it by the addition of the power [grace] of God. God works together with willing souls. But if the person abandons his eagerness, the Spirit from God is also restrained. To save the unwilling is the act of one using compulsion; but to save the willing, that of one showing grace.[15]

Although the human will is fallen, it is not obliterated. If it were, none of the righteous Old Testament figures could have chosen to follow the will of God. Although human nature is fallen, human persons made in the image of God still have the capacity to seek God and do His will. Human nature does not exist in the abstract (this is a Western idea); it does not exist apart from a subject. Human nature only exists in the form of specific human persons who have free will, can choose to move in the direction of God's image, and through faith can uncover and purify that image.

In St. Paul's Epistle to the Romans—the premier source for the Protestant doctrine of justification by faith alone—we read, "Do you not know that to whom you present yourselves slaves to obey, you are that one's slaves whom you obey, whether of sin *leading* to death, or of obedience *leading* to righteousness?" (6:16). It is clear from this passage that obedience to God leads to righteousness. One is "justified [made righteous] by faith" because faith is always expressed as obedience to God. As St. Clement of Rome (AD 30–96) wrote, "For what reason was our

---

15   Quoted from David W. Bercot, *Will the Real Heretics Please Stand Up: A New Look at Today's Evangelical Church in the Light of Early Christianity* (Tyler, TX: Scroll Publishing Company, 1989), p. 54.

father Abraham blessed? Was it not because he worked righteousness and truth through faith?"[16]

When we study the early Church Fathers, we understand they did not see justification by faith as the Reformers later did. Once in a chiropractor's office I picked up a book with an intriguing title: *Will the Real Heretics Please Stand Up.* As it turned out, the book was written by an evangelical Christian who had devoted much time to reading the early Church writers on this very issue. He was greatly surprised to find a theology very different from what he had always been taught and believed.[17] In the book he shares his findings regarding faith and works. The following passages are illuminating:

> You may be saying to yourself, "I'm confused. Out of one side of their [the early Christian writers'] mouths they say we are saved because of our works, and out of the other side they say we are saved by faith or grace. They don't seem to know what they believed!
>
> Oh, but they did. Our problem is that Augustine, Luther, and other Western theologians have convinced us that there's an irreconcilable conflict between salvation based on grace and salvation conditioned on works or obedience. They have used a fallacious form of argumentation known as the "false dilemma," by asserting that there are only two possibilities regarding salvation: it's either (1) a gift from God or (2) it's something we earn by our works.

---

16 First Epistle to the Corinthians, 1.13.

17 While the author concludes that Protestantism is at odds with the pre-Nicene Church and needs to revise some of its beliefs, he also claims the Church's theology fell into corruption beginning with the Emperor Constantine. However, this only strengthens the argument. He is not simply a cheerleader for Catholics or Orthodox, but he still recognizes that the early Church did not believe as Protestants do on these issues.

The early Christians would have replied that a gift is no less a gift simply because it's conditioned on obedience. Suppose a king asked his son to go to the royal orchard and bring back a basket full of the king's favorite apples. After the son had complied, suppose the king gave his son half of his kingdom. Was the reward a gift, or was it something the son had earned? The answer is that it was a gift. The son obviously didn't earn half of his father's kingdom by performing such a small task. The fact that the gift was conditioned on the son's obedience doesn't change the fact that it was still a gift.

The early Christians believed that salvation is a gift from God but that God gives His gift to whomever he chooses. *And He chooses to give it to those who love and obey him.*

Is their understanding really that strange? I so often hear evangelical Christians say that welfare should only be given to those persons who are truly *deserving.* When they say that certain poor persons are "deserving," do they mean that welfare constitutes wages earned by such persons? Of course not. They still consider welfare to be a gift. Simply because a person is selective in his giving, it doesn't change the gift into a wage.[18]

THE HOLY SCRIPTURES ON JUSTIFICATION BY FAITH

Justification by faith is indeed a biblical teaching. As Orthodox Christians, we should not make the mistake of acting as if it were not part of the apostolic teaching and scriptural witness. The questions surrounding the topic of justification are primarily a matter of biblical interpretation. Therefore, our efforts should be focused on correcting the innovative and false

---

18   Bercot, *op. cit.*, pp. 61–62.

notions of what the words *justification* and *faith* really mean by placing them within the context of the whole of the Scriptures.

When we do that, we discover that justification (or salvation) is not a legal matter, but an issue of one's openness to God and His grace and of placing one's whole being in harmony with God's will. We will also find that faith is not a mere mental assent or emotional experience leading to belief in God. Rather, it is an orientation, a conviction, and a whole way of life consistent with His teachings—that is, the life of grace.

Yet we should not try to counter justification by faith alone with another false idea that we are saved by works. While in the Scriptures salvation is dependent upon one's works, it is only so because those works (when done with faith) make our souls receptive to grace. Christ calls us to follow the commandments of God not merely to impose a morality on us but to dispose our hearts to the Holy Spirit, who will then come and abide in us. Through our works we have fellowship (i.e., communion) with light or with darkness. The Apostle Paul admonishes, "have no fellowship with the unfruitful works of darkness" (Eph. 5:11), precisely because such deeds by their very nature darken the soul rather than bringing light.

The following are only some of many scriptural quotes that are very difficult to harmonize with the narrow and overly technical Protestant understanding of justification by faith alone.

Justification/salvation related to what we do

Matt. 12:37: "For by your words you will be justified, and by your words you will be condemned."

Matt. 16:27: "For the Son of Man will come in the glory of His Father with His angels, and then He will reward each according to his works." (NIV: "... what they have done")

Luke 18:13–15: "And the tax collector, standing afar off, would not so much as raise *his* eyes to heaven, but beat his breast, saying, 'God, be merciful to me a sinner!' I tell you, this man went down to his house justified *rather* than the other; for everyone who exalts himself will be humbled, and he who humbles himself will be exalted."

John 5:28–29: "Do not marvel at this; for the hour is coming in which all who are in the graves will hear His voice and come forth—those who have done good, to the resurrection of life, and those who have done evil, to the resurrection of condemnation."

Rom. 2:3–11: And do you think this, O man, you who judge those practicing such things, and doing the same, that you will escape the judgment of God? Or do you despise the riches of His goodness, forbearance, and longsuffering, not knowing that the goodness of God leads you to repentance? But in accordance with your hardness and your impenitent heart you are treasuring up for yourself wrath in the day of wrath and revelation of the righteous judgment of God, who "will render to each one according to his deeds": eternal life to those who by patient continuance in doing good seek for glory, honor, and immortality; but to those who are self-seeking and do not obey the truth, but obey unrighteousness—indignation and wrath, tribulation and anguish, on every soul of man who does evil, of the Jew first and also of the Greek; but glory, honor, and peace to everyone who works what is good, to the Jew first and also to the Greek. For there is no partiality with God.

Rom. 2:13: For not the hearers of the law are just in the sight of God, but the doers of the law will be justified.

1 Cor. 7:19: Circumcision is nothing and uncircumcision is nothing, but keeping the commandments of God *is what matters.*

2 Cor. 5:10: For we must all appear before the judgment seat of Christ, that each one may receive the things *done* in the body, according to what he has done, whether good or bad.

2 Cor. 11:15: Therefore it is no great thing if his ministers also transform themselves into ministers of righteousness, whose end will be according to their works.

Col. 3:25: But he who does wrong will be repaid for what he has done, and there is no partiality.

2 Tim. 4:14: Alexander the coppersmith did me much harm. May the Lord repay him according to his works.

Heb. 10:36: For you have need of endurance, so that after you have done the will of God, you may receive the promise.

James 2:14: What *does it* profit, my brethren, if someone says he has faith but does not have works? Can faith save him?

James 2:17: Thus also faith by itself, if it does not have works, is dead.

James 2:18: But someone will say, "You have faith, and I have works." Show me your faith without your works, and I will show you my faith by my works.

James 2:21–22: Was not Abraham our father justified by works when he offered Isaac his son on the altar? Do you see that faith was working together with his works, and by works faith was made perfect?

James 2:24–26: You see then that a man is justified by works, and not by faith only. Likewise, was not Rahab the harlot also justified by works when she received the messengers and sent *them* out another way? For as the body without the spirit is dead, so faith without works is dead also.

Rev. 2:5: "Remember therefore from where you have fallen; repent and do the first works, or else I will come to you quickly and remove your lampstand from its place—unless you repent."

Rev. 14:13: Then I heard a voice from heaven saying to me, "Write: 'Blessed are the dead who die in the Lord from now on.'" "Yes," says the Spirit, "that they may rest from their labors, and their works follow them."

Rev. 20:12: And I saw the dead, small and great, standing before God, and books were opened. And another book was opened, which is *the Book* of Life. And the dead were judged according to their works, by the things which were written in the books.

Rev. 20:13: The sea gave up the dead who were in it, and Death and Hades delivered up the dead who were in them. And they were judged, each one according to his works.

Faith does the will of God

Faith is not merely a mental process; it is a whole way of life that includes the whole human person—mind, soul, spirit, and body.

Gal. 6:15: For in Christ Jesus neither circumcision nor uncircumcision avails anything, but a new creation.

Justification at Baptism (the great act of faith)

1 Cor. 6:9–11: Do you not know that the unrighteous will not inherit the kingdom of God? Do not be deceived. Neither fornicators, nor idolaters, nor adulterers, nor homosexuals, nor sodomites, nor thieves, nor covetous, nor drunkards, nor revilers, nor extortioners will inherit the kingdom of God. And such were some of you. But you were washed, but you were sanctified, but you were justified in the name of the Lord Jesus and by the Spirit of our God.

Titus 3:5: Not by works of righteousness which we have done, but according to His mercy He saved us, through the washing of regeneration and renewing of the Holy Spirit.

Good works distinguished from works of the law or dead works

Rom. 3:20: Therefore by the deeds of the law no flesh will be justified in His sight, for by the law *is* the knowledge of sin.

Rom. 8:13: For if you live according to the flesh you will die; but if by the Spirit you put to death the deeds of the body, you will live.

Gal. 2:16: That we might be justified by faith in Christ and not by the works of the law.

Eph. 2:10: For we are His workmanship, created in Christ Jesus for good works, which God prepared beforehand that we should walk in them.

Col. 3:9-10: Do not lie to one another, since you have put off the old man with his deeds, and have put on the new *man* who is renewed in knowledge according to the image of Him who created him.

1 Tim. 6:18-19: *Let them* do good, that they be rich in good works, ready to give, willing to share, storing up for themselves a good foundation for the time to come, that they may lay hold on eternal life.

Titus 1:16: They profess to know God, but in works they deny *Him*, being abominable, disobedient, and disqualified for every good work.

Titus 2:6-8: Likewise, exhort the young men to be sober-minded, in all things showing yourself *to be* a pattern of good works; in doctrine *showing* integrity, reverence, incorruptibility, sound speech that cannot be condemned, that one who is an opponent may be ashamed, having nothing evil to say of you.

Titus 2:14: Who gave Himself for us, that He might redeem us from every lawless deed and purify for Himself *His* own special people, zealous for good works.

Heb. 6:1: Therefore, leaving the discussion of the elementary *principles* of Christ, let us go on to perfection, not laying again the foundation of repentance from dead works and of faith toward God.

Heb. 9:14: How much more shall the blood of Christ, who through the eternal Spirit offered Himself without spot to God, cleanse your conscience from dead works to serve the living God?

Heb. 10:23–25: Let us hold fast the confession of *our* hope without wavering, for He who promised *is* faithful. And let us consider one another in order to stir up love and good works, not forsaking the assembling of ourselves together, as *is* the manner of some, but exhorting *one another*, and so much the more as you see the Day approaching.

THE CHURCH FATHERS ON JUSTIFICATION

The following quotes clearly show that the early Church Fathers understood justification by faith differently from what was formulated at the time of the Protestant Reformation. They did not separate justification from obedience, righteousness, and sanctification but understood all as part and parcel of the life of faith.

Keep in mind that they read and understood the Greek of the Scriptures not only as their first language but as the very atmosphere in which they lived. To believe that the Church Fathers were unaware of some other "true" understanding of justification by faith is to believe that the most essential doctrine regarding man's salvation was universally misunderstood or lost in a matter of one or two generations, only to be recovered over a thousand years later.

St. Clement of Rome (c. AD 30–96)

For what reason was our father Abraham blessed? Was it not because he worked righteousness and truth through faith? (*First Epistle to the Corinthians*, Bercot, *op. cit.*, ANF vol. 1., p. 31)[19]

Let us, then, not only call Him Lord, for that will not save us. For He says, "Not everyone who says to Me, Lord, Lord, will be saved, but he that works righteousness." For that reason, brethren, let us confess Him by our works, by loving one another. (*Second Epistle to the Corinthians*, 4.1–3)

Therefore, brethren, by doing the will of the Father, and keeping the flesh holy, and observing the commandments of the Lord, we will obtain eternal life. (*Op. cit.*, 8:4)

St. Ignatius of Antioch (c. AD 35–108)

Faith cannot do the works of unbelief, nor unbelief the works of faith. (*Epistle to the Ephesians* 8)

St. Polycarp of Smyrna (c. AD 69–155)

They know that "by grace you have been saved, not of works," but by the will of God through Jesus Christ. . . . But He who raised Him up from the dead will raise us also—if we do His will, and walk in His commandments, and love what He loved, keeping ourselves from all unrighteousness. (*Epistle to the Philippians*, 1.3–2.2)[20]

---

19 According to early church historians, Clement of Rome was a disciple of St. Paul and is the Clement mentioned in Phil. 4:3. His epistle was considered as Scripture by many in the early Church.

20 St. Polycarp, the saintly Bishop of Smyrna, was a direct disciple of the Apostle John and was martyred for faith in Christ at age 86.

St. Justin the Martyr (AD 100–165)

"Blessed is the man to whom the Lord does not impute sin" (Ps. 32:2). That is, having repented of his sins, he can receive remission of them from God. But this is not as you [Jews] deceive yourselves, and some others who resemble you in this. For they say, that even though they remain sinners, the Lord will not impute sin to them, because they know God. (*Dialogue with Trypho*, Bercot, *op. cit.*, ANF vol. 1, p. 270)

Each man goes to everlasting punishment or salvation according to the value of his actions. (*Op. cit.*, p. 166)

For it is not those who make profession, but those who do the works, who will be saved. (*Op. cit.*, p. 168)

St. Irenaeus of Lyons (c. early second century–AD 202)

To believe in Him is to do His will. (*Against Heresies*, Bercot, *op. cit.*, ANF vol. 1, p. 468)

Clement of Alexandria (c. AD 150–c. 215)

"For by grace we are saved"—but not, indeed, without good works. Rather, we must be saved by being molded for what is good, acquiring an inclination for it. . . . For this, we have the greatest need of divine grace, of right teaching, of holy susceptibility, and of the drawing of the Father to Himself. (*The Stromata*, Bercot, *op. cit.*, ANF vol. 2, p. 445)

It is the will of God that he who repents of his sins and is obedient to the commandments should be saved. (*Op. cit.*, p. 363)

Eusebius of Caesarea (c. AD 260/265–339/340)

Some of the [heretics] . . . simply deny the Law and the Prophets for the sake of their lawless and impious doctrine. And under the pretense of grace, they have sunk down to the lowest abyss of perdition. (*Fragments of Caius*, Bercot, *op. cit.*, ANF vol. 5, p. 602)

St. Cyprian of Carthage (c. AD 200–258)

Abraham believed in God and it was accounted to him as righteousness. Assuredly, then, whoever believes in God and lives in faith is found righteous and is already blessed in faithful Abraham. (*Epistle LXII*, Bercot, *op. cit.*, ANF vol. 5, p. 359)

CHAPTER 5

Tradition & Scripture

Therefore, brethren, stand fast and hold the traditions which you were taught, whether by word or our epistle. (2 Thess. 2:15)

Now that the new Gentile converts have been received into the "apostles' . . . fellowship" (Acts 2:42), being baptized into the Body of Jesus Christ, they have begun to encounter the tangible, daily pattern of the Church. The blessed Peter had told them they were now part of a "royal priesthood" and "holy nation" (1 Pet. 2:9), but they had not really known exactly what that meant.

The apostle had asked Cornelius and family to spend an extended period of time with the church in Jerusalem so that they might experience the Christian way of life firsthand and learn to "walk according to this rule" (Gal. 6:16) of life in Christ. It was not long before they realized this way touched every aspect of daily life and engaged body, mind, spirit, and all their senses in the glorification of God.

Along with the believers in Jerusalem, "they continued steadfastly in the apostles' doctrine and fellowship, in the breaking of [the] bread, and in [the] prayers" (Acts 2:42). It was becoming clear to them that this was an all-encompassing life of spiritual exercise and worship of God that was designed to bring them into unity with Christ and one another.

Cornelius realized this was not of human design but revealed to the apostles through their association with the Lord. It was what the brethren called "the tradition of the apostles," a saving way of life that had been infused in them by Jesus Himself and inspired by the Holy Spirit. The apostles were now passing down and delivering this way to those who had come to believe through their preaching.

As Cornelius was now seeing for himself, this way of life was centered each day by a schedule of prayer, worship, and instruction, highlighted by and culminating in the gathering for the breaking of the bread, or the Supper of the Lord. Here especially, the Lord's words, which Cornelius heard repeated on several occasions, came alive: "For where two or three are gathered together in My name, I am there in the midst of them" (Matt. 18:20). These and other sayings of Jesus were kept alive and passed down by word of mouth.

This pattern of prayer, doctrine, and discipline, Cornelius learned, was established wherever the apostles' preaching bore fruit. Some of the apostles might spend years in one place in order to firmly establish the tradition of Christ there (see Acts 20:31). During that time the apostle acted as *episcopos*, or "overseer," presiding at all the gatherings of the church and handing down that which was the "custom" in all "the churches of God" (1 Cor. 11:16). Only after instructing, ordaining, and mentoring "faithful men" who would be "able to teach others also" (2 Tim. 2:2) did they depart, returning regularly to ensure the "good order" (Col. 2:5) of the new community's faith.

In the daily services of prayer, Cornelius and his family heard the scriptures, the Law of Moses, the Psalms, and the Prophets. These writings foretold the salvation that was to come in Christ and a new covenant "written not with ink but by the Spirit of the living God, not on tablets of stone but on tablets of flesh, that is, of the heart" (2 Cor. 3:3).

Introduction

This chapter on Tradition and Scripture is in some sense an extension of the first chapter on the Church, because the controversies surrounding the relationship between the Bible and Holy Tradition are directly related to how one understands and believes in the Church. In the simplest terms, one must decide: Which came first—the Church and her apostolic Tradition or the Scriptures? Does the Church with her Tradition give birth to the Bible, or does the Bible make and validate the Church?

The modern controversy pitting Tradition against Scripture was unknown for the first sixteen hundred years of church history, until the moral and doctrinal corruptions of the Roman Church prompted a reaction by those we now call the Protestant Reformers. One such corruption was the teaching that the Scripture could be interpreted correctly only by the "Magisterium" (i.e., the pope with his bishops), because they alone were privy to the Tradition of the Church and thus to the correct interpretation of Holy Scripture. As the Catholic Catechism still teaches, "The task of interpreting the Word of God authentically has been entrusted solely to the Magisterium of the Church, that is, to the Pope and to the bishops in communion with him."[1]

This position encouraged the idea that both the Scriptures and the Church's oral Tradition were secret and inaccessible to the faithful. The lack of transparency was often perceived

---

1   *Catechism of the Catholic Church,* 2nd ed. 1997, pt. 1, sect. 1, ch. 2, art. 2, III [#100].

as an opportunity to control and manipulate the lay Christian by appealing to this unknown tradition. It also helped to fuel negative feelings of clericalism, with all power coming from the top down.

In practice, the laity were discouraged from reading or interpreting Scripture themselves. Due to the rise of various heresies, the Councils of Toulouse (1229) and Tarragona (1234) both prohibited the laity from reading the Bible, at least in their indigenous languages. In 1564, the Council of Trent declared generally that allowing the laity to read the Scriptures would cause "more harm than good."[2]

A combination of this attitude of excluding the greater portion of the faithful from direct knowledge of the Scriptures, a growing suspicion toward Church Tradition, and the invention of the printing press culminated in Martin Luther and others championing the cause of all Christians having access to the Bible. While Martin Luther did not intend to do away with all Church Tradition (but only various corrupt traditions of the Catholicism of his day), it was only a matter of time before he and others began disavowing much of legitimate Tradition.

Within this context, both among Catholics and Protestants, Scripture and Tradition began to be seen as two distinct and separate sources of the Christian faith. Increasingly, the Church Tradition came to be understood as something *extraneous* to the Bible, even something manmade, as opposed to God's revealed Word found in the Holy Scriptures.

For Protestants, tradition—this purely human and added

2   *Council of Trent: Rules on Prohibited Books,* approved by Pope Pius IV, 1564. Quoted from http://www.justforcatholics.org/a198.htm.

component of the corrupt Roman Church system—was *the* problem. To the battle cries "faith *alone*" and "saved by grace *alone*" was added "*sola scriptura*" (Scripture *alone*).[3] After all, did not Christ condemn "the tradition of men" (Mark 7:8) during His earthly ministry?

For the more radical Reformers, *all* Church Tradition came to be equated with a deceitful and corrupt tradition of men also warned against by the Apostle Paul (see Col. 2:8). Evangelical Christians, who are inheritors of the radical Reformed tradition, typically believe they adhere to *no* tradition whatsoever but follow the Bible exclusively. Evangelicals believe the Bible is the "only ultimate and infallible authority for faith and practice."[4]

And so it was that Protestants lost faith in the Church and yet sought to recover the truth from the Church's book, a product of Church Tradition. Because, however, they were products of a church body already detached for centuries from the authentic Church Tradition, they did this without an organic connection to the Bible. The result was that they inadvertently reinvented Church Tradition according to their various and conflicting interpretations of Scripture. In the end, sola scriptura could not produce *sola ecclesia* (one Church), but only a continuous proliferation of differing factions or denominations, the result of opposing interpretations of Scripture.

---

3   Please see the excellent and comprehensive article "Sola Scriptura: An Orthodox Examination of the Protestant Teaching" by Fr. John Whiteford at: http://orthodoxinfo.com/inquirers/tca_solascriptura.aspx

4   For example see: http://www.theriveracademy.org/index.php?option=com_content&task=view&id=15&Itemid=31

Tradition and the Church

As we have seen, for Orthodox Christians the Church is "the pillar and ground of the truth" (1 Tim. 3:15); that is to say, the Church is the living repository and source of the whole apostolic faith of Jesus Christ that brings man into communion with God. Because the Church is the Body of Christ, it breathes forth and communicates the grace of the Holy Spirit. As St. Irenaeus declared, "For where the Church is, there is the Spirit of God; and where the Spirit of God is, there is the Church and every kind of grace."[5] The Church is such a definitive spring of revelation that it even imparts wisdom and truth to the angels (1 Pet. 1:12).

From earliest times, the term used for the deposit of faith manifest in the Church was "tradition" (1 Cor. 11:2; 2 Thess. 2:15; 3:6). The word *tradition*, in Greek *paradosis* and in Latin *traditio*, means literally "to hand down" or "to deliver." Thus, St. Paul prefaces his confession of faith with the words, "For I *delivered* to you first of all that which I also *received*" (1 Cor. 15:3, emphasis added).

Not only the great apostle but the successors of the apostles received the Tradition of the Church from those who came before them. As St. Cyprian, bishop of Carthage (+258), affirms:

> You must diligently observe and keep the practice delivered from divine tradition and apostolic observance, which is also maintained among us and almost throughout all the provinces.[6]

This Church Tradition, or *Holy* Tradition, is to be distinguished from the "tradition of men" condemned by the Lord and His

---

5   *Against Heresies,* 3:24.1.
6   Letters 75.3, 5371.

apostle (Mark 7:8; Col. 2:8). The source and inspiration for Holy Tradition is the teaching of the apostles and the continual guidance of the Holy Spirit in the Church (John 16:13).

Church Tradition is both old and new at the same time—it preserves the faith as received but is always made alive in the Church by the Spirit of God, as particularly expressed in the lives of the saints. Those who experience the uncreated grace and light of God in each new generation remain in complete fidelity to the one apostolic Tradition, yet they incarnate it and express it in a fresh and personal way.

While we say that Church Tradition is alive and thus always new, it is never *innovative* but is always faithful to the past. The Orthodox do not subscribe to the idea of the development of doctrine. There is nothing truly new or added to Holy Tradition over time but only fresh reiterations and expressions of the same faith. The Lord said, "Behold, I make all things new" (Rev. 21:5); He did not say, "I make *new things*."

Holy Tradition, then, is the living expression and practice of the Church's apostolic doctrine and way of life. It is like a blueprint that can be seen and touched or an original garment on which other garments are modeled. St. Paul calls it a "pattern" (2 Tim. 1:13). Church Tradition is the pattern that leads to spiritual health and union with God, the blueprint for abiding in the Holy Spirit as revealed by God in Jesus Christ.

This original garment, known as the apostolic Tradition of the Church, is a tapestry woven with a number of sacred and indispensable threads. No one of these threads can be taken alone without diminishing the whole garment of faith, for all of them are authoritative witnesses of the Church's Tradition.

Among the first is the Bible, the Old and New Testaments, the most important written tradition of the Church. Tradition also includes the liturgical practice of the Church (the Eucharist and other services of prayer), much of which predates the writings of the New Testament and influenced their content. Other threads in this tapestry are the dogmatic formulations of the Ecumenical Councils along with their disciplinary canons, which are prescriptions and guides for healthy and normative Christian life. The writings of the Church Fathers and lives of the saints are also faithful witnesses to the Tradition, for they express and exhibit the apostolic faith. Iconography, hymnography, and church architecture also affirm the liturgical, doctrinal, and spiritual traditions of the Church.

From this we see that the Bible is *one* element of the whole body of Church Tradition. Scripture itself is Tradition and is an expression of the Tradition. It is the book of the Church, written within the Church, by the Church, and for the Church. The Scriptures bear witness to the life of this Church.

Christ did not come to establish a book, but His Church, His Body. As St. John Chrysostom notes, the Lord Himself did not impart anything to His disciples in writing.[7] This is significant. As the New Hieromartyr of Russia St. Hilarion Troitsky explains, "Christianity itself is not a teaching but a *new life*, established in mankind by the Holy Spirit on the basis of the Incarnation of the Son of God." He continues:

> It was the incarnation of the Son of God that was necessary
> for the salvation of mankind, and not a book. No book is able,

---

7   *Homilies on the Gospel according to St. Matthew*, NPNF, 1.10, p. 1.

nor could it ever have been able to save mankind. Christ is not [mainly] the *Teacher* but precisely the *Savior* of mankind.[8]

The Church thrived well before any of the writings of the New Testament existed. It was the Church that determined which writings would be included in the canon of Scripture. These determinations were made in councils of the Church, made up of bishops of the Church. In fact, the canon of the New Testament was not universally agreed upon before the fifth century and officially only by the seventh century.

If, therefore, one accepts the authority of the compilation determined by the Church, one implicitly accepts the authority (and inspiration of the Holy Spirit) of the Church that compiled it. In the end, the writings that were included in the canon of Holy Scripture were chosen because they bear witness to the Tradition that was *already* practiced and taught within the Church.

The Church, not the Scriptures, is the source of divine truth. As the Apostle Paul declares in the Scriptures, the Church is the "pillar and ground of truth" (1 Tim. 3:15).

St. Irenaeus (125–202) also provides us with the proper perspective:

> We should not seek from others the truth which can easily be received from the Church. For in her, as in a rich treasury, the Apostles placed in fullness all that belongs to the truth, so that whoever wishes can receive from her the water of life. She is the entrance to life.[9]

---

8   *Holy Scripture and the Church,* trans. by Igor Radev, p. 1.
9   *Against Heresies,* 3:4.

It is significant that in the Nicene Creed, one of the most ancient expressions of the apostolic faith, we do not confess, "I believe in one Bible," but "I believe in one holy, catholic, and apostolic *church*." The Church, not the Bible, is (after Christ Himself) the source of truth and the object of faith for the Christian.

The Bible is a testament to the faith and Tradition of the Church. But it is not the complete Tradition. It was never meant to be. For this reason, St. Paul wrote, "Therefore, brethren, stand fast and hold the traditions which you were taught, *whether by word or our epistle*" (2 Thess. 2:15, emphasis added). Only when a man knows the Church Tradition will he begin to see the whole reflected within and emanating from the Scriptures.

Without an organic understanding and living experience of the Church and her Tradition, the Scriptures are more likely to be twisted, misconstrued, and misinterpreted.[10] The devil himself consistently quoted Scripture in an effort to tempt the Lord Jesus Christ from His divine mission (see Matt. 4:5–6).

As we have seen from Chapters 1 and 2, the Church is the source of salvation because it is the source of grace, the new life that Christ came to give. In the Acts of the Apostles, we see that those who were being saved were "added to the church" (Acts. 2:47). "Why was it essential to be added to the Church?" asks St. Hilarion. "It is because special grace-bearing power is needed

---

10   The ancient heretics used Scripture to promote their teachings but had a difficult time appealing to the actual practice and prayer of the Church. In St. Basil's writings against those who denied the divinity of the Holy Spirit, he primarily uses the liturgical prayers (i.e., Tradition) as a witness to the Holy Spirit's equality with the Father and the Son. This was a particularly strong argument, since the heretics themselves used these prayers. St. Basil also enumerates many important apostolic traditions that are not included in the Bible.

for salvation, and this power can only be possessed by those who participate in the life of the Church." He concludes, "Thus, Holy Scripture is one of the manifestations of the common grace-filled life of the Church."[11]

Tradition (and therefore Holy Scripture) is not the possession of disconnected individuals; it resides within a community, the Church. When Jesus promises that the Holy Spirit "will guide *you* into all truth" (John 16:13), He speaks in the plural, to the community of the apostles, and through them to the churches that are united in their Tradition. Tradition is therefore the bond of unity in the Church. It is through Holy Tradition that the Church speaks "with one mind and one mouth" (Rom. 15:6).

St. Irenaeus again attests to this understanding of Holy Tradition:

> As I said before, the Church, having received this preaching and this faith, although she is disseminated throughout the whole world, yet guarded it, as if she occupied but one house. She likewise believes these things just as if she had but one soul and one and the same heart; and harmoniously she proclaims them and teaches them and hands them down, as if she possessed but one mouth. For, while the languages of the world are diverse, nevertheless, the authority of the tradition is one and the same.[12]

As the source for the Faith that binds the members of the Body of Christ together, Tradition is also the guardian against "destructive heresies," (2 Pet. 2:1), teachings and practices that

---

11 New Hieromartyr Hilarion Troitsky, "Holy Scripture and the Church," trans. Igor Radev, in *The Orthodox Word*, Vol. 45, Nos. 1–2 (264–5), January–April 2001, pp. 9–10.

12 *Against Heresies* 1:10:2.

are outside the "pattern of sound words" (2 Tim. 1:13), i.e., the apostolic Faith. For this reason the Church calls her Faith not merely traditional, or a tradition, but Holy or Sacred Tradition. The Tradition of the Church is not an imprisoning set of archaic rules, but a light revealing the path of holiness and salvation.

The Relationship of Tradition and Scripture

The Church Fathers and the Orthodox Church do not separate Scripture and Tradition into two distinct categories but instead understand the Scriptures to be the most honored, canonical written expression of Church Tradition. Thus, Scripture *is* tradition and can only be fully understood from within the experience of the whole Tradition. The Church Tradition, as the very source and context of Scripture, is clearly attested to in them. As the product of the living and active presence of the Holy Spirit in the Church, Tradition cannot be reduced to the written word.

These points are summarized below.

TRADITION IS SCRIPTURAL

Both the term and the fundamental understanding of Church Tradition are attested to in the New Testament Scriptures. Tradition cannot be explained away as a late development, as two of these references are from St. Paul's earliest epistles—those to the Thessalonians.

> Therefore, brethren, stand fast and hold the traditions which you were taught, whether by word or our epistle. (2 Thess. 2:15)

> But we command you, brethren, in the name of our Lord Jesus Christ, that you withdraw from every brother who walks disor-

derly and not according to the tradition which he received from us. (2 Thess. 3:6)

Now I praise you, brethren, that you remember me in all things and keep the traditions just as I delivered *them* to you. (1 Cor. 11:2)

The word translated from the Latin as "tradition" is *paradosis* in Greek. It means "that which is passed down" or "handed on." Tradition is literally something that has been received from another and passed on to others.

For I delivered [*paredoka*] to you first of all that which I also received: that Christ died for our sins according to the Scriptures, and that He was buried, and that He rose again the third day according to the Scriptures, and that He was seen by Cephas, then by the twelve. After that He was seen by over five hundred brethren at once. . . . After that he was seen by James, then by all the apostles. Then last of all He was seen by me also, as by one born out of due time. (1 Cor. 15:3–8)

For I received from the Lord that which I also delivered [*paredoka*] to you: that the Lord Jesus on the *same* night in which He was betrayed took bread. (1 Cor. 11:23)

Not only do we see that Holy Tradition is scriptural, but it is of the utmost importance, a matter of life and death. For the apostle also anathematizes anyone who changes the teaching and Tradition of the Church:

If we, or an angel from heaven, preach any other gospel to you than what we have preached to you, let him be accursed. (Gal. 1:8)

SCRIPTURE IS TRADITION

In what has become the Western understanding, Tradition and Scripture are set against one another as two separate and distinct sources of Christian doctrine. Tradition, therefore, is understood to be an *addition* to Scripture, and Scripture is understood to be something *other than* tradition. Whether one accepts or rejects Church Tradition, he does so on that basis. The question becomes whether one understands Tradition as a legitimate addition to Scripture or as a competing contradiction.

However, for Orthodox Christians, Scripture *is* Tradition. There is only *one* source of truth, and that is the Tradition of the Church, from which the Scriptures issued forth and of which they form a vital part. As Clement of Alexandria sums up, "The tradition of the apostles was one."[13]

The early teacher and scriptural commentator, Origen (AD 185–254), attests to the common understanding of Tradition as the Christian criterion of truth.

> The teaching of the Church has indeed been handed down through an order of succession from the apostles and remains in the churches even to the present time. That alone is to be believed as the truth which is in no way at variance with ecclesiastical and apostolic tradition.[14]

Since the Church existed before the writing and compilation of the New Testament Scriptures, it must be concluded that it is the Tradition handed down from the apostles that guides the Church. The Scriptures reflect the living Tradition of the Church, whether in doctrine or worship or spirituality or gov-

13   *Miscellanies*, 2.555.
14   *The Fundamental Doctrines*, 1:2 [AD 225].

ernment. We can see many examples of this in the Scriptures themselves.

For instance, the New Testament quotes hymns and creeds that were already in use in the Church prior to its writing and were therefore part of oral tradition. Examples include Ephesians 5:14; Philippians 2:6–11; 1 Timothy 3:16; 6:15–16; 2 Timothy 2:11–13.

Other liturgical phrases or doxologies found in the New Testament reflect the liturgical practice and tradition of the Church, and some are used to this day in Orthodox worship:

» "For of Him and through Him and to Him are all things, to whom be glory unto the ages. Amen." (Rom. 11:36)

» "The grace of our Lord Jesus Christ be with you." (1 Cor. 16:23)

» "The grace of our Lord Jesus Christ, and the love of God, and the communion of the Holy Spirit be with you all." (2 Cor. 13:14)

» "To whom be glory unto ages of ages. Amen." (Gal. 1:5)

» "To Him be glory in the church by Christ Jesus to all generations unto ages of ages. Amen." (Eph. 3:21)

» "Now to our God and Father be glory unto ages of ages. Amen." (Phil. 4:20)

» "Now to the King eternal, immortal, invisible, to God who alone is wise, be honor and glory unto ages of ages. Amen." (1 Tim. 1:17)

» "To Him be glory unto ages of ages. Amen." (2 Tim. 4:18)

» "That in all things God may be glorified through Jesus Christ, to whom belong the glory and the dominion unto ages of ages. Amen." (1 Pet. 4:11)

» "To Him be the glory and the dominion unto ages of ages. Amen." (1 Pet. 5:11)

St. Paul's invitation at the end of many of his letters to "Greet one another with a holy kiss" (Rom. 16:16; 1 Cor. 16:20; 2 Cor. 13:12) is a direct reference to the "kiss of peace," a formal liturgical rite that is exchanged by the faithful just prior to the celebration of the Eucharist.

We also see from Holy Scripture that the Church discerns and further articulates the depths of Holy Tradition when clarification is required. While the Church's faith "was once for all delivered to the saints" (Jude 1:3), it is also dynamic and must respond to new challenges and questions.

When the apostles and presbyters came together in council to consider the question of circumcision for the Gentiles, their conclusion uncovered and expressed the truth given by the Holy Spirit in the Church: "For it seemed good to the Holy Spirit, and to us" (Acts 15:28). They did not appeal to Scripture (which did not provide clear answers) but to the living experience and consensus of grace within the Church.

In this case, the decision of the council was written down and disseminated among the churches and recorded for us in what has become the New Testament (see Acts 15:22–29). Later councils of the Church, particularly those called "ecumenical," or universal, continued this work and discernment of the Holy Spirit on behalf of Christ's Body. The decisions of these councils, like those of the one in Jerusalem, faithfully articulate what has always been believed by the Church—that is, Church Tradition.

TRADITION IS BOTH WRITTEN AND UNWRITTEN

From earliest times the primary distinction was not between Tradition and Scripture, but between oral and written tradition. So the Apostle Paul commands the Thessalonians, "hold the traditions which you were taught, *whether by word or our epistle*" (2 Thess. 2:15, emphasis added). Several hundred years later, St. Epiphanius (AD 320–403) attests to the same reality:

> It is needful also to make use of [unwritten] tradition, for not everything can be gotten from sacred Scripture. The holy apostles handed down some things in the scriptures, other things in [oral] tradition.[15]

A distinction was also made between the *kerygma*, or public preaching of Christ, which could be written down for public consumption, and *dogma*, which was considered appropriate only for those who were baptized into the Church. The kerygma consisted of the preaching of the good news of Christ crucified and raised from the dead, the need for repentance and reconciliation with God, and the remission of sins in Christ through baptism (see Acts 2:32–38). That which pertained to this preaching was to be proclaimed and preached boldly and publicly.

Generally, however, *dogma* was neither preached to unbelievers nor written down for fear that it would be misunderstood, trivialized, and mocked, subjected to petty curiosity that is demeaning to holy things. As St. Basil the Great puts it, "Reverence for the mysteries is best encouraged by silence."[16]

Although counterintuitive to our modern minds, the Church was very reticent to "throw pearls to swine" (Matt. 7:6), lest that

15 *Medicine Chest Against All Heresies,* 61:6.
16 *On the Holy Spirit,* ch. 27, 66.

which is holy be trampled upon. The dogmas of the Church reflect the inner mystery of life in Christ that cannot be appreciated or embraced except by those illumined by divine grace and joined to the family of God. The inner life of the Body of Christ can be understood and received spiritually by participation and experience, not merely by logical reasoning.

Therefore the dogmas of the Church were purposely kept discreet and unwritten. Catechumens were instructed not to write down on paper what they were hearing and not to share dogma with unbelievers. The Church's more intimate teachings and many of her practices were taught only by word of mouth or not spoken of at all until one had entered the Church and experienced her inner life. Even the Lord's Prayer was not taught to catechumens (let alone unbelievers) until after or just prior to their baptism. For how can one call God Father when he has not been adopted as a son of God through baptism?[17]

Jesus Himself spoke in parables to the multitudes and did not reveal the mysteries of the Kingdom to all. He spoke of the mysteries of the Kingdom of God to His disciples but not to the multitudes.[18] Even the disciples did not understand many of Christ's words until they were baptized by the Holy Spirit on the Day of Pentecost (see Mark 9:32; Luke 2:50; John 2:21).

So we can also speak of the *public* Tradition and the *inner* Tradition of the Church. These generally correspond to the kerygma and dogma, respectively. "Dogma is one thing," explains St.

17   St. Basil: "The uninitiated were not even allowed to be present at the mysteries; how could you expect these teachings to be paraded about in public documents?" (*On the Holy Spirit,* ch. 27, 66).
18   "And He said, 'To you it has been given to know the mysteries of the kingdom of God, but to the rest it is given in parables, that "Seeing they may not see, / And hearing they may not understand"'" (Luke 8:10).

Basil, "kerygma another; the first is observed in silence, while the latter is proclaimed to the world."[19]

Today this distinction has been blurred for a variety of reasons. The dogmatic teachings of the Church are largely written and accessible to anyone. While this may be positive in some ways, we must be vigilant to maintain the proper attitude of reverence for the inner Tradition of the Church. St. Basil warns, "We have unwritten tradition so that the knowledge of dogma might not become neglected and scorned through familiarity."[20]

The New Testament primarily belongs to the category of kerygma. Noticeably missing are details regarding the Church's corporate life such as prayers used for the services of baptism and ordination, instructions for celebrating the Eucharist along with the prayers of consecration, prayers offered for the departed faithful, and so on.

The Synoptic Gospels, Matthew, Mark, and Luke, are particularly kerygmatic in nature. It is significant that the Church begins reading the Gospel of John corporately only after the celebration of the Resurrection. The Gospel of John alludes more deeply to the inner Tradition of the Church with sacramental overtones more readily recognizable and understandable to the baptized. Since those preparing for baptism were received just before Pascha,[21] they were now prepared to remain in church for the celebration of the Eucharist and experience the inner mysteries of the Church.

In his work on the Holy Spirit, St. Basil writes on the

---

19 *On the Holy Spirit,* ch 27, 66.

20 *Ibid.*

21 The Greek term for "Passover," used from earliest times for the celebration of the Resurrection of Christ. St. Paul calls Christ "our Passover" (1 Cor. 5:7).

significance of the unwritten Tradition and provides us with a summary of some of the most prominent of these essential practices of the Church, which are not mentioned explicitly in Holy Scripture.

> Of the dogmas and sermons preserved in the Church, certain ones we have from written instruction, and certain ones we have received from the Apostolic [oral] Tradition, handed down in secret [i.e., discreetly]. Both the one and the other have one and the same authority for piety, and no one who is even the least informed in the decrees of the Church will contradict this. For if we dare to overthrow the unwritten customs as if they did not have great importance, we shall thereby imperceptively do harm to the Gospel in its most important points. And even more, we shall be left with the empty name of the Apostolic preaching without content.
>
> For example, let us especially make note of the first and commonest thing: that those who hope in the Name of our Lord Jesus Christ should sign themselves with the Sign of the Cross. Who taught this in Scripture? Which Scripture instructed us that we should turn to the east in prayer? Which of the saints left us in written form the words of invocation during the transformation of the bread of the Eucharist and the Chalice of blessing? For we are not satisfied with the words which are mentioned in the Epistles or the Gospels [for the Eucharistic prayers], but both before them and after them we pronounce others also as having great authority for the Mystery, having received them from the unwritten teaching. By what Scriptures, likewise, do we bless the water of Baptism and the oil of anointing and, indeed, the one being baptized himself? Is this not the silent and secret tradition? And what more? What written word has taught us this anointing with oil itself? Where is the triple immersion and all the rest that has to do with baptism,

the renunciation of Satan and his angels to be found? What Scripture are these taken from? Is it not from this unpublished and unspoken teaching which our Fathers have preserved in a silence inaccessible to curiosity and scrutiny, because they were thoroughly instructed to preserve in silence the sanctity of the Mysteries [i.e., Sacraments]? For what propriety would there be to proclaim in writing a teaching concerning that which it is not allowed for the unbaptized even to behold?[22]

SCRIPTURE IS TO BE INTERPRETED IN THE LIGHT OF TRADITION

From the earliest times, Holy Tradition has always been the source and criterion for apostolic Christian faith. It should not surprise anyone, then, that Holy Scripture has always been read and interpreted within the perspective of Church Tradition, that is, what the Church has always believed. As the Apostle Paul submitted the content of his preaching to St. Peter and the larger Church, so we must submit our personal interpretations of the Scriptures to the wisdom of the mind of the whole Church from all ages. For "no prophecy of Scripture is of any private interpretation" (2 Pet. 1:20). Clement of Alexandria reiterates this point: "It is necessary for men to abandon impious opinion and turn from there to the true tradition."[23]

Our personal interpretations are to be crucified, so to speak, by the light of what has been handed down. This does not mean that each scriptural passage has one "official" interpretation or meaning. On the contrary, the Church has found multiple layers and levels within each word and passage of Scripture. She

---

22 *On the Holy Spirit*, 27, 66.
23 *Miscellanies*, 2.530.

also has allowed for various interpretive approaches to the holy text—literal, moral, mystical, typological, allegorical, etc. Yet all of these layers and methods are judged as to whether they resonate or are otherwise dissonant with the Tradition and consensus of interpretation.

This does not mean that an institutional "elite" within the Church dictates the proper interpretation of Scripture. It simply means that any interpretation of Holy Scripture is held up to the light of "that faith which has been believed *everywhere, always, by all*"[24] to ensure that it does not fall outside the bounds of the apostolic faith. Church Tradition is the consensus of the Church throughout the world, in all ages, and by the majority of her most holy and reputable members. This can be likened to the Church's collective "memory," guarded and preserved by the Holy Spirit.

"The Holy Spirit . . . will bring to your remembrance all things that I said to you [plural]." (John 14:26)

Therefore, when He had risen from the dead, His disciples remembered that He had said this to them. (John 2:22)

Do you not remember that when I was still with you I told you these things? (2 Thess. 2:5)

---

24 St. Vincent of Lérins (d. 445), *Commonitory*, 2: "This rule we shall observe if we follow universality, antiquity, consent. We shall follow universality if we confess that one faith to be true, which the whole Church throughout the world confesses; antiquity, if we in no wise depart from those interpretations which it is manifest were notoriously held by our holy ancestors and fathers; consent, in like manner, if in antiquity itself we adhere to the consentient definitions and determinations of all, or at the least of almost all priests and doctors."

This subjection of Holy Scripture to the light of what the Church has always believed protects against the sprouting of false teachings and a diluting and fracturing of the faith. For conflicting doctrines are a sign of a corrupt interpretation and use of the Scriptures: "Where diversity of doctrine is found, *there*, then, must the corruption both of the Scriptures and the expositions thereof be regarded as existing."[25]

In the Orthodox Church, there is no singular leader or personality who has the authority to alter the tradition or "discover" a new teaching. The Church is governed in a conciliar fashion, meaning that nothing of significance can be done without the assent of the brotherhood of bishops, and through them, the whole flock of Christ. Church history is replete with defenders of the faith, such as St. Athanasius of Alexandria (a deacon at the First Ecumenical Council), St. Maximos the Confessor (a monk), and St. Basil the Great (a bishop), whose heroic fidelity to the sacred Tradition saved the Church from the shipwreck of heresy and compromise.

CLARIFICATIONS

The Orthodox Church has, in general, always encouraged the faithful to personally and fervently read Holy Scripture.[26] She

---

25 Tertullian (AD 160–220), *The Prescription Against Heretics*, 38.
26 It is true that the Synod of Jerusalem in 1692, under the leadership of Patriarch Dositheus, sought to exclude those who have "not inquired into the deep things of the Spirit" and are ignorant of the life and Tradition of the Church, comparing such to infants unable to eat meat. The catalyst for this was the chaos caused by the Protestant Reformation and the multiplicity of interpretations of Scripture that had arisen. (See *Confession of Dositheus*, Question I, Willits, CA: Eastern Orthodox Books.)

has only warned against private interpretation that falls out-side the bounds of Holy Tradition, which even the Scriptures themselves do (see 2 Pet. 1:20). To the contrary, the saints and fathers of the Church, both ancient and recent, exhort the faith-ful to regularly and reverently read the Scripture and apply it in their way of life. As an example, St. John Chrysostom (fourth–fifth century), Archbishop of Constantinople, preaches inces-santly about the need for all Christians to read Holy Scripture. In his *Homilies on Genesis,* preached in the church of Antioch, he remarks:

> Reading the holy Scriptures is like a treasure. With a treasure, you see, anyone able to find a tiny nugget gains for himself great wealth; likewise in the case of Sacred Scripture, you can get from a small phrase a great wealth of thought and immense riches. The Word of God is not only like a treasure, but is also like a spring gushing with everflowing waters in a mighty flood.[27]

His conviction about the benefits of the knowledge of the Holy Scriptures is so great that he quips, "The ignorance of Scripture is the source of all evil."[28]

In the seventh century, St. John of Damascus teaches the following:

> To search the Scriptures is a work most fair and most profitable for souls. For just as the tree planted by the channels of waters, so also the soul watered by the Divine Scripture is enriched and gives fruit in its season, viz., Orthodox belief, and is adorned with evergreen leafage, I mean actions pleasing to God. For

27 Robert C. Hill, *Homilies on Genesis,* 1–17 (The Fathers of the Church, Vol. 74, Catholic University of America Press, 1986), p. 39.
28 Homily 9, On Colossians.

through the Holy Scriptures we are trained to action that is pleasing to God, and untroubled contemplation. For in these we find both exhortation to every virtue and dissuasion from every vice.[29]

St. Ignatius Brianchaninov, a bishop and theologian of nineteenth-century Russia, echoes these sentiments, encouraging the faithful not only to read the Scriptures but to do so with attentiveness in a spirit of adoration:

> Read the Gospel with the greatest reverence and attention. Do not consider anything in it of little importance, little worthy of consideration. Every iota of it emits a gleam of life. Neglect of life is death.[30]

It is worth noting that for the bulk of church history the Scriptures were not often available to the average believer. Rather, Christians heard the Scriptures as they were read in church (see Col. 4:16; 1 Thess. 5:27). The Scriptures were then expounded upon by those gifted and ordained to preach and teach. So, keeping in mind the great value of reading Holy Scripture, we should also be reminded that not all have the gift of teaching (see 1 Cor. 12:27–30) and that Scripture comes alive in the gathering and worship of the whole church.

While it is true that the bishop (and through him the priest) has an official responsibility for teaching within the Body, the Orthodox recognize a charismatic gift of teaching that may be given to any one of the faithful, but particularly to those who have reached great sanctification.[31] In Orthodoxy, theology is

---

29 "Exposition of the Orthodox Faith," NPNF, 9:89.

30 http://orthodoxinfo.com/praxis/xc_home.aspx.

31 While this is true, we must also recognize that such a gift must be recognized both by the faithful and by the bishop responsible for such a person. In the

not mainly the result of intelligence or schooling or office; it is the fruit of true prayer and a pure heart. In the early Church, bishops were distinguished by their holiness and purity of life. The office of bishop was not thought of in institutional terms but as a charismatic gift of the Spirit of which a man must be worthy and to which he must remain faithful. In other words, the man must embody the Tradition of the Church through his own personal experience of the life of grace. It was also assumed that candidates for the episcopacy were purified of sinful passions and illumined by the Holy Spirit. For this reason, after the persecutions ended, it was determined that bishops would be taken from the ranks of holy monks who had shown themselves as men of great spiritual stature.

THE HOLY SCRIPTURES ON SCRIPTURE & TRADITION

While there are no passages in Scripture that teach sola scriptura, there are many passages that reveal that Tradition is authoritative for Christians. Furthermore, the Tradition not only includes doctrines to be believed but encompasses the whole way of life that brings salvation. This way of life, which was taught and modeled by the apostles, is not completely and explicitly delineated in Holy Scripture. The Christian forms of worship, for instance, are not made explicit in the New Testament.

Orthodox Church we place humility and obedience above spiritual gifts or talents. A very gifted person may lose his salvation due to pride expressed by unwillingness to submit to the authority that God ordained within the Church. The Scriptures clearly teach that not all Christians are called to be teachers (1 Cor. 12:29).

Many verses show that one can be led astray by misinterpreting the Scriptures. The failure of the sola scriptura doctrine is clearly seen by its fruits—the continual splintering of denominations, all claiming to interpret the Scriptures correctly without reference to Church Tradition.

Tradition (written or unwritten) is authoritative

2 Thess. 2:15: Therefore, brethren, stand fast and hold the traditions which you were taught, whether by word or our epistle.

2 Thess. 3:6: But we command you, brethren, in the name of our Lord Jesus Christ, that you withdraw from every brother who walks disorderly and not according to the tradition which he received from us.

1 Thess. 4:1: . . . just as you received from us how you ought to *walk* and to please God.

1 Cor. 11:2: Now I praise you, brethren, that you remember me in all things and keep the traditions just as I delivered *them* to you.

1 Cor. 15:3-4: For I delivered [passed on, "traditioned"] to you first of all that which I also received: that Christ died for our sins according to the Scriptures, and that He was buried, and that He rose again the third day according to the Scriptures.

1 Cor. 11:23: For I received from the Lord that which I also delivered ["traditioned"] to you: that the Lord Jesus on the *same* night in which He was betrayed took bread.

2 Tim. 1:13: Hold fast the pattern of sound words which you have heard from me, in faith and love which are in Christ Jesus.

Gal. 1:8: But even if we, or an angel from heaven, preach any other gospel to you than what we have preached to you, let him be accursed.

The Scriptures are often misused or misinterpreted

Matt. 4:5–6: Then the devil took Him up into the holy city, set Him on the pinnacle of the temple, and said to Him, "If You are the Son of God, throw Yourself down. For it is written: 'He shall give His angels charge over you,' and, 'In *their* hands they shall bear you up, / Lest you dash your foot against a stone.'"

John 5:39: "You [the Jews] search the Scriptures, for in them you think you have eternal life; and these are they which testify of Me."

Acts 8:30–31: So Philip ran to him [the Ethiopian Eunuch], and heard him reading the prophet Isaiah, and said, "Do you understand what you are reading?" And he said, "How can I, unless someone guides me?" And he asked Philip to come up and sit with him.

2 Pet. 3:16: [There] are some things hard to understand [in St. Paul's Epistles], which untaught and unstable *people* twist to their own destruction, as *they do* also the rest of the Scriptures.

Scripture is to be interpreted within the Church community

2 Pet. 1:20–21: Knowing this first, that no prophecy of Scripture is of any private interpretation, for prophecy never came by the will of man, but holy men of God spoke *as they were* moved by the Holy Spirit.

Non-canonical Old Testament writing becomes New Testament Scripture

Jude 14–15: Now Enoch, the seventh from Adam, prophesied about these men also, saying, "Behold, the Lord comes with ten thousands of His saints, to execute judgment on all, to convict all who are ungodly among them of all their ungodly deeds which they have committed in an ungodly way, and of all the harsh things which ungodly sinners have spoken against Him."

Sola scriptura *should be judged by its fruit*

Matt. 7:15-20: "Beware of false prophets, who come to you in sheep's clothing, but inwardly they are ravenous wolves. You will know them by their fruits. Do men gather grapes from thornbushes or figs from thistles? Even so, every good tree bears good fruit, but a bad tree bears bad fruit. A good tree cannot bear bad fruit, nor *can* a bad tree bear good fruit. Every tree that does not bear good fruit is cut down and thrown into the fire. Therefore by their fruits you will know them."

THE CHURCH FATHERS ON SCRIPTURE & TRADITION

St. Hegesippus (c. AD 110–180)

When I had come to Rome, I [visited] Anicetus, whose deacon was Eleutherus. And after Anicetus [died], Soter succeeded, and after him Eleutherus. In each succession and in each city there is a continuance of that which is proclaimed by the law, the prophets, and the Lord. (*Memoirs*, cited in Eusebius, *Ecclesiastical History* 4:22 [AD 180])

Letter to Diognetus (c. AD 150–190)

I am not speaking of things that are strange to me, nor is my undertaking unreasonable, for I have been a disciple of apostles, and now I am becoming a teacher of the Gentiles. The things that pertain to the tradition I try to minister fittingly to those who are becoming disciples of the truth. (2:11)

St. Irenaeus of Lyons (c. early second century–AD 202)

As I said before, the Church, having received this preaching and this faith, although she is disseminated throughout the whole world, yet guarded it, as if she occupied but one house. She likewise believes these things just as if she had but one soul and one and the same heart; and harmoniously she proclaims them and teaches them and hands them down, as if she possessed but one mouth. For, while the languages of the world are diverse, nevertheless, the authority of the tradition is one and the same. (*Against Heresies* 1:10:2 [AD 189])

Clement of Alexandria (c. AD 150–215)

Well, they preserving the tradition of the blessed doctrine derived directly from the holy apostles, Peter, James, John, and Paul, the sons receiving it from them . . . came by God's will to us also to deposit those ancestral and apostolic seeds . . . according as they delivered it. For such a sketch as this, will, I think, be agreeable to a soul desirous of preserving from loss the blessed tradition. (*Miscellanies* 1:1 [AD 208])

The dogmas taught by strange sects will be brought forward. And against these dogmas will be opposed all those things that should be premised in accordance with the profoundest contemplation of the knowledge that will advance to our view, as we proceed to the renowned and venerable canon of tradition. (*Miscellanies* 2.302)

It is necessary for men to abandon impious opinion and turn from there to the true tradition. (*Miscellanies* 2.530)

He, who has spurned the ecclesiastic tradition and darted off to the opinions of heretical men—he has ceased to be a man of God and to remain faithful to the Lord. (*Miscellanies* 2.551)

St. Cyprian of Carthage (c. AD 200–258)

Know that we do not depart from the tradition of the Gospel and of the apostles. Rather, with constancy and firmness, we ... maintain the discipline of the church. (*Letters* 75.3, 5.357)

You must diligently observe and keep the practice delivered from divine tradition and apostolic observance, which is also maintained among us and almost throughout all the provinces. (*Letters* 75.3, 5.371)

CHAPTER 6

The Eucharist & Liturgical Worship

"I am the living bread which came down from heaven. If anyone eats of this bread, he will live forever; and the bread that I shall give is My flesh, which I shall give for the life of the world." (John 6:51)

Through the mouth of the Prophet Malachi, the Lord had foretold a "pure offering" that would one day be made "among the Gentiles . . . in every place" (1:11). As the first Gentile among the followers of Christ, Cornelius held this prophecy especially dear. The prophet had testified of the Lord's displeasure with the priests of Israel who had departed from His way and who "offer defiled food on My altar" (1:7).

Cornelius learned that this prophecy was fulfilled in Jesus Christ through His apostles. For having entered into the communion of the Church through the rebirth of baptism, he and his household, the first Gentile Christians, are now encountering the "pure offering" Malachi foretold. Among God's people it is known as the Lord's Supper, or simply "the breaking of the bread."

As have all his brethren in Christ, Cornelius has come to know this Supper as the central and defining act of Christ's Church.

This offering of praise, made in the form of bread and wine offered on the altar, is the ultimate means of communion with God through Christ by the action of the Holy Spirit. It is the most perfect offering of thanksgiving (Eucharist) to God, because through it Christians "remember," that is, relive, the one, perfect offering of the Lord Jesus, the source of all thanksgiving.

Cornelius still marvels and rejoices at the glorious mystery: how this humble offering of bread and wine by God's grace becomes the flesh and blood of the Lord who was crucified and is risen. He has heard that this teaching is from the mouth of Jesus Himself: "He who eats My flesh and drinks My blood abides in Me, and I in him" (John 6:56).

On the Lord's Day, called by Gentiles the day of the sun, all the Christians, Gentile or Jew, gather together for the breaking of the bread. It is not only their means of unity with Christ, but it is what binds them together and makes them the Body of Christ. Cornelius has been instructed that no Christian can be absent from this gathering without reasonable cause, for it is the source of grace and the fulfillment, not only of Malachi's prophecy, but of God's purpose in Christ.

What Is the Holy Eucharist?

Eucharist (Greek for *thanksgiving* or *gratitude*) became the most common term used to embody the central act of Christian worship. It was in wide use by the successors of the apostles, such as St. Ignatius of Antioch and St. Justin Martyr, and perhaps by the apostles themselves (see Heb. 13:15). It is used to refer to both the liturgical service of Holy Communion and the Holy Gifts themselves, the Body and Blood of Christ.

On the eve of His Passion, the Lord ate a Passover meal with His disciples. Instead of the prayers of thanksgiving for God's blessings normally offered over first the bread and then the wine, Jesus transformed the Jewish meal by inserting the reality of His coming death and Resurrection, saying explicitly, "Take, eat; this is My body," and "Drink from it, all of you. For this is My blood of the new covenant, which is shed for many for the remission of sins" (Matt. 26:26–28). For this reason the Eucharist is also called the Lord's Supper or Mystical Supper.

In the Orthodox Church, the entirety of the liturgical service through which we give thanks to God and receive His Body and Blood is called the Divine Liturgy. The Divine Liturgy includes, like a seamless garment, the liturgy of the Word, followed usually by the homily or sermon, and then the liturgy of the Eucharist.

The Eucharist is also called Communion or more properly Holy Communion, as St. Paul intimates to the Corinthians: "The cup of blessing which we bless, is it not the communion of the blood of Christ? The bread which we break, is it not the communion of the body of Christ?" (1 Cor. 10:16).

What can we learn from these four titles—Eucharist, Lord's Supper, Divine Liturgy, and Holy Communion—regarding the nature of this Christian act of offering?

EUCHARIST

First, we call this service to God "Eucharist" because it is the ultimate offering of thanksgiving to God. Gratitude is the natural state of one who loves God and has faith in Him.

This was the condition of Adam and Eve in paradise. The Holy Fathers teach us that our first parents were in a constant and natural state of prayer and conversation with God, a condition of illumination. Adam and Eve were able to experience the living presence of God in the depths of their hearts, as the eye of their soul, or *nous,* was not darkened by sins. In their natural state, all their human energies were focused and directed toward the contemplation of God living within them. God had breathed the Holy Spirit into them at the time of their creation (Gen. 2:7), and they were made in God's image—that is, made like His Son, Jesus Christ, who therefore resided in the depths of their being.

Man, as created by God, was a eucharistic being. He saw all things as they are—a gift and blessing from God given freely for no other reason except His overflowing love for His creation. In response to God's gifts and abounding grace, Adam and Eve could only give thanks to God. They used God's creation, not as an end in itself or for self-centered gratification, but as a means of offering gratitude to God. And this giving of thanks only increased their experience of God's grace.

As the only creatures of God both material and spiritual, Adam and Eve had the vocation to be the priests of creation. Their work was to offer the material creation as a sacrifice of praise to the Creator, to offer the food and drink of this world to God on the altar of a pure heart. Their whole existence was to be a never-ending eucharistic liturgy whereby they would offer God's own gifts back to Him in a spirit of thanks. As the priest proclaims when he lifts up the offering of the bread and wine in the Divine Liturgy, "Thine own of Thine own, we offer unto Thee." And they were to do this not as isolated and self-enclosed individuals but "on behalf of all and for all." Their priestly ministry was to spread this grace and thanksgiving from paradise into the whole creation.

But, as we know, Adam and Eve turned away from their vocation; they lost their priesthood; they lost their natural communion with God. The first-created succumbed to temptation and ate of the forbidden tree, not as a means of communion with God but to circumvent Him. They essentially made an offering of ingratitude. By sinning (the Greek word for *sin* means literally "missing the mark"), this eucharistic liturgy was interrupted and stalled, sending reverberations throughout all creation. The consequence of this was corruption (decay, pain, suffering, sickness, etc.), which ultimately leads to physical death.

But God, wishing to restore man to his true dignity and renew His image, sent His Son, Jesus Christ, to become Man, to show us what it means to be in communion with God, allowing Him to give Himself as an offering to God on our behalf, overcoming corruption and death by His Resurrection. In offering His own Body, His Flesh and Blood, He Himself has become our Eucharist, our Thanksgiving and Communion, through whom we have communion with God.

By being joined to His Body, the Church, we are restored to communion with God and to the eucharistic way of life. This life is most perfectly communicated to us through our participation in the Divine Liturgy and Holy Communion, to the extent we truly desire it, participate in it, and live it.

The center of the Divine Liturgy is our thanksgiving to God for all His gracious gifts and blessings, but especially for His salvation through Jesus Christ. In the Liturgy we become eucharistic beings again, like Adam and Eve in Paradise:

Priest: Let us lift up our hearts!
People: We lift them up unto the Lord.

Priest: Let us give thanks unto the Lord.
People: It is meet and right.

The priest then begins the great eucharistic prayer, which recounts and gives thanks for the wonderful works of God, culminating in the coming of His Only-begotten Son:

> It is meet and right to hymn Thee, to bless Thee, to praise Thee, to give thanks unto Thee and to worship Thee in every place of Thy dominion; for Thou art God, ineffable, inconceivable, invisible, incomprehensible, ever-existing and eternally the same, Thou and Thine Only-begotten Son and Thy Holy Spirit. Thou it was who didst bring us from nonexistence into being and when we had fallen away didst raise us up again, and didst not cease to do all things until Thou hadst endowed us with Thy kingdom which is to come. For all these things we give thanks unto Thee, and to Thine only-begotten Son and to Thy Holy Spirit.[1]

In the Eucharist, Christ the High Priest offers Himself *on our behalf*, "for the life of the world," as the perfect thanksgiving to God. He perfects what Adam failed to do and allows us to share in His victory and triumph over the devil (the most *ungrateful* of all creatures).

Since in the end we have nothing worthy to offer to God, we are taken up into the one sacrifice of praise to the Incarnate Lord, Jesus Christ. In the Eucharist, we offer this fallen world to God, and He returns it to us as the fruit of His perfect Offering, the "pure offering" of His own Flesh and Blood, as the means of communion with Him.

We offer our imperfect thanks to God and in return are given

---

1   The Eucharist Prayer of St. Basil the Great spells out in great detail God's redemptive activity among His people.

Christ, the perfect Eucharist. We offer our lives to God in the form of the bread and wine, but we receive the life of God in the form of the life-giving Flesh and Blood of His Son. We offer our sinful selves to God and are graced by God to receive the Sinless One. We offer earthly food and receive the Food of the Kingdom of God. We offer earthly bread to God but receive it from Him as the Bread from heaven. We lift up our hearts, and He comes down to abide in them, with the Father and the Spirit. For this there can be only one response—thanksgiving.

LORD'S SUPPER

The first Eucharist, just prior to the Lord's Passion, was celebrated in the context of a meal or supper. Just as our first parents' fall from communion with God occurred because of food, so the celebration of the Mystery of God's abiding with and in us is given in the form of food.

Jesus celebrated this first Eucharist with His apostles within the context of a Passover meal. This was a ritual or liturgical meal with a definite structure that was accompanied by particular prayers. The rabbi or the eldest or most respected participant presided, leading the chanting of specific, assigned prayers of blessing and thanksgiving to God. The one who presided first took bread and said the prayer of blessing. He then broke and distributed the bread to the others. After the rest of the meal, he took a cup of wine mingled with water and prayed the assigned blessing for the cup. He then drank of it and offered it to all present.

We know from the Scriptures that in this case Jesus changed at least some of the designated prayers. For after He blessed and broke the bread, and as He distributed it, He identified it as His own Body: "Take, eat; this is My body" (Mark 14:22). And when He distributed the cup of wine He referred to it as His Blood, which was being shed for the whole world: "This is My Blood of the new covenant, which is shed for many" (Mark 14:24). The Gospels of Saints Matthew and Mark note that the meal ended with a hymn.

Therefore, the Lord's Supper was not an impromptu, improvised, casual dining experience, but a liturgical rite featuring bread and wine as offerings for God's bountiful blessings in thanksgiving for His work of redemption among His people. Jesus, then, inserted something *new*—the greatest and final redemptive work He was about to accomplish through the Cross. As St. John Chrysostom notes, "He both sketched out the Passover that was a type and added in the true Passover."[2]

As God, knowing what was to come, He offered the bread mystically as His Body that would be broken and offered to God for our salvation. He identified the cup as the Blood that He would shed for the remission of sins and for our reconciliation and union with God. Thus, the rite is called the "Mystical Supper," a sacramental supper, because through it we participate in His death and Resurrection in a real but mystical way that transcends time and space.

---

2   Hieromonk Gregorios, *The Divine Liturgy: A Commentary in the Light of the Fathers,* trans. Elizabeth Theokritoff (Columbia, MO: Newrome Press, 2009), p. 3. St. John says that at the supper Christ celebrated "both the Passover that was the type and the Passover that was the reality. Christ was doing exactly what an artist does when on the same canvas he first draws an outline and puts in the shading, and then adds the actual colours. At the very same table, He both sketched out the Passover that was a type and added in the true Passover."

It is not by accident that the Lord instituted a meal as the means of uniting Himself with His people. As we have said, it was by food that man fell. But it was also by food—that is, the Tree of Life—that he was to be perfected in God's likeness. Man is a *hungry* being. But he can only be satisfied and satiated by union with God. Yet even this satisfaction serves to heighten his hunger for God.

Adam and Eve sinned inasmuch as they misdirected this God-given hunger and yearning, attempting to find satisfaction in created things apart from God, making the created world the object of their hunger. Being deceived, they traded spiritual fulfillment for sensual pleasure.

In the Eucharist we once again have access to the food of Paradise through the resurrected and deified Body of Jesus Christ, the "Tree of Life" from which Adam and Eve were barred after their sin (Gen. 3:24).[3] When we feed upon this imperishable food, we are filled with life eternal. By it our flesh is united to the undying and incorruptible Flesh and Blood of the God-Man, Jesus Christ.

We abstain from all other food and drink before receiving the Eucharist so that our hunger and thirst might be redirected from this fallen world to Christ, the "bread from heaven" (John 6:32). We then find that our true appetite can only be satisfied through communion with God in the heavenly food of the Eucharist. This was a permanent condition for St. Ignatius of Antioch, who had attained to a spiritual height akin to that of Adam before the Fall:

---

3   According to the Church Fathers, they were barred not as a punishment from God but by His mercy, so that they would not partake of the Tree after their Fall and live eternally in sin, corruption, and sorrow.

I have no taste for corruptible food nor for the pleasures of this life. I desire the Bread of God, which is the flesh of Jesus Christ, who was of the seed of David; and for drink I desire his blood, which is love incorruptible.[4]

Divine Liturgy

The whole service that includes and leads up to the Eucharist has come to be known by Orthodox Christians as the "Divine Liturgy." This description provides us with more clues about the nature of the Church's Eucharist.

As we've seen, the Eucharist is not the invention of man but the revelation and commandment of the Lord. Just as God personally revealed the specific forms and meaning of worship through Moses to His people of the Old Testament (see Ex. 24—30), He did the same to the Church through the Person of His Incarnate Son by means of the eucharistic meal He shared with His disciples. The Lord Jesus not only revealed this worship, but He commanded it: "*Do* this" (Luke 22:19; 1 Cor. 11:24–25).

The Christian Eucharist is therefore called "divine," as its source is God Himself. For Orthodox Christians, worship is not created by man according to his own ideas or logic; rather it has been received from the Lord through His apostles and their successors. St. Paul prefaces his teaching on the institution of the Eucharist with these words: "For I received from the Lord[5] that which I also delivered to you" (1 Cor. 11:23).

The Eucharist, along with the worship of the Church in gen-

---

4   *Letter to the Romans* 7:3.
5   St. Paul's phrase, "received from the Lord," most likely refers to the apostolic Tradition of the Church, which he received through membership in the Church, confirmed by St. Peter and others.

eral, is *liturgical*. The Eucharist therefore follows a fixed pattern received from Christ and the apostles. Corporate Christian worship is not, as some imagine, an unstructured, spontaneous, freeform activity to be altered at the whim of leaders or congregants. In about the year AD 160, St. Justin the Martyr provided us with a skeletal pattern of the Eucharist received from the apostles:

> And on the day which is called Sunday, all who live in the cities or in the country gather together in one place and the memoirs of the apostles and the writings of the prophets are read as long as time permits. Then the reader concludes, and the president verbally instructs and exhorts us to the imitation of these excellent things, then we all rise together and offer up our prayers; and as I said before when we have ended our prayer, bread is brought and wine and water; and the president in like manner offers up prayers and thanksgivings according to his ability and the people give their assent by saying "Amen"; and there is a distribution and a partaking by everyone of the Eucharist and to those who are absent a portion is brought by the deacons.[6]

Here we have the basic pattern for the Divine Liturgy still in use today in the Orthodox Church:

The Liturgy of the Word
Reading of Scriptures
Homily (Sermon)
Prayer (intercessory)
The Liturgy of the Eucharist
Offering of Bread and Wine
Eucharistic Prayers
Distribution of Holy Communion

---

6 *Apology* 1, 67.

Since the apostles were Jews, and Jewish worship was liturgical, it is not surprising that Christian worship followed a similar pattern. It is clear that the apostles did not reject the liturgical worship Israel received from God as they continued "daily with one accord *in the temple*" (Acts 2:46, emphasis added). Only the breaking of the bread (the Eucharist) was done apart from the normative liturgical life of Judaism, as this rite was exclusive to those who had accepted Jesus as Messiah and received Christian baptism. This is confirmed in the writings of St. Justin the Martyr.

> This food is called Eucharist with us, and only those are allowed to partake who believe in the truth of our teaching and have received the washing for the remission of sins and for regeneration [baptism]; and who live in accordance with the directions of Christ.[7]

The New Testament Scriptures do not contain instructions for Christian worship or specific prayers to be used in worship. However, they do attest to the liturgical nature of Christian worship. For example, Saul and Barnabas were ordained to the ministry within the context of liturgical prayer, probably within the Eucharist, as is still the practice of the Orthodox Church today. As Acts 13:2 records, "As they ministered (Greek, *leitourgounton*) to the Lord and fasted, the Holy Spirit said, 'Now separate to Me Barnabas and Saul for the work to which I have called them.'"

The only corporate prayer recorded in the Book of the Acts of the Apostles (4:24–30) also follows a liturgical pattern. It may even have been a specific form of prayer used for occasions of

---

7   *First Apology*, 66.

persecution, as the text implies it was said corporately ("they raised their voice to God with one accord"). As do many Orthodox prayers, it quotes from the Psalms. Here is the complete prayer:

> Lord, You *are* God, who made heaven and earth and the sea, and all that is in them, who by the mouth of Your servant David have said:
> "Why did the nations rage,
> And the people plot vain things?
> The kings of the earth took their stand,
> And the rulers were gathered together
> Against the LORD and against His Christ." (Ps. 2:1–2)
> For truly against Your holy Servant Jesus, whom You anointed, both Herod and Pontius Pilate, with the Gentiles and the people of Israel, were gathered together to do whatever Your hand and Your purpose determined before to be done.
>
> Now, Lord, look on their threats, and grant to Your servants that with all boldness they may speak Your word, by stretching out Your hand to heal, and that signs and wonders may be done through the name of Your holy Servant Jesus.

HOLY COMMUNION

The Eucharist is also known by the name "Holy Communion." In our English Bibles, the word for "communion" (Greek, *koinonia*) is often translated "fellowship," reducing its meaning to a mere social gathering, apart from any reference to the Eucharist. But the biblical and Orthodox experience embodied by the word "communion" is much more than that. It signifies the real communion of faith that exists and is energized by the Eucharist.

God Himself is the source and the model of the Church's life of communion. God is a communion of Persons—Father, Son, and Holy Spirit. He exists as Community in a perfect union of life, will, and activity. Because God is perfect communion, He is also perfect love.

In the Church, this communion of love and truth is available by God's grace, and particularly through the Eucharist, or Holy Communion. Communion with God can only be real when it is rooted in *orthodoxy*, that is, true doctrine and true worship, because true doctrine leads us to true worship or glorification of God—communion with Him. And true worship promotes and reinforces an authentic faith and understanding that also leads to communion with Him.

We could say there are three elements that exist together where there is real Christian communion:

» a common confession and understanding of the faith
» a common way of worship and living ("spirituality")
» crowned by a common Eucharist, which confirms and enlivens true faith, worship, and life.

We see this holy communion of the Church clearly in the description of the first Christian community in Jerusalem: "And they continued steadfastly in the apostles' doctrine and fellowship, in the breaking of [the] bread [Eucharist], and in [the liturgical] prayers" (Acts 2:42). The Scriptures also show us that oneness of faith and prayer naturally creates community or communion.

> Now the multitude of those who believed were of one heart and one soul; neither did anyone say that any of the things he possessed was his own, but they had all things in common. (Acts 4:32–33)

In this way they led a eucharistic life, a life that leads to communion with God and one another. Practically speaking, the life led by the early Church was akin to Orthodox monastic life, except that it included married couples.

There are two aspects or dimensions of our life of communion in the Church. We could call these two dimensions *vertical* and *horizontal*. The first and most obvious dimension of the Eucharist is the vertical. In Holy Communion we have union with God. In his first letter to the Corinthians, the Apostle Paul expresses the nature of the Eucharist as communion with the Lord:

> The cup of blessing which we bless, is it not the fellowship [communion] of the blood of Christ? The bread which we break, is it not the fellowship [communion] of the body of Christ? (10:16)

The Apostle Paul also testifies that the Eucharist is communion among the individual members of the Church: "For we, *though* many, are one bread *and* one body; for we all partake of that one bread" (1 Cor. 10:17).

Here St. Paul expresses the horizontal direction of Holy Communion. The horizontal dimension is our unity with the apostles and with all who are joined to the apostles, past, present, and future. Holy Communion is not only communion with Jesus Christ but also with the members of His Body, the Church. We come to communion with God through the Church. The Apostle John expresses this when he writes:

> That which we have seen and heard we declare to you, that you also may have fellowship [communion] with us; and truly our fellowship [communion] *is* with the Father and with His Son Jesus Christ. (1 John 1:3)

In this horizontal aspect of communion we also include the departed saints, who are "with Christ" (Phil. 1:23). Because they are truly united to Jesus, we have communion with them through Him. (See Chapter 10, "Intercession of the Saints.") We know from the Scriptures that the saints, "the spirits of just men made perfect," commune with us in the Holy Eucharist (Heb. 12:23).

We do not come to Christ as isolated or separated individuals. We cannot have communion with an isolated Christ, for He is never alone. He is always with His Body or Bride, the Church. Therefore, those who desire communion together must have a complete communion of faith and life, as in a marriage.

We know that the Lord intended and desired that His flock be one. He expressed this desire before His Passion when He prayed to the Father, "that they may be one as We *are*" (John 17:11). This oneness Jesus prayed for is not a partial unity, or a unity in the basics; it is not paying lip service to a philosophy or ideology from a safe distance. As He Himself expressed it, it is nothing less than the perfect communion He shares with His Father: "that they all may be one, as You, Father, *are* in Me, and I in You; that they also may be one in Us" (John 17:21).

Both the vertical (human-to-God) and the horizontal (human-to-human) dimension of Holy Communion come alive together in and through the Church. These are two distinct but interrelated and inseparable movements of unity that intersect like a cross in the Eucharist. A horizontal communion alone is merely a club or a commune—or, in a political context, communism. But attempting to isolate the vertical from the horizontal dimension creates an individualistic, churchless, self-serving "spirituality" based on personal opinions and preferences.

A prayer from the Liturgy of St. Basil the Great, which comes just after the consecration of the Holy Gifts of Communion, provides us with a beautiful expression of the communion among the members of the Church.

> And as for us, partakers of the one bread and of the [one] cup, do Thou unite all to one another unto communion of the Holy Spirit, and grant that no one of us may partake of the holy Body and Blood of Thy Christ unto judgment or unto condemnation, but rather that we may find mercy and grace with all the holy ones who through the ages have been well pleasing unto Thee.

Mystery of Mysteries

The Holy Eucharist is the Mystery of mysteries and Sacrament of sacraments. It is the highest mountain within the landscape of the sacramental life of the Church. The Eucharist is also the source of the sacramental life. Why? Because through it we are joined to Christ's crucified, resurrected, and ascended Body. And this is *salvation*—to be grafted into the Flesh of the Savior and thus be filled with the uncreated and divine grace and energies of God. As He Himself said, "He who eats My flesh and drinks My blood abides in Me, and I in him" (John 6:56).

This was the very reason for the Incarnation, the loving purpose for which God "gave His only begotten Son" (John 3:16). It is the purpose for which God created the universe—to unite Himself perfectly with His creation.

The Church *is* this unity of God with His creation. It continues Christ's Incarnation by uniting more and more people to the Body of Christ and by nourishing them with the Body of Christ. As the Fathers of the Third Ecumenical Council affirm, "For He is the life according to His nature as God, and when He became united to His flesh, He made it also to be life-giving."[8]

The Church is the new Paradise with the Tree of Life (i.e., Christ on the Cross) in its midst. The Eucharist continuously feeds and renews the Church—Christ's Body—with His Body. The Eucharist actualizes the Church, and the Church continually discovers Her true nature in the Eucharist.

Because the Eucharist is communion with the incarnate Son, it is the source of grace and the fountainhead of all the other sacraments.[9] The Lord Himself has revealed that without the Eucharist, there is no real life. "Most assuredly, I say to you, unless you eat the flesh of the Son of Man and drink His blood, you have no life in you" (John 6:53).

The Eucharist is the Mystery of mysteries and source of life because through it we remember Christ's redemptive offering and sacrifice. The Lord commanded, "Do this in remembrance of Me" (Luke 22:19). But in the language of the Bible, "remembrance" (Greek, *anamnesis*) is not a simple mental recollection of the past. Rather, anamnesis transports a past event into the present moment. This kind of remembrance implies participation in the full reality and force of that which is being remembered. It is a re-presentation, a real experience in the present of what has been.

---

8   Session 1, *Letter of Cyril to Nestorius* [AD 431].
9   This is why almost all the other mysteries of the Church were originally performed in the midst of the eucharistic gathering, including baptism, marriage, ordination, funeral, etc. And both baptism and confession are also a prerequisite for the Eucharist.

In the Eucharist, then, we are not merely reminded of Christ's Incarnation, death, and Resurrection; we experience and partake of it in the here and now. The Eucharist re-presents or presents anew the life-giving and saving acts of God through Christ through the agency of the Holy Spirit. The Divine Liturgy is therefore not a re-sacrifice of Christ (an unfortunate but popular description used in the Roman Church at the time of the Reformation). It is not a new Lord's Supper but the very same sacrifice on the Cross, "once *for all*" (Heb. 10:10), and the same Supper wherein Christ shared His broken Body and spilled Blood with the disciples. In the words of St. John Chrysostom, "The sacrifice that was offered then, we offer now too."[10] And again, "that very same Supper at which Christ was present is accomplished. The eucharistic Supper does not differ from that Supper in any way."[11]

Through the mystery of this remembrance and because His saving acts are not confined to the past but are eternally present realities, the faithful participate not only in His sacrificial death but also in His glorious Resurrection. Chrysostom expresses this as well in another homily:

> The Mystery we celebrate at Easter contains nothing additional to what we celebrate now [in the Sunday Eucharist]. It is one and the same, the same grace of the Holy Spirit. It is always Easter.[12]

In the Eucharist the Church transcends created time and space, entering into the timeless and heavenly liturgy. For this reason

---

10   *The Divine Liturgy*, p. 18.
11   *Ibid.*
12   *Ibid.*

our hymnography speaks of past events as present: "*Today* Christ is born," "*Today* Christ is ascended," and so forth. All of these historical acts of the Lord who accomplished our salvation within history are simultaneously present in the heavenly liturgy, where all of history exists at once.

In God's "time" *all* is present *all* the time. For instance, in St. John's Apocalypse, Jesus is presented as "the Lamb slain from the foundation of the world" (Rev. 13:8). In the heavenly vision of Isaiah (6:6), it is the resurrected Christ who is seen as the "live coal" taken from the altar that cleanses the sins of the prophet (itself a foreshadowing of Holy Communion).

Since the Eucharist is all of this, it communicates not the fallen and corruptible life of this world, but eternal life. "Whoever eats My flesh and drinks My blood has eternal life, and I will raise him up at the last day. For My flesh is food indeed, and My blood is drink indeed" (John 6:54–55).

Holy Communion is the food of eternal life, heavenly food. It is food, because in the Incarnation Christ assumed material creation. It is heavenly, because He was raised never to die again but ascended back to His Father. "I am the living bread which came down from heaven. If anyone eats of this bread, he will live forever; and the bread that I shall give is My flesh, which I shall give for the life of the world" (John 6:51).

Medicine of Immortality

Realizing all the above, we should also recognize that the Eucharist is the healing of our soul and body. It is a medicine to be received as a cure for the sickness of sinful passions. Holy Communion is meant to be medicine to bring our fallen humanity back to its original and natural health, in which all our God-given energies are concentrated and consecrated in Christ for incorruptible life. St. Ignatius of Antioch affirms the eucharistic food as "the medicine of immortality" when he encourages the Ephesian Christians to "obey the bishop and the presbytery with undisturbed mind, breaking one loaf, which is the medicine of immortality, the antidote which results not in dying but in living forever in Jesus Christ."

But the Eucharist is not a magic pill. Holy Communion does not cure us without our cooperation and faith. Our participation must be accompanied by a life of repentance with the help of the Sacrament of Confession and the struggle to "crucify the flesh" (Gal. 5:24)—to redirect our soul's sinful energies by an ascetical effort to keep the commandments of God. This in turn opens us to God's grace and energizes us further toward virtue and love of God and neighbor.

In essence, what we are saying is that the liturgical and eucharistic life does not work without the ascetical life and effort. The grace of God in the Eucharist cannot force itself upon a heart that is hardened or unwilling to struggle to repent. So it is possible to partake regularly of Holy Communion without an increase in grace and virtue, because there is no ascetical effort to open the heart to receive it.

St. Mary of Egypt received the Eucharist only twice in her life, once at the beginning of her repentance and then at the end of her life. However, her repentance was such that the grace of the Body and Blood of Christ was retained and moved her to even greater struggles for the sake of the love of God. That single drop of Holy Communion at the beginning of her life in

Christ was enough to bring her to the heights of sanctification due to her continual cooperation with God's grace through repentance.

Thus the Eucharist works upon each person according to his or her spiritual condition. While the Eucharist is undoubtedly the Body and Blood of the Savior, it does not automatically sanctify us against our will. As Clement of Alexandria warns, "Into the impure soul, the grace of God finds no entrance."[13] On the contrary, it is clear from the Scriptures and Church Tradition that Holy Communion may be received in a manner that does not benefit or is even harmful to the soul. This is why the prayers prescribed to be said before Holy Communion beseech God that we would not partake "unto condemnation."

Just as strong medicine, like chemotherapy, can only be received if the body is healthy enough to endure it, so the fire of the Eucharist can burn or weaken us spiritually when we are unprepared or approach unworthily. This very phenomenon occurred in the Corinthian church. St. Paul addresses the issue head-on in his first epistle. He ascribes the recent illnesses and deaths in the community to the judgment that naturally follows when Holy Communion is approached casually:

> Therefore whoever eats this bread or drinks *this* cup of the Lord in an unworthy manner will be guilty of the body and blood of the Lord. But let a man examine himself, and so let him eat of the bread and drink of the cup. For he who eats and drinks in an unworthy manner eats and drinks judgment to himself, not discerning the Lord's body. For this reason many *are* weak and sick among you, and many sleep [i.e., have died]. (1 Cor. 11:27–30)

---

13   Bercot, *op. cit.,* ANF vol. 2, p. 595.

The apostle says elsewhere, "Our God is a consuming fire" (Heb. 12:29). Fire can either warm and comfort or burn and destroy. The Church applies this same understanding to Holy Communion, through which we receive the fire of divinity in Christ's Body. If the soul has become weak and brittle through sin and neglect, there is danger that the eucharistic fire, instead of burning away our sins, may expose them. "For what fellowship has righteousness with lawlessness? And what communion has light with darkness?" (2 Cor. 6:14). The Apostle Peter understood this intuitively when, overwhelmed by the power of Jesus, he fell down before Him, saying, "Depart from me, for I am a sinful man, O Lord!" (Luke 5:8).

For this reason, father confessors may suggest that a person who has sinned abstain from communion for a time so that the soul might be strengthened first through repentance and faith. This is not a punishment but a medicine for the healing of soul and body.

But when we are actively striving to live a life of repentance by faith in God, Holy Communion is for us the source and pinnacle of communion with Jesus Christ, for "He who eats My flesh and drinks My blood abides in Me, and I in him" (John 6:56).

The Eucharist and the Reformation

There exists today a rather broad spectrum of Protestant doctrine regarding the nature of the Eucharist. What developed historically is the result of trends in Western theology and practice along with the individual notions of various reform movements. Several developments or abuses related to the celebration of the

Roman Mass (the Roman word for the Divine Liturgy) became sources of objections and helped to form the Protestant attitudes toward the Eucharist. Let's look briefly at several of the most important of these.

PURGATORY AND INDULGENCES

First, the Mass was connected to the doctrine of purgatory and the buying and selling of indulgences.[14] For indulgences could (and still can) be acquired for attending Mass on certain days and could be gained on behalf of departed loved ones by having a Mass said for the dead.[15]

Hence private masses were solicited from clergy with the incentive of a financial offering. The high demand for masses created by the prospect of lessening a relative's time in Purgatory seems to be the origin of the current practice of allowing a single priest to serve multiple masses on the same day, something previously forbidden by the Church canons (and still forbidden in the Orthodox Church). In Luther's Eighty-third Thesis he alludes to these transactions:

> Why should funeral and anniversary masses for the dead continue to be said? And why does not the pope repay, or permit to be repaid, the benefactions instituted for these purposes?[16]

---

14 The Council of Trent established reforms in the practice of granting indulgences. Also, due to previous abuses, in 1567 Pope Pius V "canceled all grants of indulgences involving any fees or other financial transactions" (*Catholic Encyclopedia*, Indulgences: Traffic in Indulgences, http://www.newadvent.org/cathen/07783a.htm).

15 An act done to acquire a plenary indulgence also requires that one make confession and attend Mass within a certain number of days.

16 Martin Luther's 95 Theses, 83, https://carm.org/luthers-95-theses.

THE MASS AS MERIT

For the Reformers, the practice of indulgences was an abomination. It was viewed as a means of earning salvation through good works instead of by God's grace through the work of Christ. Luther also complained that the Roman Mass had come to be viewed through the lens of works, merits, and indulgences. For him this effectively nullified the purpose of Christ's one-time sacrifice for sin.

> Furthermore, they do not regard Christ's body and blood as a sacrifice of thanksgiving, but as a sacrifice of works in which they do not thank God for His grace, but obtain merits for themselves and others . . . we want to win grace ourselves through our works.[17]

At the time of the Reformation and up to the present day, the Mass has been intimately intertwined with the teaching of indulgences as a means of receiving satisfaction for the remission of temporal punishment. The prerequisites for a plenary indulgence are the Sacraments of Confession and Communion. The Mass itself is a means of acquiring the merits of Christ and the saints. As explained by a participant in *Catholic Answers*, a discussion forum for the teachings of the Roman Catholic Church:

> Christ's Sacrifice is infinite, but its merits must be applied to us, hence the need for the Holy Sacrifice of the Mass. Since Christ's Sacrifice has gained for the Church a superabundance of merits, these are applied to remit temporal punishments due to sin via indulgences.[18]

---

17 E. Theodore Bachmann, ed., *Luther's Works: Word and Sacrament IV*, Vol. 38, pp. 117–118.

18 http://forums.catholic.com/showthread.php?t=510679&high-

To miss the Mass on Sunday or other obligatory holy days is considered a mortal sin (unless excused for serious reason). As such, it brings on the guilt of eternal punishment that must be removed through sacramental confession. In that case, the temporal punishment would need to be satisfied by penance or indulgences.

"LOW" MASS

Another unfortunate eucharistic practice that became normative for many centuries up to relatively recent times was the use of the "low Mass" (also called "private Mass"). This was a simplified and shorter version of the Eucharist that was characterized most notably by the lack of participation by the laity. The priest intoned or simply said the service quietly and, for the vast majority of the congregation, inaudibly. One server sang or said the responses normally assigned to the people. Not only was there was no sermon, but preaching was often forbidden by church authority.

Unable to hear or participate in the service, the lay people became spectators or more often used the Mass as a time for personal devotions. The corporate sense of the Eucharist was lost. It was the priest who "did" the Eucharist while the people watched. Their participation was limited to the moment they came forward to receive communion.

Luther complains about this lack of participation by the average Christian, saying that the Mass has become

---

light=Christ%27s+Sacrifice+is+infinite%2C+but+its+merits+must+be+applied+to+us%2C+hence+the+need+for+the+Holy+Sacrifice+of+the+Mass.+Since+C what the priest does alone at the altar, to which no ordinary Christian or layman adds anything. For they indeed know that no layman or ordinary Christian can celebrate mass and they will not allow it. Nor do they allow it to be or to be called a mass when a layman receives the sacrament; but they . . . alone celebrate mass; all other Christians simply receive the sacrament and do not celebrate mass.[19]

Thus the original sense of the Eucharist as the joyful communal celebration of the Body of Christ with the Lord and His saints in their midst was reduced largely to private, individual religious experience.

Martin Luther was not a fan of this inaudible form of the Mass, in which one could not even hear the Words of Institution so central to the Eucharist, especially for the West. Apparently it was even taught by some that it was not proper for the laity to hear these holy words:

But see what they have made of the mass! In the first place, they have hidden these words of the testament and have taught that they are not to be spoken to the laity, that these are secret words to be spoken only by the priest. Has not the devil here in a masterly way stolen from us the chief thing in the mass and put it to silence?[20]

LAITY EXCLUDED FROM COMMUNION

By Luther's day, the laity were also no longer offered the chalice, the Blood of the Lord, but only the consecrated Body. This has continued to be the standard practice in the Catholic Church up to the present. However, when masses were said at the behest

---

19   *Ibid.*
20   *Ibid.*, vol. 35, p. 90.

of certain individuals for their own special "intentions," other congregants present were excluded from *both* elements, and the Body and Blood were offered only to the one who requested the service. This raised the ire of Luther.

> What kind of peddling is this, yes, what thievery and robbery when I am robbed of the body and blood of Christ which by right ought to be given to me freely, and when in exchange for my money and goods, I am offered the sacrifice and work of a godless, miserable man? I would call that robbing me of my nourishment and, moreover, selling refuse for money.[21]

SACRIFICE OR WORK?

Martin Luther saved his most vehement criticism for the designation and teaching of the Mass as a sacrifice. To understand this, it is helpful to remember that at that time the popular characterization of the Mass was dominated by a myopic focus on the gruesomeness of the Crucifixion and rather gross literalism in the understanding of the consecrated host.

That the Mass was a participation in the sacrifice of Christ was indeed an authentic characterization. But since the common explanation of the atonement had now come to mean that Christ was offered as a victim to satisfy or appease God's justice, to speak of the Mass as a sacrifice or re-sacrifice of Jesus conjured up horrid images.

To associate the Mass, and specifically the elements of Communion, with the bloody mutilation of the body of Jesus, punished at the hands of God the Father, was too much. It was enough that it happened once in history and, said the Reform-

---

21 *Ibid.*, vol. 38, p.159.

ers, that alone atones for and justifies sinners who have come to faith in Jesus. It is within this context that the Reformers objected to the idea of the Mass as a sacrifice and a "work" rather than an act of faith and grace.

It is also in this context that the Reformers rejected the doctrine of *transubstantiation* (Latin, *transsubstantiatio*), the term used to describe the change of the bread and wine into the Body and Blood of Christ. The word first appeared in relation to the Eucharist in the tenth century. By the twelfth century, it had become the prevalent description for the change of the Gifts offered in the Eucharist. In the early thirteenth century, the Fourth Lateran Council—considered an "ecumenical council" by the Roman Catholic Church—used this term in its official declaration of faith. Since that time, transubstantiation has become the operative explanation of what happens to the bread and wine in the Eucharist.

The doctrine holds that the whole substance of the bread and wine are transubstantiated (changed in substance) into the literal Body and Blood of Jesus. This also means that the substance of the bread and wine no longer exist, but only the "accidents" of the elements (their appearance, taste, smell, etc.) remain the same. The Orthodox view, by contrast, holds that the elements are indeed changed, but in a mystical sense rather than a literal one.

DIFFERING PROTESTANT VIEWS

While they agreed that they disagreed with transubstantiation, the Reformers could not agree among themselves regarding the nature of the Eucharist.

Martin Luther took the most literal position among the Reformers, confessing that the Eucharist is truly the Body and Blood of Christ "in the forms of" bread and wine. Instead of describing the change as "transubstantiation," he referred to a "sacramental union" of Christ with the consecrated elements. His main disagreement with Rome's doctrine of transubstantiation was in that he insisted the bread and wine retain their actual properties. Luther placed great emphasis on the Words of Institution and on one's belief in them to effect the remission of sins.

In contrast, John Calvin rejected the idea of a sacramental unity with Christ and the Lutheran position that the Body and Blood are present "in, with, and under" the forms of bread and wine. Generally he understood the sacraments as "signs" associated with God's promises. He believed that the Holy Spirit is the only vehicle of communion with God, but emphasized that through the activity of the Holy Spirit, God uses the Eucharist to strengthen and nourish those who partake in faith. To his credit, Calvin confessed that the Eucharist is "a secret too sublime for my mind to understand or words to express. I experience it rather than understand it."[22]

Ulrich Zwingli held a largely symbolic view that sparked an intense dialogue with Luther. He affirmed the presence of Christ in the Eucharist only in a general sense, primarily because of His presence "where two or three are gathered" in His name (Matt. 18:20). In Zwingli's terminology, the Mass is only a "memorial" (reminder) of Christ's sacrifice, and the bread and wine are figurative or symbolic of the Lord's Body and Blood.

---

22   Kilian McDonnel, *John Calvin, the Church, and the Eucharist* (Princeton: Princeton University Press, OCLC, 1967), p. 206.

Zwingli's heretical view of the Incarnation—that Christ's humanity did not participate in His divinity—influenced his opinion that Christ's Body and Blood could not be present in bread and wine. At any rate, Christ's Body could not be present in the Eucharist, as it is now found only in one place, at the right hand of the Father. He did speak of Christ's Body being eaten in a "spiritual manner."

The Anabaptists,[23] who rejected certain elements of Zwingli's teachings, took his position to its logical conclusion. To them, the Lord's Supper is not a sacrament but a symbol, or sign, and a remembrance or commemoration of Christ's sufferings. Over and against any belief in the real presence of Christ in the Eucharist, they held simply that He was *not* present in the bread and wine.

The position taken by the Anabaptist movement (also known as the "Radical Reformation") is representative of that of the majority of evangelical Christians today. The bread and wine are seen as purely symbols that call to mind what Jesus did on the Cross for our salvation. The significance of the Lord's Supper is highly subordinated to the preaching of the word of God in the sermon. Services of communion in evangelical churches bear little resemblance to the eucharistic liturgy of the historical Church.

In the evangelical Christian teaching, there is no objective reality or presence of Christ in the symbols of the bread and wine, and so communion is simply another way to engage one's own personal faith in Jesus. It is not uncommon to hear an

---

23   The Anabaptist movement is represented by the following groups: Amish, Hutterites, Baptists, Mennonites, Church of the Brethren, Quakers, and Brethren in Christ.

admonishment from the preacher to this effect before the commencement of the ceremony. Since communion has little significance for believers and the community, it is usually served infrequently—four times per year or even once a year.

THE HOLY SCRIPTURES ON THE EUCHARIST

Matt. 26:26–28: And as they were eating, Jesus took bread, blessed and broke *it,* and gave *it* to the disciples and said, "Take, eat; this is My body." Then He took the cup, and gave thanks, and gave *it* to them, saying, "Drink from it, all of you. For this is My blood of the new covenant, which is shed for many for the remission of sins." (See also Mark 14:22–24; Luke 22:19–20.)

John 6:48–51: "I am the bread of life. Your fathers ate the manna in the wilderness, and are dead. This is the bread which comes down from heaven, that one may eat of it and not die. I am the living bread which came down from heaven. If anyone eats of this bread, he will live forever; and the bread that I shall give is My flesh, which I shall give for the life of the world."

John 6:53: Then Jesus said to them, "Most assuredly, I say to you, unless you eat the flesh of the Son of Man and drink His blood, you have no life in you."

John 6:54–55: "Whoever eats My flesh and drinks My blood has eternal life, and I will raise him up at the last day. For My flesh is food indeed, and My blood is drink indeed."

John 6:56: "He who eats My flesh and drinks My blood abides in Me, and I in him."

1 Cor. 10:16: The cup of blessing which we bless, is it not the communion of the blood of Christ? The bread which we break, is it not the communion of the body of Christ?

1 Cor. 11:23-26: For I received from the Lord that which I also delivered to you: that the Lord Jesus on the *same* night in which He was betrayed took bread; and when He had given thanks, He broke *it* and said, "Take, eat; this is My body which is broken for you; do this in remembrance of Me." In the same manner *He* also *took* the cup after supper, saying, "This cup is the new covenant in My blood. This do, as often as you drink *it*, in remembrance of Me." For as often as you eat this bread and drink this cup, you proclaim the Lord's death till He comes.

1 Cor. 11:27: Therefore whoever eats this bread or drinks *this* cup of the Lord in an unworthy manner will be guilty of the body and blood of the Lord.

1 Cor. 11:28-30: But let a man examine himself, and so let him eat of the bread and drink of the cup. For he who eats and drinks in an unworthy manner eats and drinks judgment to himself, not discerning the Lord's body. For this reason many *are* weak and sick among you, and many sleep.

THE CHURCH FATHERS ON THE EUCHARIST

St. Ignatius of Antioch (c. AD 35–108)

Take note of those who hold heterodox opinions on the grace of Jesus Christ which has come to us, and see how contrary their opinions are to the mind of God. . . . They abstain from the Eucharist and from prayer because they do not confess that the Eucharist is the flesh of our Savior Jesus Christ, flesh which suffered for our sins and which that Father, in his goodness, raised up again. They who deny the gift of God are perishing in their disputes. (*Letter to the Smyrnaeans* 6:2—7:1)

St. Justin Martyr (AD 100–165)

Moreover, as I said before, concerning the sacrifices which you at that time offered, God speaks through Malachi [1:10–12]. . . . It is of the sacrifices offered to Him in every place by us, the Gentiles, that is, of the bread of the Eucharist and likewise the cup of the Eucharist. (*Dialogue with Trypho* 41)

We call this food Eucharist, and no one else is permitted to partake of it, except one who believes our teaching to be true and who has been washed in the washing which is for the remission of sins and for regeneration [baptism] and is thereby living as Christ enjoined. For not as common bread nor common drink do we receive these; but since Jesus Christ our Savior was made incarnate by the word of God and had both flesh and blood for our salvation, so too, as we have been taught, the food which has been made into the Eucharist by the Eucharistic prayer set down by him, and by the change of which our blood and flesh is nurtured, is both the flesh and the blood of that incarnated Jesus. (*First Apology* 66 [AD 151])

St. Irenaeus of Lyons (c. early second century–AD 202)

For as the bread, which comes from the earth, receives the invocation of God, and then it is no longer common bread but Eucharist, consists of two things, an earthly and a heavenly; so our bodies, after partaking of the Eucharist, are no longer corruptible, having the hope of the eternal resurrection. (*Against Heresies* 4:28 [AD 189])

Clement of Alexandria (c. AD 150–215)

"Eat my flesh," [Jesus] says, "and drink my blood." The Lord supplies us with these intimate nutrients, he delivers over his flesh and pours out his blood, and nothing is lacking for the growth of his children. (*The Instructor of Children* 1:6:43:3 [AD 191])

St. Cyprian of Carthage (c. AD 200–258)

He Himself warns us, saying, "Unless you eat the flesh of the Son of man and drink his blood you shall not have life in you." Therefore do we ask that our Bread, which is Christ, be given to us daily, so that we who abide and live in Christ may not withdraw from His sanctification and from His Body. (*The Lord's Prayer* 18)

Aphrahat the Persian Sage (c. AD 280–345)

After having spoken thus [at the Last Supper] . . . with his own hands the Lord presented his own body to be eaten, and before he was crucified he gave his blood as drink. (*Treatises* 12:6 [AD 340])

St. Cyril of Jerusalem (c. AD 313–386)

The bread and the wine of the Eucharist before the holy invocation of the adorable Trinity were simple bread and wine, but the invocation having been made, the bread becomes the body of Christ and the wine the blood of Christ. (*Catechetical Lectures* 19:7 [AD 350])

Blessed Augustine of Hippo (AD 354–430)

I promised you [new Christians], who have now been baptized, a sermon in which I would explain the sacrament of the Lord's Table. . . . That bread which you see on the altar, having been sanctified by the word of God, is the body of Christ. That chalice, or rather, what is in that chalice, having been sanctified by the word of God, is the blood of Christ. (*Sermons* 227 [AD 411])

MARTIN LUTHER ON THE EUCHARIST

Who ever read in the Scriptures, that "my body" is the same as "this is a sign of my body"? . . . Not one of the Fathers, though so numerous . . . ever said, "It is only bread and wine"; or, "the body and blood of Christ is not there present." Surely it is not credible . . . that they should never . . . so much as once, say . . . "It is bread only" or "the body of Christ is not there," especially it being of great importance, that men should not be deceived. Certainly in so many Fathers, and in so many writings, the negative might at least be found in one of them had they thought the body and blood of Christ were not really present: but they are all of them unanimous. (*Luther's Collected Works*, Wittenburg Edition, no. 7, p. 391, cited from https://bfhu.wordpress.com/2011/05/13/martin-luther-on-the-real-presence/)

CHAPTER 7

Ordination & the Priesthood

Because of the grace given to me by God, that I might be a minister
[liturgist] of Jesus Christ to the Gentiles, ministering the gospel of
God, that the offering of the Gentiles might be acceptable, sanctified
by the Holy Spirit. (Rom. 15:15–16)

As Cornelius and his household are integrated into the family of God in the Church and into the Church's life of communion centered in the celebration of the Eucharist, they also encounter an order within the community. It is an order that is ordained by God and originates in the life of God, the Holy Trinity. It maintains the apostolic nature of the Church, nurtures a life of communion with God, and protects it from wolves who would seek to devour or distort it.

Cornelius especially sees this order, which promotes the balance and harmony of the Body, reflected beautifully in the celebration of the Eucharist. As there is one God, there is also one who presides at the altar as the expression of the unity and fullness of the whole Church. There are others who surround him, concelebrating with him and sharing in his apostolic ministry. And there are those who assist him and are servants for the sake of the Body.

As the nature of the Church is unfolding for him, the new Gentile Christian learns that these men have been called out from within the Church, having first been tested and qualified through an irreproachable life, to share in a unique way in the priestly ministry of Jesus Christ, the heavenly and eternal High Priest. They have been ordained by the apostles of Christ as shepherds for His flock, teaching and "rightly dividing the word of truth" (2 Tim. 2:15), to be the liturgists who lead in the offering of pure worship (Rom. 15:16), "stewards of the mysteries of God" (1 Cor. 4:1), and even "fathers" in the faith (1 Cor. 4:15).

Others serve on a smaller scale and tend to practical needs, looking out for the weaker members of the family. Certain widows and virgins are called to a special consecrated service to God. The whole congregation of the baptized, together with those in leadership, have become "a holy priesthood," offering up "spiritual sacrifices acceptable to God through Jesus Christ" (1 Pet. 2:5).

This is the Christian community, the "body of Christ" (1 Cor. 12:27), made up of many members, each equally "members of the body" (1 Cor. 12:22) and "of one another" (Rom. 12:5; Eph. 4:25), but with a diversity of ministries (1 Cor. 12:5), functions (Rom. 12:4), and gifts (Rom. 12:6–8) within the Body. Cornelius sees that all things are done "decently and in order" (1 Cor. 14:40) for the glory of God and edification of all, not for personal gain or glory (Titus 1:11; 1 Pet. 5:2).

Only a generation later, one of the most prominent leaders of the Church in his day, a bishop and martyr for Christ, St. Ignatius of Antioch, would describe this apostolic pattern of ordering the Body of Christ as a harmonious choir:

For your presbytery—worthy of fame, worthy of God—is attuned to the bishop like strings to a lyre. Therefore by your unity and harmonious love Jesus Christ is sung. Each of you must be part of this chorus so that, being harmonious in unity, receiving God's pitch in unison, you may sing with one voice through Jesus Christ to the Father. (*To the Ephesians*, 4)[1]

Ordination in Protestantism

There is a fundamental difference between the Protestant and Orthodox conceptions of ordination. The Protestant, and especially evangelical, understanding of church leadership is primarily functional. The church leader is a "pastor" or a "minister" because that is what he *does*, i.e., he pastors and ministers. It is often the case that once a pastor is no longer active in ministry, he is no longer considered or considers himself a pastor.

There is nothing of any essential nature bestowed upon the man in the rite of ordination itself; rather, he is recognized or authorized to act as leader of a community. Depending on the denomination, this authority is given either by some form of church leadership, or by a congregation, or by virtue of the completion of studies or attainment of an academic degree.

Put another way, in the evangelical Protestant view, there is no objective or ontological reality imparted in the act of ordination. Therefore, the one ordained is not in any essential way different from what he was before ordination or from the members of his congregation, except that he now functions in a role of leadership. The underlying concern that shaped this theological perspective was the Protestant Reformation's rejection of the particular priesthood (see "The Priesthood of All Believers" below).

This rejection was largely a reaction to the extreme clericalism existing in Roman Catholicism at the time of the Reformation.

---

1   *Apostolic Fathers*, p. 78.

Even the language of the time betrayed this attitude in that the clergy and monastics were referred to as the "religious" with everyone else categorized as "non-religious." The many abuses in the Roman Church and corrupt theological explanations regarding clerical orders solidified a Protestant reaction against priesthood and distrust of hierarchical order within the Church in general.

A more fundamental and profound reason for the Protestant position is the lack of a sacramental view of the Church. If by "church" we mean merely an organization, an institution, an assembly of like-minded believers, rather than the real, mystical Body of Christ and the source of divine grace in this world, then the actions of such a church, including ordination, are also not understood as sacramental and transformational. If the Church is not rightly understood as the divine–human organism of Christ's own resurrected and victorious Body, uniting the heavenly and earthly realms, and thereby as the conduit for the participation of created matter in the divine life of God, then sacraments and the sacramental nature of the Church cannot exist.

Ordination in the Orthodox Church
ORDINATION AS SACRAMENT AND GRACE
Ordination, or Holy Orders, is a Mystery of the Church in which God brings about a real change, as He does also in the other sacramental actions of the Church. (For example, in baptism one is reborn, the old man dies and the new man, Christ, is put on; in marriage a man and woman are made "one flesh," and so forth.) It is a gift from God through Jesus Christ by the power of the Holy Spirit, something given through the mystical power

of Christ's Body, resulting in a tangible gift of divine grace. We see this in St. Paul's exhortation to Timothy to maintain the gift of ordination given by the laying on of hands of the presbyters: "Do not neglect the gift that is in you, which was given to you by prophecy with the laying on of the hands of the eldership" (1 Tim. 4:14).

This gift is not an external, institutional authority, an appointment to a position, or merely a job to be performed. An appointment or selection is a necessary preliminary precursor to the process, but it is not the ordination itself, which is accomplished through prayer and the invocation of the Holy Spirit by the laying on of hands in the eucharistic liturgy. Rather, the Church's act of ordination bestows a spiritual grace that previously did not exist in that man but now exists and acts within him who receives it. "Therefore I remind you to stir up the gift of God which is in you through the laying on of my hands" (2 Tim. 1:6).

QUALIFICATIONS FOR MINISTRY

Since ordination is not essentially a function to be performed but a gift or *charism* to be lived up to and executed with holiness and purity, the qualifications for ordination are not based only on practical abilities or talents such as public speaking. More importantly, the Church requires spiritual qualities that express stability, maturity, and godly virtue.

> A bishop then must be blameless, the husband of one wife, temperate, sober-minded, of good behavior, hospitable, able to teach; not given to wine, not violent, not greedy for money, but gentle, not quarrelsome, not covetous; one who rules his own

house well, having *his* children in submission with all reverence (for if a man does not know how to rule his own house, how will he take care of the church of God?); not a novice, lest being puffed up with pride he fall into the *same* condemnation as the devil. (1 Tim. 3:2–6)

These qualifications are not only concerned with the character of the candidate and his good repute among the members of Christ, but also with the reputation of the Church among non-believers, so that he does not bring scandal upon her. "Moreover he must have a good testimony among those who are outside, lest he fall into reproach and the snare of the devil" (1 Tim. 3:7).

St. Ignatius writes similarly, in this case speaking specifically of those ordained as deacons: "For they are not ministers of food and drink but servants of the church of God; therefore they must guard themselves from accusations as from fire" (*To the Trallians,* 2).[2]

These scriptural instructions are also expressed and clarified in later canons of the Church in order to preserve the principles they stipulate. Because the clergy represent Jesus Christ and the Church in a very official and visible manner, the Church maintains a strictness of expectation regarding them. While all Orthodox Christians are called to live according to the great grace of their baptism, the ordained, who have received the grace to participate sacramentally in the headship of Jesus Christ, have an even greater responsibility to live in a way that is consistent with the gift within them.

---

2   *Apostolic Fathers,* p. 93.

THREEFOLD MINISTRY OF THE CHURCH

This ordained ministry of leadership in the Church is expressed by three major orders of ministry. These three are attested to in the Holy Scriptures and throughout the history of the Church.

First there is the office of bishop,[3] in Greek *episcopos*, meaning "overseer." As the title implies, the bishop's ministry is to oversee and order the church or churches within a specific city or region. This is the office of an apostle or direct successor of the apostles. When the apostles were gathered together after the Resurrection, they selected Matthias to fill the apostolic ministry of Judas, the betrayer of Christ. They quoted Psalm 109:8, "Let another take his office." The word translated "office" here is *episcopen*, the Greek word from which we get our English word "bishop."

In antiquity, the term *episcopos* was used to designate the chief servant in a large household. This is an apt description of an Orthodox bishop, for "If anyone desires to be first, he shall be last of all and servant of all" (Mark 9:35). The unique ministry of the bishop is to preside as the focal point of unity in the assembly of the church community, teaching the apostolic faith and guarding the faith from error. He is to embody the faith of the Church as handed down from the apostles, both in teaching and in his way of life. As the overseer in his region, he maintains the good order of the churches and their various ministries, ordains presbyters and deacons and lower clergy, and takes part in the consecration of brother bishops. He is to be an image and imitator of the Good Shepherd among his flock.

The second major order of ordained leadership is that of

---

3   In the New Testament, the office of bishop is specifically mentioned in Phil. 1:1; 1 Tim. 3:1–2; Titus 1:7. Jesus is called Bishop (or "Overseer") in 1 Pet. 2:25.

presbyter, or elder. It is important to note that the New Testament uses the terms "bishop" and "presbyter" interchangeably, and for good reason. In terms of ordination, there is qualitatively no difference between the two. A bishop is the head presbyter or eldest in rank among presbyters. When a new bishop is made, we say not that he is ordained but that he is *consecrated,* that is, set apart among the presbytery for the ministry of apostolic oversight. Therefore the bishop is still a presbyter, as were the apostles. After exhorting the presbyters in his first letter, the Apostle Peter calls himself "a fellow elder" (1 Pet. 5:1; see 2 John 1:1; 3 John 1:1). St. Timothy was made a bishop "with the laying on of the hands of the eldership" (1 Tim. 4:14), which we know included the Apostle Paul himself (2 Tim. 1:6).

Like the bishop, the presbyter is ordained to preside at the altar, leading a local congregation in worship, preaching, teaching, and ministry, as delegated and overseen by the bishop. The quality of his ordination is identical to that of the bishop, and his ministry reflects similarly that of the apostles. However, he cannot ordain others, and he serves in submission to his local bishop. In St. Ignatius's day, every local church community had a bishop, along with presbyters and deacons all serving in their own capacity. But in time, as the church grew rapidly, a bishop became the overseer of several or many local churches, with the presbyters under his care serving the Eucharist and ministering. This occurred even in the first century, as St. Ignatius relates. "A valid Eucharist is to be defined as one celebrated by the bishop or by a representative [presbyter] of his" (*Letter to the Smyrnaeans,* 8).[4]

---

4   *Apostolic Fathers,* pp. 112–118.

Like the bishop, the presbyter is also a "priest,"[5] as he is a partaker in the priesthood of Jesus Christ by grace through ordination. He is not a priest according to human lineage as in the Old Testament priesthood, but according to the spiritual and eternal Priesthood of Christ. He is ordained in this priesthood to lead the people in offering up "spiritual sacrifices" (1 Pet. 2:5) and most especially the bloodless sacrifice of the Holy Eucharist. Of course, this is not a re-sacrifice of Christ but a participation in the one perfect sacrifice of the Lord. The earthly priest "lends his tongue [voice] and offers his hand"[6] to Jesus Christ, the eternal High Priest, who is always the real Celebrant of the Eucharist, since it is in fact always His self-offering. It is only ours by participation and grace. As St. John Chrysostom teaches:

> This Sacrifice . . . is always the same as that which Christ gave His disciples and which priests now offer . . . because it is not men who sanctify the offering of today; it is the same Christ who sanctified His own.

Here we should note that the place of the bishop or priest among his people is that of a father. Hence the practice of the Church has always been to refer to the ordained clergy as fathers.

This practice is an apostolic one, despite what seems like a clear teaching of the Lord: "Do not call anyone on earth your father; for One is your Father, He who is in heaven" (Matt. 23:9). For even the Apostle Paul refers to himself as the spiritual father

---

5   St. Clement, Bishop of Rome from AD 92–99, uses the term "priest" for the presbyter: "Thus to the high priest [bishop] have been appointed his proper services, to the priests [presbyters] their own place assigned, upon the Levites [deacons] their proper duties imposed; and the layman is bound by the rules for laymen" (*Apostolic Fathers,* p. 40).

6   St. John Chrysostom, quoted in *Divine Liturgy,* p. 42.

of the Corinthians. As he admonishes them in the Lord, calling them his "beloved children," he writes, "For though you might have ten thousand instructors in Christ, yet *you do* not *have* many fathers; for in Christ Jesus I have begotten you through the gospel" (1 Cor. 4:15).

The term is also given to holy ones who have come before. The apostles refer to the saints of the Old Testament as "fathers" on numerous occasions, especially in the Book of Acts but also in the epistles (e.g., 1 Cor. 10:1). The Apostle Peter seems to use the term for Christian leaders who have fallen asleep in Christ (2 Pet. 3:3–4). Our Lord Himself does not hesitate to use the term in his parable of Lazarus and the rich man, speaking of "Father Abraham" not once but twice (Luke 16:24, 30).

Thus, the Lord's teaching in Matthew 23:9 has always been understood in a spiritual manner—as an admonition never to exalt any man to the level of God the Father, who is the true father of us all (see Eph. 4:6). If we were to apply this teaching strictly and literally, no Christian could even address his biological father with this title. In the very next verse (Matt. 23:10), the Lord also teaches us not to call any man "teacher," yet we regularly address school instructors and pastors as "teacher."

By his participation in the headship of Christ, the priest or presbyter (i.e., elder) is placed in a relationship of spiritual fatherhood among the people of God. In this way he is an icon of God the Father. St. Ignatius of Antioch consistently refers to the bishop in particular as reflecting the ministry of God the Father.

A more particular form of this spiritual fatherhood occurs when clergymen or lay monks form relationships of spiritual guidance with Christians who voluntarily become their spiritual children. Relationships of spiritual guidance can also develop with holy women monastics, who may be considered spiritual mothers.

The third office is that of *diaconos*, or deacon, meaning "servant." The ministry of the diaconate originates from the earliest years of the first Christian community in Jerusalem. It was instituted due to the need to care for the widows of the community. The apostles chose and ordained "seven men of *good* reputation, full of the Holy Spirit and wisdom" (Acts 6:3) to organize and ensure the daily distribution of food. The most prominent among the seven deacons, St. Stephen, became the first martyr of the Church (Acts 7:54–60).

The deacon's ministry is qualitatively different from that of presbyter. He is ordained, we could say, to assist the bishop or presbyter in bringing the grace of God from the altar to the people. This is very literally the case, as from earliest times the deacons brought Holy Communion to the sick and those unable to gather with the church for the Eucharist. The deacons organized the ministry to the poor as well. In the life of St. Lawrence, the deacon, the civil authorities mandated that he bring all the treasury of the local church of Rome to be confiscated. Asking for three days' time, St. Lawrence returned, having gathered all the sick and needy in the community, and declared, "Behold, the treasures of the Church!"

The deacon also assists the bishop and presbyter in the celebration of the Eucharist. He does not preside at the altar and may not serve the eucharistic liturgy. But he assists in the liturgy, leads in the prayer of the people, and may assist also in the distribution of Holy Communion.

THE ORIGIN OF THE GRACE OF ORDINATION

Each ordained ministry in the Orthodox Church has Jesus Christ and His ministry as its origin and source. The major orders of leadership in the Church—bishop, priest, and deacon—originate in the Person of Jesus Christ. By God's grace, ordination bestows upon a man a participation or share in the unique ministry of grace that flows from Him. As witnessed by the Scriptures, Jesus Himself is the model and source for all three orders of leadership in the Church.

> » Jesus is the Deacon: "For even the Son of Man did not come to be served, but to serve, and to give His life a ransom for many" (Mark 10:45).

> » Jesus is the Priest: "But Christ came *as* High Priest of the good things to come, with the greater and more perfect tabernacle not made with hands, that is, not of this creation" (Heb. 9:11). "And having been perfected, He became the author of eternal salvation to all who obey Him, called by God as High Priest 'according to the order of Melchizedek'" (Heb. 5:9–10).

> » Jesus is the Overseer (*Episcopos*, Bishop): "For you were like sheep going astray, but have now returned to the Shepherd and Overseer of your souls" (1 Pet. 2:25). "And when the Chief Shepherd appears, you will receive the crown of glory that does not fade away" (1 Pet. 5:4).

We could sum up the ministries of the three orders as follows:

Deacon: *service*
Priest: *sacrifice*
Bishop: *oversight*

THE PRIESTLY NATURE OF THE MINISTRY

We have already mentioned the priestly nature of the bishop and presbyter. While in the Old Testament the priesthood was conferred upon men who were of the tribe of Aaron, thus based on human lineage, the priesthood in the New Testament is a gift of grace in Jesus Christ, who was not of the priestly tribe, but who is a "priest forever after the order of Melchizedek" (Heb. 5:6). This Melchizedek appears on the scene seemingly without any human genealogy, as "king of Salem [Peace] and priest of the Most High God" (Gen. 14:18). He brings with him bread and wine and blesses Abram, offering thanksgiving to God on his behalf for the victory over his enemies. Melchizedek disappears as mysteriously as he appeared, and there is no mention of his death.

According to the Epistle to the Hebrews, Melchizedek is a type of Christ, whose priesthood never ends, since He Himself has no end. As foreshadowed in Melchizedek, Jesus' priesthood is eternal, transcending any human lineage, having its origin in the Godhead but inaugurated on Earth by His self-offering on the Cross. Therefore, he who is ordained through the grace of the Holy Spirit in the Church does not receive a priesthood based on the bloodline of Aaron, which dies along with him, but rather a portion in the eternal priesthood of Jesus Christ, through His Blood shed on the Cross and His victory over death.

Therefore, the New Covenant priesthood established by Christ is far superior to that of the Old Covenant, as Christ is superior to Moses and grace is superior to the Law. This priesthood is completed and perfected in the Person of Jesus, who is "High Priest" (Heb. 3:1, 9:11) by nature, and then is extended by grace and participation to His apostles, and through them to others (see 2 Tim. 2:2). The gift is bestowed on many, but the priesthood itself is one and eternal, since it is nothing less than a continual participation in the one high priesthood of Christ. Like the Holy Eucharist, the priesthood is also "divided yet never disunited."[7]

The experience of the Church is that the grace and dignity received in ordination constitute a great, exalted, and fearful mystery that is worthy of great reverence and awe. The priest is an icon of the priestly office of the Lord Jesus. When we meet the priest, we encounter Christ Himself through the mystery of ordination. St. John Chrysostom describes the priesthood as an angelic and heavenly ministry that by the Holy Spirit is exercised on earth:

> For the priestly office is indeed discharged on earth, but it ranks amongst the heavenly ordinances; and very naturally so, for neither man, nor angel, nor archangel, nor any other created power, but the Paraclete Himself instituted this vocation, and persuaded men while still abiding in the flesh to represent the ministry of angels.[8]

The same saint reminds us that without the existence and grace of the priesthood there is no baptism or Eucharist, and thus, according to the words of the Savior Himself, no salvation:[9]

---

7 The priest says these words in the eucharistic liturgy at the breaking of the consecrated Body of Christ.

8 St. John Chrysostom, "On the Priesthood," NPNF, First Series, Vol. 9, p. 46.

9 The early Church Fathers unapologetically held that schismatics and heretics did not have the priesthood and therefore did not have valid baptism, Eucharist, etc.

For transparent madness it is to despise so great a dignity, without which it is not possible to obtain either our own salvation, or the good things which have been promised to us. For if no one can enter into the kingdom of Heaven except he be regenerate through water and the Spirit, and he who does not eat the flesh of the Lord and drink His blood is excluded from eternal life, and if all these things are accomplished only by means of those holy hands, I mean the hands of the priest, how will any one, without these, be able to escape the fire of hell, or to win those crowns which are reserved for the victorious?[10]

The biblical, historical, and patristic Christian teaching is that ordination is a Holy Mystery in which is bestowed a tangible gift of grace by the Holy Spirit. In ordination a man is *transformed*, just as the bread and wine are transformed in the Divine Liturgy and as a man and woman are transformed to become one flesh in the Sacrament of Marriage. As the prophet Samuel declared to Saul, "Then the Spirit of the Lord will come upon you, and you will . . . be turned into another man" (1 Sam. 10:6).

This is not magic, an indelible power that can be bestowed and discharged without regard to godliness and the faith of the Church. The grace of the priesthood flows from the grace that is in the Church. The same Church can make this grace ineffectual. Yet it is an objective and transformative gift given through the power of the Holy Spirit to be "stirred up," nurtured and deepened. "Therefore I remind you to stir up the gift of God which is in you through the laying on of my hands" (2 Tim. 1:6).

---

10   "On the Priesthood," p. 47.

ORDAINED AND LAY PRIESTHOOD

One of the hallmarks of Protestantism is a conscious rejection of an ordained New Testament priesthood. While various groups have retained different titles for leaders (bishop, presbyter, minister, pastor, elder, etc.) and systems of organizational structure (from presbyterianism to congregationalism), all have eliminated any understanding of ordained priesthood. This is the result of several factors.

First, the Reformers loathed any association of the Eucharist with a sacrifice. If there is no sacrifice, there is no need for a priest to offer it.

Next was the clericalism that was so dominant at the time. In the medieval Roman Church there existed an exaggerated and unhealthy chasm between clergy and laity. All power resided with the clergy, who seemed pompous, detached, and untouchable.

Finally, the moral corruption among the clergy was rampant and conspicuous. This perhaps had the greatest effect on the perception of the priesthood at the time of the Reformation. In some places, it was an accepted norm that most of the nominally celibate clergy would have concubines and even sire children. The Catholic monarch Isabella I, Queen of Castile, confirms the magnitude of the situation in November of 1500:

> The dissolution is such, that souls entrusted to the clergy receive great damage, for we are told that the majority of the clergy are living in open concubinage, and that if our justice intervenes in order to punish them, they revolt and create a scandal, and that

they despise our justice to the point that they arm themselves against it.[11]

As a new priest, Martin Luther was appalled by the vulgarity and blasphemy that went on among clergy even during the proceedings of the holy services. The moral character of the priests of this period appeared worse than that of the heathen to the Reformers.

> Today there is no order of men more notorious in excess, effeminacy, voluptuousness, in short, in all sorts of lusts; in no order are there masters more adept or skillful in every deceit, fraud, treason and treachery; nowhere is there as great cunning or boldness to do harm.[12]

Interestingly, John Calvin remarks on the dissonance between the behavior of the clergy and the standard of the church canons:

> There is scarcely a bishop, and not one in a hundred parish priests, who, if his conduct were to be judged according to the ancient canons, would not be subject to excommunication or at least deposition from office.[13]

This failure of spiritual purity and uprightness leads him to conclude that "the order that they have, it is clear, is neither from Christ, nor from the Apostles, nor from the Fathers, nor from the ancient Church."

Instead of an ordained ministry of priesthood, the Reformers,

---

11   Justo L. González, *The Story of Christianity: The Reformation to the Present Day*, vol. 2 (New York: HarperOne, 1995), p. 6.

12   *Institutes*, vol. 4, 5:14.

13   *Institutes of the Christian Religion*, IV, 5, 14, cited from http://www.catholic-culture.org/culture/library/view.cfm?recnum=2976.

desirous to revive the dignity of the lay Christians, spoke of "the priesthood of all believers." It is unfortunate that in recognizing a legitimate quality of all the baptized they should have dispensed with the ordained priesthood, which is just as genuine and ancient.

The Orthodox Church has always maintained both priesthoods—the royal priesthood of all the faithful given in their "ordination" by the Holy Spirit at baptism, and the particular ordination of those chosen from within the community of the Church to exercise the priestly ministry of Christ with and on behalf of the faithful. Blessed Augustine attests to the legitimacy of both priesthoods:

> To the words, "In them the second death hath no power," are added the words, "but they shall be priests of God and Christ, and shall reign with Him a thousand years" (Rev. 20:6) and this refers not to the bishops alone, and presbyters, who are now specially called priests in the Church; but as we call all believers Christians on account of the mystical chrism, so we call all priests because they are members of the one Priest.[14]

This same double priesthood existed in the Old Covenant. For the Lord declared through Moses to all the people of Israel: "And you shall be to Me a kingdom of priests and a holy nation" (Ex. 19:6). Yet He also instituted the ecclesial priesthood through Aaron for the carrying out of His prescribed worship (Ex. 29:1–37).

Every baptized Orthodox Christian is to exercise his priestly ministry of offering within his rank as layman. He is to do this through a whole life of service and offering to God and also in

---

14   *The City of God,* NPNF, 1st Series, Book XX, ch. 10, vol. 2, p. 432.

conjunction with the ordained priesthood in the offering of the Eucharist and other worship of the Church.

THE HOLY SCRIPTURES ON ORDINATION & THE PRIESTHOOD

In our English New Testaments, the word "elder" is typically used for the Greek word *presbyteros* ("presbyter"), from which the word "priest" is derived. In the earliest Church, the titles of presbyter and bishop (Greek, *episcopos*) were often synonymous. In our English Bibles, the word *episcopos* is usually translated as "overseer." The bishop, then and now, is simply the head or "eldest" priest.

Acts 14:23: So when they had appointed elders in every church, and prayed with fasting, they commended them to the Lord in whom they had believed.

Acts 15:2, 4, 6: They determined that Paul and Barnabas and certain others of them should go up to Jerusalem, to the apostles and elders, about this question. . . . And when they had come to Jerusalem, they were received by the church and the apostles and the elders; and they reported all things that God had done with them. . . . Now the apostles and elders came together to consider this matter.

Acts 15:22–23: Then it pleased the apostles and elders, with the whole church, to send chosen men of their own company to Antioch with Paul and Barnabas. . . . They wrote this *letter* by them: The apostles, the elders, and the brethren, To the brethren who are of the Gentiles in Antioch, Syria, and Cilicia: Greetings.

Acts 16:4: And as they went through the cities, they delivered to them the decrees to keep, which were determined by the apostles and elders at Jerusalem.

Acts 20:17: From Miletus he [Paul] sent to Ephesus and called for the elders of the church.

Acts 20:28: Therefore take heed to yourselves and to all the flock, among which the Holy Spirit has made you overseers, to shepherd the church of God which He purchased with His own blood.

Phil. 1:1: Paul and Timothy, bondservants of Jesus Christ, To all the saints in Christ Jesus who are in Philippi, with the bishops and deacons.

1 Thess. 5:12–13: And we urge you, brethren, to recognize those who labor among you, and are over you in the Lord and admonish you, and to esteem them very highly in love for their work's sake.

1 Tim. 3:1: This *is* a faithful saying: If a man desires the position of a bishop, he desires a good work.

1 Tim. 4:14: Do not neglect the gift that is in you, which was given to you by prophecy with the laying on of the hands of the eldership.

1 Tim. 5:17: Let the elders who rule well be counted worthy of double honor, especially those who labor in the word and doctrine.

1 Tim. 5:22: Do not lay hands on [ordain] anyone hastily, nor share in other people's sins; keep yourself pure.

1 Tim. 6:12: Fight the good fight of the faith, lay hold on eternal life, to which you were also called and have confessed the good confession in the presence of many witnesses [his confession of faith at his ordination].

2 Tim. 1:6: Therefore I remind you to stir up the gift of God which is in you through the laying on of my hands.

2 Tim. 1:13: Hold fast the pattern of sound words which you have heard from me, in faith and love which are in Christ Jesus.

2 Tim. 1:14: That good thing which was committed to you, keep by the Holy Spirit who dwells in us.

Titus 1:5: For this reason I left you in Crete, that you should set in order the things that are lacking, and appoint elders in every city as I commanded you.

James 5:14: Is anyone among you sick? Let him call for the elders of the church, and let them pray over him, anointing him with oil in the name of the Lord.

1 Pet. 5:1: The elders who are among you I exhort, I who am a fellow elder and a witness of the sufferings of Christ, and also a partaker of the glory that will be revealed.

1 Pet. 5:2: Shepherd the flock of God which is among you, serving as overseers, not by compulsion but willingly, not for dishonest gain but eagerly;

Rev. 5:8: Now when He had taken the scroll, the four living creatures and the twenty-four elders fell down before the Lamb, each having a harp, and golden bowls full of incense, which are the prayers of the saints.

THE CHURCH FATHERS ON ORDINATION & THE PRIESTHOOD

St. Clement of Rome (c. AD 30–96)

We ought to do, in order, everything that the Master has commanded us to perform at the appointed times. Now he commanded the offerings and services to be performed diligently, and not to be done carelessly or in disorder, but at designated times and seasons. . . . For to the high priest [bishop] the proper services have been given, and to the priests [presbyters] the proper office has been assigned, and upon the Levites [deacons] the proper ministries have been imposed. The layman is bound by the layman's rules. (*First Epistle to the Corinthians* 40:1–5)

The apostles received the gospel for us from the Lord Jesus Christ. . . . So, preaching both in the country and in the towns, they appointed their first fruits, when they had tested them by the Spirit, to be bishops and deacons for the future believers. (*Op. cit.,* 42:1–4)

Our apostles likewise knew, through our Lord Jesus Christ, that there would be strife over the bishop's office. . . . For it will be no small sin for us, if we depose from the bishop's office those who have offered the gifts blamelessly and in holiness. Blessed are those presbyters who have gone on ahead, who took their departure at a mature and fruitful age, for they need no longer fear that someone might remove them from their established place. (*Op. cit.,* 44:1, 4–5)

St. Ignatius of Antioch (c. AD 35–108)

Now, therefore, it has been my privilege to see you in the person of your God-inspired bishop, Damas; and in the persons of your worthy presbyters, Bassus and Apollonius; and my fellow-servant, the deacon, Zotion. What a delight is his company! For he is subject to the bishop as to the grace of God, and to the presbytery as to the law of Jesus Christ. (*Letter to the Magnesians,* 2:1)

Take care to do all things in harmony with God, with the bishop presiding in the place of God, and with the presbyters in the place of the council of the apostles, and with the deacons, who are most dear to me, entrusted with the business of Jesus Christ, who was with the Father from the beginning and is at last made manifest. (*Op. cit.,* 6:1).

It was the Spirit who kept preaching these words, "Do nothing without the bishop, keep your body as the temple of God, love unity, flee from divisions, be imitators of Jesus Christ, as he was imitator of the Father." (*Letter to the Philadelphians* 7:1–2)

St. Irenaeus of Lyons (c. early second century–AD 202)

And all the apostles of the Lord are priests, who do inherit here neither lands nor houses, but serve God and the altar continually. (*Against Heresies, Book* 4, 8:3)

Clement of Alexandria (c. AD 150–215)

A multitude of other pieces of advice to particular persons is written in the holy books: some for presbyters, some for bishops and deacons; and others for widows, of whom we shall have opportunity to speak elsewhere. (*The Instructor of Children* 3:12:97:2 [AD 191])

Even here in the Church the gradations of bishops, presbyters, and deacons happen to be imitations, in my opinion, of the angelic glory and of that arrangement which, the scriptures say, awaits those who have followed in the footsteps of the apostles and who have lived in complete righteousness according to the gospel. (Miscellanies 6:13:107:2 [AD 208])

St. Hippolytus, Bishop of Rome (AD 170–235)

As often as a bishop takes of the sacred mysteries [Eucharist], let the deacons and presbyters be gathered together, clothed in white robes, brilliant in the view of all the people; and in like manner with a reader. (*On the Apostolic Tradition, Appendix, Canon* 37)

Origen (AD 184/185–253/254)

So, too, the apostles, and those who have become like apostles, being priests according to the Great High Priest and having received knowledge of the service of God, know under the Spirit's teaching for which sins, and when, and how they ought to offer sacrifices, and recognize for which they ought not to do so. (*On Prayer* 18)

St. Cyprian of Carthage (AD 200–258)

But if [the apostolic succession] was with Cornelius, who succeeded the bishop Fabian by lawful ordination, and whom, beside the honour of the priesthood, the Lord glorified also with martyrdom, Novatian is not in the Church; nor can he be reckoned as a bishop, who, succeeding to no one, and despising the evangelical and apostolic tradition, sprang from himself. For he who has not been ordained in the Church can neither have nor hold to the Church in any way. (*Epistle* 75:3)

Christ, who says to the apostles, and thereby to all chief rulers, who by vicarious ordination succeed to the apostles: "He that heareth you, heareth me; and he that heareth me, heareth Him that sent me; and he that despiseth you, despiseth me, and Him that sent me" (Luke 10:16). (*Epistle* 68:4)

For which reason you must diligently observe and keep the practice delivered from divine and apostolic observance . . . that for [the proper celebration of ordinations] all the neighboring bishops of the same province should assemble with that people for which a prelate is ordained. (*Epistle* 67:5)

On which account it is fitting, that with full diligence and sincere investigation those should be chosen for God's priesthood whom it is manifest God will hear. (*Epistle* 67:2)

Eusebius of Caesarea (c. AD 260/265–339/340)

Moreover, he made the priests of God his counselors, and deemed it incumbent on him to honor the God who had appeared to him with all devotion. (*Life of Constantine* 1:32)

Pope Peter I of Alexandria (martyred AD 311)

Since I have found out that Meletius acts in no way for the common good, for neither is he contented with the letter of the most holy bishops and martyrs. (*Fragments* 1)

St. Athanasius the Great of Alexandria (c. AD 296–373)

Added to this he (Saint Anthony) was tolerant in disposition and humble in spirit. For though he was such a man, he observed the rule of the Church most rigidly, and was willing that all the clergy should be honoured above himself. For he was not ashamed to bow his head to bishops and presbyters, and if ever a deacon came to him for help he discoursed with him on what was profitable, but gave place to him in prayer, not being ashamed to learn himself. (*Life of St. Anthony* 67)

For if all were of the same mind as your present advisers, how would you have become a Christian, since there would be no bishops? Or if our successors are to inherit this state of mind, how will the Churches be able to hold together? (*Letter* 49:4)

Ordination Prayer of St. Hippolytus, Bishop of Rome (from AD 215)

God and Father of our Lord Jesus Christ, Father of mercies and God of all consolation, you who live in the highest, but regard the lowest, you who know all things before they are, you who gave the rules of the Church through the word of your grace, who predestined from the beginning the race of the righteous through Abraham, who instituted princes and priests, and did not leave your sanctuary without a minister; who from the beginning of the world has been pleased to be glorified by those whom you have chosen, pour out upon him the power which is from you, the princely Spirit, which you gave to your beloved Son Jesus Christ, which he gave to your holy apostles, who founded the Church in every place as your sanctuary, for the glory and endless praise of your name. Grant, Father who knows the heart, to your servant whom you chose for the episcopate, that he will feed your holy flock, that he will wear your high priesthood without reproach, serving night and day, incessantly making your face favorable, and offering the gifts of your holy church; in the spirit of high priesthood having the power to forgive sins according to your command; to assign lots according to your command; to loose any bond according to the authority which you gave to the apostles; to please you in mildness and a pure heart, offering to you a sweet scent, through your son Jesus Christ, through whom to you be glory, power, and honor, Father and Son, with the Holy Spirit, in the Holy Church, now and throughout the ages of the ages. Amen. (*Apostolic Tradition*, ch. 3, from http://www.bombaxo.com/hippolytus.html)

CHAPTER 8

Confession & Repentance

If we confess our sins, He is faithful and just to forgive us our sins and to cleanse us from all unrighteousness. (1 John 1:9)

Not only do the newly baptized begin to experience the order in the Christian community, their relationship to the leaders of the family of God begins to form and deepen. Their saintly and humble bishop, a friend and disciple of the apostle who baptized them and himself an apostle, one of the seventy, seems accessible and present to all. His fatherly warmth and profound Christlike virtue are expressed by his gentleness and compassion as well as his uncompromising adherence to truth. Often his silence is more powerful than even his words, and he acts with an unspoken authority. There are times when his words seem to pierce Cornelius's heart and lovingly expose even his secret thoughts.

Cornelius's family has been placed under the spiritual wings of one elderly presbyter, Demetrios. The community affectionately refers to him as Papa Demetrios, and he is fast becoming a true spiritual father to these newborn members of Christ's Church. It is evident to Cornelius that this servant of God, meek and obedient, genuinely seeks to "imitate the faith" (1 Cor. 4:16; 11:1; Heb. 6:12; 13:7) of his holy bishop.

This faithful man of priestly rank is coming to know each unique soul in Cornelius's household and the particular struggles and temptations by which the devil seeks to tear each of them from unity with the Lord and His Church. Cornelius himself has now had several lengthy talks with Papa on matters ranging from the upbringing of his children to the sinful inclinations that still cling to his soul.

Although he "was buried" and "died with Christ" in holy baptism (Rom. 6:1–8), Cornelius has not completely "put off the old man" (Col. 3:9) and has found that "the evil I will not *to do,* that I practice" (Rom. 7:19). He has shed tears of repentance as he confides in his spiritual father regarding the days of his youth as a Gentile and the "sinful passions" (Rom. 7:5) of the flesh that have not yet been fully "crucified" (6:6). He also seeks his pastor's counsel on the apostolic way of life and how he might "walk in the light" (1 John 1:7).

Papa Demetrios's fatherly advice is both consoling and challenging. He is stern at times, like a strong medicine that burns momentarily before bringing relief and healing. But Cornelius knows and feels that these words are given in love so that Christ might be formed in him (Gal. 4:19). This life of repentance sometimes seems to be a difficult and narrow path (Matt. 7:14). Once his spiritual father asked him to fall to his knees before his wife and ask her forgiveness for his impatience and stubbornness. Cornelius felt a change in his heart at that difficult moment and thanked his dear papa when he saw him next.

Introduction

It can be very difficult to convey to others the Orthodox Christian vision and experience of the Sacrament of Confession. The idea of confessing one's sins in the presence of a priest can conjure up frightening images and uncomfortable emotions. We have seen too many movies where a desperate sinner hurriedly speaks to an anonymous clergyman in a darkened booth. The priest may offer a few words of advice before dispassionately mumbling a formula of forgiveness while still separated from the penitent by a partial wall. The sinner, who is looking for relief from guilt through absolution, then jumps right back into the worldly drama that is his or her life.

In other depictions, confession becomes a benign counseling session with the minister playing the part of psychologist. He offers nothing different from what can be found in a self-help book or in the echo chamber of modern pop psychology. Orthodox Christian confession is something quite different. As we shall see, this is due to a different theological perspective from what has developed in the history of Western Christendom.

In Orthodoxy, confession is more a return home from college than a visit to the dentist. In some cases it is a weekly experience with one's spiritual father, who, like a physical father, knows when to be a little more forceful with his child out of love for him or her. There is no "penalty box," but an open church with a heavenly atmosphere, where the penitent is surrounded by images of saints, some of whom were once terrible sinners themselves.

Priest and penitent stand side by side before the icon of Jesus Christ, who is the One receiving the confession and forgiving the sins. The priest also confesses to his spiritual father in a similar fashion. There may be a stand with a book holding the four Gospels along with a hand cross depicting Christ peacefully and voluntarily rescuing all of humanity from the sting of death.

Confession is not like a court session for a traffic violation. The priest often begins with familiar prayers, some of which are part of the daily prayers said at home, which help to bring us into a place of shelter spiritually and encourage us to be bold and honest in confessing everything that God already knows anyway. These prayers are a reminder that we stand before God, and God is the One who hears and receives the confession.

In the Orthodox mind the Church is home, but it is also the spiritual hospital, a place of healing for sinners. Christ is the Great Physician of our souls and bodies, and the priest is the Physician's assistant. He shares and bears the Priesthood of Christ, cooperating and participating in Christ's ministry.

Penitents are not there to check off a grocery list of sins that need to be absolved so they can escape punishment. Of course sin needs forgiveness from the Lord, but there is more to it than that. We go to confession to expose and receive healing for the sources of sin that have rooted themselves in our hearts. These are the passions (Rom. 1:26; 7:5; Gal. 5:24): God-given desires or energies of the soul that have become distorted and misdirected through the fallen condition and our own personal sinfulness. The passions become "gods," competing with God for our love, our hearts. The passions, then, are a disease or sickness of the soul. They are the means by which the devil tempts us. They promise pleasure and fulfillment and then enslave and control us against our will. They must be redirected. This is the primary work of the grace-filled Sacrament of Confession.

The priest may prescribe a penance—not a punishment for violations but a prescription for the passion plaguing us. This medicine is designed to redirect the energy of our souls toward

God, resulting in healing and communion with Him. The prescription is not a one-size-fits-all proposition. Each passion requires a different medicine. If the passion is pride, penance seeks to facilitate humility. If it is anger, the medicine prescribed is active kindness and love, by which the passion of anger is healed.

All of this is a very practical way of re-forming us into the likeness of God, so that we will not be "conformed to this world, but be transformed by the renewal of [our] *mind*" (Rom. 12:2). The target here is not our brains or merely our thoughts, but the *nous*, the spiritual "eye of the soul" that has become darkened by sin. To the extent that this darkness is cleared and God's grace brings in the light, we begin to see clearly and experience a real union with the Holy Trinity (see Matt. 6:22–23).

As each of us stands with the priest, we realize that there is something greater going on than what the earthly eyes can see. It is not just our part (the confession) and the priest's part (spiritual guidance and encouragement). God's presence, His mercy, His power, even His loving rebuke at times, are palpable; the Holy Spirit intercedes, softening and opening our hearts, directing the words of the priest, contributing the greatest and most important part of the confession.

When all has been said, the penitent kneels as the priest places the stole he wears over the penitent's head, like a spiritual cover and confirmation. There is both a spiritual and material connection now as the priest reads the prayer of absolution as Christ's steward, affirming God's forgiveness and sending the penitent on his or her way with gratitude to God.

CONFESSION IN THE WEST

Protestant views on the Sacrament of Confession have varied from the inception of the Reformation. Martin Luther embraced traditional confession with a priest as helpful for all Christians (although he did not consider it a sacrament), whereas John Calvin vehemently rejected the practice. Interestingly, Calvin's strong preference was for public confession before the whole church. Zwingli and the Anabaptists did away with any form of public confession.

In some Protestant denominations, a time of silent confession is assigned within regular worship. In the Anglican Church a confession of sin takes place in the context of the Eucharist, where congregants are asked to confess silently to God. As to personal confession with a priest, an oft-quoted saying summarizes the current practice in Anglicanism: "All *may*, none *must*, some *should*."

In practice, confession is rarely a feature of church life even within denominations that have not rejected it outright. Among nondenominational evangelicals, no formal confession exists, although one hears at times of the practice of accountability partners, a sort of lay confession between two persons. Pentecostals do often emphasize a need for a more public confession of sins, but they have no standard practice.

As usual, the Protestant attitudes toward confession were formed in reaction against the practices of the Roman Church. We have already mentioned the rampant immorality and corruption among many ordained priests during this period. One can only imagine that trust in the Sacrament of Confession suffered greatly under these circumstances.

Yet it was not only the popular practice of the sacrament that suffered abuse; the underlying theological presumptions had undergone change as well. These theological distortions advanced a new trajectory of understanding and practice of confession that differs subtly but substantially from the earliest and Orthodox Christian tradition.

THE AUTHORITY OF THE PRIESTHOOD

The first change relates to the gift and authority of the priesthood. In the Roman Catholic scheme, the pope, as successor to St. Peter, has been given the power to bind and to loose: "Whatever you bind on earth will be bound in heaven, and whatever you loose on earth will be loosed in heaven" (Matt. 16:19). The source of his priestly authority was derived from a kind of transfer of power from the Person of Christ directly to the pope (through the apostle Peter), to whom Christ had given the "keys of the kingdom of heaven," providing him the power and prerogative to exercise supreme authority over the Church.

The pope then also delegated this power to other bishops and to priests for the purposes of absolving the faithful from the guilt of sin. This authoritarian system made the power to bind and loose seem like a power that could be used almost independently from God. The pope, and the priest by extension, did not facilitate the ministry of Christ, but replaced Christ.

While it is true that Christ had extended to the apostles and their successors the gift and responsibility to "bind" and "loose" and "forgive" or "retain" sins, in the early Church this was understood as the priest's cooperation with God's action of either forgiving or withholding forgiveness. This was also the perspective of Martin Luther when he was still a Catholic priest: "The pope himself cannot remit guilt, but only declare and confirm that it has been remitted by God."[1]

The grace to bind and loose is not an external power to be exercised over the Church. The power of the priesthood is a gift from within the Church as Christ's Body, and it is also for the Church in concert with the will of God. The Church, not the pope, is the source of the grace of the priesthood.[2] For Christ is the Head of the Church (Eph. 5:23; Col. 1:18), and the Holy Spirit (John 14:26; 15:26) activates His presence and authority in the Church.

Here it is helpful to remember Simon, the sorcerer, from the record of the Acts of the Apostles. When he saw the grace the apostles possessed to impart the Holy Spirit through the laying on of hands, he understood it externally. "Give me this power also," he said, offering the apostles money as an incentive, as if grace were a commodity to be traded (Acts 8:14–19).

The priest's apostolic "ministry of reconciliation" (2 Cor. 5:18) is authoritative inasmuch as he lives and acts within the authority of the faith and apostolic Tradition of Christ's Church. The priest is Christ's agent or "steward" (1 Cor. 4:1) through whom the sinner's authentic repentance is confirmed and God's forgiveness affirmed. His authority is not so much a power to be dispensed as it is a gift and responsibility to be discerned and employed. Authority in the Church comes from

---

1   95 Theses, Thesis 6, https://carm.org/luthers-95-theses.
2   The Church Fathers teach that the "rock" (Matt. 16:18) Christ said He would build the Church upon was not Peter himself but his confession of faith. The early Church, as articulated by St. Cyprian of Carthage, viewed every bishop of the Church as "Peter" within his appointed region.

within, from the Holy Spirit, "the Spirit of truth" (John 14:17).

Therefore, according to the teaching of the Orthodox, in the Sacrament of Confession the penitent is forgiven by God, through the priest (i.e., the grace of the Priesthood of Christ), not by the priest. To this day, this important theological distinction is expressed clearly in the formulations of the two prayers of absolution. For the Roman Catholic prayer, said by the priest after the penitent confesses, states, "*I* absolve you," whereas in the Orthodox Church the wording reflects the original understanding: "May *God* forgive you, through me, a sinner."[3]

Because of the theology of Rome, the argument about confession during the Reformation focused on whether a priest can forgive sins or whether only God can do so. In other words, it was about who was doing the forgiving, with emphasis on who had the power to do so. If the priest has the power to forgive sins, then one needs to confess to the priest. But if God alone forgives (Mark 2:7), the sacrament requiring the priest becomes superfluous. Following this line of thinking, John Calvin comments, "Since it is the Lord who forgives, forgets, and wipes out sins, let us confess our sins to him in order to obtain pardon."[4]

Because of the Roman understanding of the power of the priesthood, confession is understood as being made to the priest. In the Orthodox tradition, the theological perspective is that confession is made to Jesus Christ (although the penitent speaks to the priest).

This is by no means a demeaning or diminishing of the true

---

3   The formulation "I absolve you" was adopted by the Russian Orthodox Church but is a late Western importation.

4   *Institutes of the Christian Religion*, ch. 4:9, http://www.ccel.org/ccel/calvin/institutes.v.v.html.

authority of the priesthood; it is merely a proper placement of the priest's authority. The Orthodox believe that in ordination a man receives something objective and real, the very grace of Christ's Priesthood (see Chapter 7). The power and grace of the priesthood are indeed real, but it is still Christ's power, and it can be deactivated and essentially removed also by Him through His Church. The Roman Catholic Church holds to a doctrine of the indelible priesthood, whereby through ordination a man's soul is indelibly marked forever. His priesthood can never be eradicated. This teaching is unknown among the early Church Fathers, and the canons of the Church make it clear that a defrocked priest is returned to the rank of layman.

We want to affirm that the power of the Sacrament of Confession is also very real. Consider the following story from a man who witnessed it.[5] An experienced Orthodox priest was carrying out an exorcism at a church in Greece. However, the demon refused to come out. When asked "Why?" persistently by the priest, the demon pointed out one of the bystanders, who had not confessed a certain sin. After some reflection, the faithful Orthodox man indeed realized that he had failed to confess this sin. The priest immediately took the man and confessed him, saying the prayer of absolution, after which the demon departed from the possessed person.

SIN AND PENANCE

In the medieval Roman Church, a new understanding of sin and penance had also become normative. This stemmed in part from Anselm's satisfaction theory of atonement, which quickly

5   Told to me directly by the priest who personally witnessed it.

became the exclusive explanation of God's redeeming work in the Christian West. According to this view, the sin of Adam was an offense against God that required a just "satisfaction," or compensatory act, to restore God's honor and consequently allow Him to extend forgiveness to mankind. Because the offense was against the infinite God, only an infinite satisfaction would suffice. But since no mere man could make an adequate payment, God sent His Son to become Man and to die on the Cross.

Thomas Aquinas advanced Anselm's teaching by making punishment an essential element in the equation. Not only was satisfaction necessary, but a satisfactory punishment was required. The punishment for sin was satisfied by Christ's death, and therefore the debt was paid for past sins. But future sins would be satisfied by the overabundance of grace that Christ merited for His Passion and death. This extra grace (or "treasury of satisfactions") was accessible through the sacraments of the Church (and later, as we have seen, through indulgences). Aquinas's formulation had become the accepted Catholic teaching by the time of the Protestant Reformation.

Thomas Aquinas's formulation of satisfactory punishment also applied to the sins committed by Christians after baptism. For this reason penance (also called "satisfaction") is given to repentant sinners at the time of confession to satisfy their debt of sin.

Whereas in the early Church penance was understood primarily as a means of healing the soul in order to bring one back into relationship with God, now it took on a more juridical or legal purpose. Aquinas defined penance as "the payment of the temporal punishment due on account of the offence committed against God by Sin."[6]

Later, penances became associated with the doctrine of purgatory as well. As explained in the *Catholic Encyclopedia*, after the guilt of sin is expiated through the Sacrament of Confession,

There remains . . . some indebtedness to Divine justice which must be cancelled here or hereafter [i.e., in purgatory]. In order to have it cancelled here, the penitent receives from his confessor what is usually called his "penance," usually in the form of certain prayers which he is to say, or of certain actions which he is to perform, such as visits to a church, the Stations of the Cross, etc. Alms deeds, fasting, and prayer are the chief means of satisfaction, but other penitential works may also be enjoined.

The Council of Trent went so far as to condemn those who claimed "the entire punishment is always remitted by God together with the guilt."[7]

The Reformers reacted somewhat violently to the Roman view of confession and penance. They rejected the idea that penance is required to remove the debt of divine justice and countered that the debt of sin was expiated once for all by grace through Christ's redemptive work on the Cross. All the while, their fundamental views of sin, satisfaction, and atonement were Roman Catholic in nature, and they failed to return to the early patristic and Orthodox teaching.

---

6 *Summa Theologica*, Supplement 12.3. From the *Catholic Encyclopedia* online (http://www.newadvent.org/cathen/11618c.htm, "Satisfaction")
7 *Ibid.*

CRIME AND PUNISHMENT

In the Roman Church, the Sacrament of Confession became shrouded in a theology of authoritarianism and legalism. To this day confession is defined as

> a sacrament of the New Law instituted by Christ in which forgiveness of sins committed after baptism is granted through the priest's absolution to those who with true sorrow confess their sins and promise to satisfy [i.e., make penance] for the same . . . it is said to take place in the "tribunal of penance," because it is a judicial process in which the penitent is at once the accuser, the person accused, and the witness, while the priest pronounces judgment and sentence.[8]

Sin and forgiveness became a matter of crime and punishment, injury and restitution. And penance became a payback or reparation for sins. According to the *Catholic Encyclopedia*, penance is "an act of justice whereby the injury done to the honour of God is required, so far at least as the sinner is able to make reparation."

Confession and absolution removed the guilt and eternal punishment but not the temporal punishment due for sin. In the eyes of the average layperson, the sacrament then became a means of escaping eternal punishment, and penance or indulgences the means to escape purgatory. The clergy became an elite class apart from the people, the dispensers of the treasury of satisfactions with the power to bind and loose one's sins, perhaps at their own individual whim.

The result is that the sinner might come to confession without real repentance in order to obtain legal absolution of guilt

---

8   *Catholic Encyclopedia* (http://www.newadvent.org/cathen/11618c.htm).

and release from eternal damnation. Martin Luther noted and complained that absolution was being given before the appropriate penances were given or fulfilled.[9] To make matters worse, instead of fulfilling penances and thus exhibiting the fruits of repentance, penitents simply purchased indulgences, which many clergy were more than happy to sell.

All of the above circumstances have contributed to the view that one need not (and should not) confess sins to a priest.

The Authentic Practice of Confession

CONFESSION IS BIBLICAL

In the Scriptures, it is clear that the heart of the matter of repentance is the heart itself—"A broken and contrite heart—these, O God, You will not despise" (Ps. 51(50):17). But in the Bible, the heart is not the seat of emotions and subjective experiences; it is the God-ordained spiritual center of the human person, by which our "whole spirit, soul, and body" are to be sanctified "completely" (1 Thess. 5:23).

True repentance extends from the heart to the whole person, just as sin begins in the heart and is eventually manifested tangibly and bodily (Matt. 15:19). As even Martin Luther taught, the meaning of repentance "is not restricted to repentance in one's heart; for such repentance is null unless it produces outward signs in various mortifications of the flesh."[10]

Since repentance involves the whole person, confession of sin is not a private experience relegated to one's "heart." Rather,

---

9   Luther's Twelfth Thesis: "In former days, the canonical penalties were imposed, not after, but before absolution was pronounced; and were intended to be tests of true contrition."

10   95 Theses, Thesis 3.

in the Scriptures the whole process of repentance is a very robust turning away from former thoughts, words, and deeds, with confession of sin and a zeal and intention to struggle to conform our lives to God's will. Repentance includes a public confession of sin.

Consider the confession of Zacchaeus, the notorious tax collector who was converted by the presence of the Lord. His confession of sin was made in the midst of a multitude of fellow Jews, his former victims, and included a self-imposed penance, which he declared publicly to the Lord in the presence of the crowds: "Look, Lord, I give half of my goods to the poor; and if I have taken anything from anyone by false accusation, I restore fourfold" (Luke 19:8).

We have another example in the parable of the prodigal son. When the younger son came to himself and had a change of heart, he immediately formulated his plan of action:

> I will arise and go to my father, and will say to him, "Father, I have sinned against heaven and before you, and I am no longer worthy to be called your son. Make me like one of your hired servants" (Luke 15:18–19).

In the New Testament, all four passages dealing with confession of sin reveal the public nature of confession (Matt. 3:6; Mark 1:5; Acts 19:18; and James 5:16). In each of these cases, the particular verb *exomologeó* is used, whereas a different word, *homologeó*, is used for occasions when a confession of faith is made.

The suffix common to both of these verbs is logos, which means "a word," "to speak or declare." Exomologeó means "to speak out or agree to declare," to confess verbally and publicly. And so when the Apostle John writes, "If we confess our sins, He is faithful and just to forgive us our sins and to cleanse us from all unrighteousness" (1 John 1:9), it is understood that this is the Church's practice of confession, a verbal acknowledgment of sin.

With this knowledge we can also recognize that those who came to St. John the Forerunner for baptism were "confessing their sins" vocally in the presence of the Baptist and those assembled (Matt. 3:6; Mark 1:5). It is hard to believe that the people first stepped aside to privately and silently confess their sins to God. In the Acts of the Apostles we also read that "many who had believed came confessing and telling their deeds" (19:18).

In the Old Testament, David acknowledged his sin verbally in the presence of Nathan the Prophet and received God's forgiveness through him (2 Sam. 12:7–13). Sins were also acknowledged and atoned for in a public manner in the temple with prescribed sin offerings (see Lev. 4—5). Since one's relationship to God was not private but existed in the context of the worshipping community, sin was also dealt with in the corporate context of the community.

CONFESSION IN THE EARLY CHURCH

The earliest records of confession in post-biblical times reveal that it was also practiced in the context of the community, that is, in the gathering of the local church. Public confessions of sin were made just prior to the commencement of the offering of the Eucharist. Since the Eucharist is the pinnacle of unity with Christ, one cannot participate worthily when experiencing serious sin or strife with other church members. This is attested to in the first-century document known as the *Didache*:

> Confess your sins in church, and do not go up to your prayer
> with an evil conscience. This is the way of life. . . . On the Lord's
> Day gather together, break bread, and give thanks, after con-
> fessing your transgressions so that your sacrifice may be pure.[11]

The same early Church practice is witnessed to in the Epistle of Barnabas: "You shall confess your sins. You shall not go to prayer with an evil conscience. This is the way of light."[12] Only after confessions were made was the kiss of peace exchanged and the Eucharist celebrated.

It is unlikely that the leaders of the local community—the bishop or presbyters—were passive onlookers in this process of repentance. It is more likely they were quite aware, having received the confession personally some time prior. For depending upon the seriousness of the sin, the clergy have always taken part in God's forgiving or retaining sin (John 20:23) and in officially restoring repentant sinners to the communion of the Church. For discernment is required in understanding the seriousness of the sin and in advising an appropriate remedy.

The third-century Christian teacher Origen makes it clear that the priest was an integral part of the process of repentance. Origen comments that a sinner should "not shrink from declaring his sin to a priest of the Lord and from seeking medicine."[13] And a bishop from the same era, St. Cyprian of Carthage, writes, "Of how much greater faith and salutary fear are they who . . . confess their sins to the priests of God in a straightforward manner and in sorrow, making an open declaration of conscience."[14]

---

11   *The Didache: The Teaching of the Twelve Apostles,* 4:14, 14:1 [AD 70].
12   *Letter of Barnabas,* 19 [AD 74].
13   *Homilies on Leviticus,* 2:4 [AD 248].
14   *The Lapsed,* 15:1–3 [AD 251].

As the Church grew, this type of public confession seemed less prudent, but the role of the bishop and priest as the apostolic guardians of the faith, the spiritual guides and teachers of the faithful, and the witnesses to sincere repentance remained.

Confession of sins in the presence of the priest as the representative of the whole church maintained the previous principles of accountability and the inherent public nature of confession. As the great defender of Christ's divinity, St. Basil, Bishop of Caesarea, explains:

> It is necessary to confess our sins to those to whom the dispensation of God's mysteries is entrusted. Those doing penance of old are found to have done it before the saints. It is written in the Gospel that they confessed their sins to John the Baptist [Matt. 3:6], but in Acts [19:18] they confessed to the apostles.[15]

The early Church also recognized that the bishops and the priests continued the apostolic ministry of binding and loosing sin, not in some magical or authoritarian sense according to their own will, but as inspired by the grace of God and bearing witness to His will. Therefore the power to bind and loose, to retain or remit sins, is a symphony between earth and heaven. It is a fulfillment of the prayer given to us by the Lord, "Your will be done, *on earth as it is in heaven*" (Matt. 6:10). According to St. John Chrysostom, the great fourth-century preacher and bishop, this power is a heavenly grace bestowed by God on His creatures.

> What great honor the grace of the Spirit has vouchsafed to priests.... For they who inhabit the earth and make their abode there are entrusted with the administration of things which are

---

15   *Rules Briefly Treated,* 288 [AD 374].

in Heaven, and have received an authority which God has not given to angels or archangels . . . and what priests do here below God ratifies above, and the Master confirms the sentence of his servants.[16]

SIN AND THE COMPONENTS OF REPENTANCE

In the Orthodox Christian understanding, sin itself is never a private, isolated event. We are all connected and related through our one human nature. Like the sin of Adam and Eve, our sin affects others and, in some way, all of creation, as a rock thrown into a pool creates ripples in every direction.

In our modern culture, it is claimed that all things should be allowable as long as they don't hurt anyone else. This is not the Orthodox approach, since it is impossible that our spiritual condition should not affect those around us. As the poet John Donne wrote, "No man is an island." By virtue of the contact we have with others, the consequences of our words and actions, or even the energy that emanates from our soul, we bring either grace or harm to others, directly or indirectly. St. Seraphim of Sarov famously expresses this when he advises, "Acquire the Spirit of peace, and thousands around you will be saved."

Sin is not essentially the breaking of a rule or law imposed on us from outside, the breaching of a moral code. The Greek word for sin, *amartia*, originated as a term in archery meaning "to miss the target." To sin is to miss the target for which we were created; it is a failure to fulfill the destiny for which God made us, which according to the Orthodox teaching is to become like Him by grace. As such, sin is a distortion of human nature, a disease that debilitates our natural capacity for communion with God.

---

16   *On the Priesthood,* 3.

Since Adam's sin, we have all missed the target to one degree or another. As St. Paul says, we all "fall short of the glory of God" (Rom. 3:23) and are in need of repentance in order to be brought back into union with Him. For this reason, both St. John the Baptist and Jesus Christ began their public ministries with the word "Repent" (Matt. 3:2; 4:17).

But repentance is not a guilt-ridden condition of morose self-loathing. It is not a mere psychological or emotional state. Nor is it a perfectionism that is born of ego. There is no despair with true repentance, because despair has given up hope in God's grace and mercy. Despair provides a second victory for the devil. St. John Chrysostom writes, "No one should despair of his salvation. Did you sin? Repent. Did you sin a thousand times? Repent a thousand times."[17]

In the words of St. John Climacus, real repentance is a "joyful sorrow" or "sorrowful joy" inspired by the movement of God's grace in the heart, a sorrow that burns away impurity and refines the soul, leaving it joyful, peaceful, alert, and sensitive to God's will. It is a spiritual realization and conviction that energizes the soul to desire to put away everything that would obstruct it from living in the light and love of God.

The Sacrament of Confession in the Orthodox Church is one of the essential aspects of repentance. First there must be self-knowledge and awareness, some level of spiritual understanding of our condition. Second, there is contrition—that is, the "godly sorrow" written about by the Apostle Paul (2 Cor. 7:10), which leads not to despair but to a desire to be changed.

---

17 Nektarios Antonopoulos, *Return: Repentance and Confession; Return to God and His Church,* ed. Anastasia A. Koutoulakis and trans. Fr. Nicholas Palis (Athens: Akritas Publication, 1999), p. 61.

Certainly, here we benefit greatly from tearful prayer and hope in God.

The third step is a sincere, verbal confession of sin to God in the presence of the father confessor with humility and honesty, and a desire to turn to Christ and fight against the sin that alienates us from Him. The verbal confession is sealed with the prayer of absolution offered by the confessor, who, through the grace of the priesthood, is given the gift of attesting to God's forgiveness for these sins.[18] This is a great mystery of God's condescension and grace by which He allows His creatures to assist and cooperate in His act of forgiveness and healing.

After his sincere confession, the penitent should depart with full faith in God's forgiveness, giving thanks for His great mercy. The fourth and final step of repentance is the transformation of our life, the fruit of real repentance. The Sacrament of Confession cannot help us unless we are open to struggling against sin. "Even if all spiritual fathers, the Patriarchs, the Hierarchs and all people forgive you," says St. Cosmas of Aetolia, "you are unforgivable, if you don't repent in action."[19] This final step also defines the whole Christian life, for repentance is a continual way of life and movement toward the inexhaustible grace of God.

ILLNESS AND CURE: CONFESSION AND PENANCE

The Orthodox Church does not view sin through the lens of guilt and punishment. We would not agree with the Roman Catholic view that the grace of the Sacrament of Confession

---

18   In some cases, and particularly for serious sins, the Prayer of Absolution may be withheld until a later date to allow for appropriate time for healing and full repentance.
19   *Return*, p. 21.

is "deliverance from the *guilt* of sin."[20] The human problem is not guilt but sin. The Orthodox Church has never held that sin requires a temporal punishment, although she has never denied that sin is accompanied by pain.[21] Instead the Fathers of the Church most often use the paradigm of illness and health in relation to sin and repentance.

Sin is an illness, and repentance is the cure. God's grace is the medicine that heals the soul's wounds and brings the sinner into spiritual health, making him, on the one hand, truly human, and thus bringing him into communion with His Creator. Just as a sick man exposes his wounds or symptoms to a physician, we come to Confession to expose the wounds of our soul in order to receive the needed medicine and be healed. "As, then, for those of us who are diseased in body, a physician is required, so also those who are diseased in soul require a healer to cure our maladies."[22]

Therefore, in the Orthodox understanding, a penance given to us by our confessor is given as medicine, as a means of healing or correcting the imbalances and passions (misdirected energies) of the soul. A physician does not give the same medicine for different diseases. In the same way, a good confessor prescribes a penance specific to the spiritual ailment, whether it be anger, lust, greed, or other passion. In this way the soul is purified and healed, made capable of receiving illumination through the grace of God.

---

20 *Catholic Encyclopedia* (http://www.newadvent.org/cathen/11618c.htm, "The Sacrament of Penance").
21 St. Maximos the Confessor articulates this most clearly. See *Questions to Thallasios.*
22 Clement of Alexandria, ANF Vol. 2, *The Instructor (Pædagogus),* Book I, ch. 1, p. 209.

THE HOLY SCRIPTURES ON CONFESSION

In The Old Testament

Num. 5:7: He shall confess the sin which he has committed. And he shall make restitution for his trespass in full, plus one-fifth of it, and give *it* to the one he has wronged.

2 Sam. 12:7–13: (See Nathan's involvement in God's forgiveness for David.)

Neh. 9:2–3: Then those of Israelite lineage separated themselves from all foreigners; and they stood and confessed their sins and the iniquities of their fathers. And they stood up in their place and read from the Book of the Law of the LORD their God *for one*-fourth of the day; and *for another* fourth they confessed and worshiped the LORD their God.

Bar. 1:14–18: And you shall read this book which we are sending to you, in order to make confession in the house of the Lord on the feast days and on the solemn days. And you shall say, "To the Lord our God belongs righteousness, but for us shame is on our faces, as it is this day for the people of Judah and to those inhabiting Jerusalem, and for our kings, for our rulers, for our priests, for our prophets, and for our fathers, have sinned before the Lord. We have disobeyed him and have refused to heed the voice of the Lord our God, to walk in the ordinances of the Lord, which He gave to us openly."

Required by St. John the Baptist

Matt. 3:6: and were baptized by him in the Jordan, confessing their sins.

Mark 1:5: Then all the land of Judaea, and those from Jerusalem, went to him and were all baptized by him in the Jordan River, confessing their sins.

In The New Testament Church

James 5:16: Confess *your* trespasses to one another, and pray for one another, that you may be healed. The effective, fervent prayer of a righteous man avails much.

Acts 19:18: And many who had believed came confessing and telling their deeds.

1 John 1:9: If we confess our sins, he is faithful and just to forgive us *our* sins and to cleanse us from all unrighteousness.

THE CHURCH FATHERS ON CONFESSION & REPENTANCE[23]

The Didache (anonymous, written in the first century)

Confess your sins in church, and do not go up to your prayer with an evil conscience. This is the way of life.... On the Lord's Day gather together, break bread, and give thanks, after confessing your transgressions so that your sacrifice may be pure. (*Didache* 4:14, 14:1)

Epistle of Barnabas (author unknown; c. AD 74)

You shall judge righteously. You shall not make a schism, but you shall pacify those that contend by bringing them together. You shall confess your sins. You shall not go to prayer with an

---

23 From http://www.catholic.com/tracts/confession.

evil conscience. This is the way of light. (*Epistle of Barnabas* 19 [AD 74])

St. Irenaeus of Lyons (c. early second century–AD 202)

[The Gnostic disciples of Marcus] have deluded many women. . . . Their consciences have been branded as with a hot iron. Some of these women make a public confession, but others are ashamed to do this, and in silence, as if withdrawing from themselves the hope of the life of God, they either apostatize entirely or hesitate between the two courses. (*Against Heresies* 1:22 [AD 189])

Tertullian (c. AD 155–c. 240)

[Regarding confession, some] flee from this work as being an exposure of themselves, or they put it off from day to day. I presume they are more mindful of modesty than of salvation, like those who contract a disease in the more shameful parts of the body and shun making themselves known to the physicians; and thus they perish along with their own bashfulness. (*Repentance* 10:1 [AD 203])

St. Hippolytus of Rome (AD 170–235)

[The bishop conducting the ordination of the new bishop shall pray:] God and Father of our Lord Jesus Christ. . . . Pour forth now that power which comes from you, from your royal Spirit, which you gave to your beloved Son, Jesus Christ, and which he bestowed upon his holy apostles . . . and grant this your servant, whom you have chosen for the episcopate, [the power] to feed your holy flock and to serve without blame as your high priest, ministering night and day to propitiate unceasingly before your face and to offer to you the gifts of your holy Church, and by the Spirit of the high priesthood to have the authority to forgive sins, in accord with your command. (*Apostolic Tradition* 3 [AD 215])

Origen (AD 184/185–253/254)

[A final method of forgiveness], albeit hard and laborious [is] the remission of sins through penance, when the sinner . . . does not shrink from declaring his sin to a priest of the Lord and from seeking medicine, after the manner of him who say, "I said, 'To the Lord I will accuse myself of my iniquity.'" (*Homilies on Leviticus* 2:4 [AD 248])

St. Cyprian of Carthage (c. AD 200–258)

But [the impenitent] spurn and despise all these warnings; before their sins are expiated, before they have made a confession of their crime, before their conscience has been purged in the ceremony and at the hand of the priest . . . they do violence to [the Lord's] body and blood, and with their hands and mouth they sin against the Lord more than when they denied him. (*The Lapsed* 15:1–3 [AD 251])

Of how much greater faith and salutary fear are they who . . . confess their sins to the priests of God in a straightforward manner and in sorrow, making an open declaration of conscience. . . . I beseech you, brethren, let everyone who has sinned confess his sin while he is still in this world, while his confession is still admissible, while the satisfaction and remission made through the priests are still pleasing before the Lord." (*Ibid.,* 28)

And again, in the Gospel, when Christ breathed on the apostles alone, saying, "Whosoever sins ye remit they are remitted unto them, and whosoever sins ye retain they are retained." Therefore the power of remitting sins was given to the apostles, and to the churches which they, sent by Christ, established, and to the bishops who succeeded to them by vicarious ordination. (*Epistle* 74:16)

Aphrahat the Persian Sage (c. AD 280–345)

You [priests], then, who are disciples of our illustrious physician [Christ], you ought not deny a curative to those in need of healing. And if anyone uncovers his wound before you, give him the remedy of repentance. And he that is ashamed to make known his weakness, encourage him so that he will not hide it from you. And when he has revealed it to you, do not make it public, lest because of it the innocent might be reckoned as guilty by our enemies and by those who hate us. (*Treatises* 7:3 [AD 340])

St. Basil the Great (c. AD 329/330–379)

It is necessary to confess our sins to those to whom the dispensation of God's mysteries is entrusted. Those doing penance of old are found to have done it before the saints. It is written in the Gospel that they confessed their sins to John the Baptist [Matt. 3:6], but in Acts [19:18] they confessed to the apostles. (*Rules Briefly Treated* 288 [AD 374])

CHAPTER 9

Icons, Veneration & Worship

He is the image of the invisible God, the firstborn over all creation.
(Col. 1:15)

As a centurion in the Italian Regiment (Acts 10:1), Cornelius has long been familiar with the deference and honor due to his superiors in the military as representatives of the Roman emperor. He has been the recipient also of this reverence from the men under his authority. Once he had the occasion of briefly standing before the emperor, before whom he made the customary bow of reverence in recognition of his station. Cornelius knew that it was only by God's providence and as "God's minister" that the king wielded the sword (Rom. 13:3–5; 1 Pet. 2:13–14).

Of much greater importance and meaning, he is now experiencing the reverence shown to the people and things of God within the Body of Christ, the Church. Christians show appropriate honor to their spiritual leaders, those who have received a special gift of grace to shepherd the rational flock of Christ. Cornelius kisses the hand of the presbyter, Demetrios, as the hand of Jesus Christ, since he shares in Christ's high priesthood. This veneration extends to all the baptized as well. Just before the eucharistic liturgy commences, Cornelius exchanges a holy kiss with his fellow congregants as a sign of their union with one another in the Lord. In general, Christians "greet one another with a holy kiss" (Rom. 16:16; 1 Cor. 16:20; 2 Cor. 13:12; 1 Thess. 5:26) as if greeting the Lord Himself, for He abides in each of them.

There are holy vessels used in the service of God, as there were in the Old Covenant. These are used and touched only by the "stewards of the mysteries of God" (1 Cor. 4:1), those ordained to minister at the holy altar. It is they who preside in worship and who distribute the Body and Blood of Jesus Christ to the faithful.

Cornelius muses on how the altar on which is placed Christ's Body, "the bread which came down from heaven" (John 6:41, 51, 58), is like the ark of old that held the jar of manna. As Joshua fell down before the ark in repentance to God (Josh. 7:6), Christians also fall down before the altar in awe and worship of the Lord, who came down from heaven and is always present in their midst (Matt. 18:20).

Even before he had come to the knowledge of Jesus Christ, Cornelius had seen the veneration shown to the holy people and things of God as he approached the faith of the first covenant. He heard how the Lord commanded Moses to remove his shoes, because the very ground he stood on in the presence of the Lord was holy. He saw how the appointed reader in the synagogue kissed the Torah before the reading. He knew how each pious Jew kissed his prayer shawl before donning it. And he heard from the holy writings themselves how God instructed His people to make holy images of cherubim on the ark of His presence. He was familiar with the veneration shown to angels and to men in the stories of the Torah.

In his travels, Cornelius had visited many synagogues, some adorned with painted or mosaic depictions of the holy ones of old and the events of God's saving acts among His people.[1] These had pulled upon his heart and had drawn him into a deeper appreciation for God's presence among His faithful people.

All of this had prepared him for an even more intensified experience of reverence in Christian worship. For through Christ, God had not just intervened in His creation as in the days of old; He had become a Creature, taking upon Himself our own flesh and blood, sanctifying His own creation, joining heaven and earth in His Body, the Church.

Introduction

In C.S. Lewis's *The Silver Chair,* from his Chronicles of Narnia series, we encounter a beautiful description of a most natural, God-inspired act of icon veneration. Finding his formerly blackened shield now immaculate and revealing the blood-red image of the lion (Aslan, Lewis's Christ figure), Prince Rilian addresses his small band of fellow travelers: "Now by my counsel, we shall all kneel and kiss his likeness, and then all shake hands one with another, as true friends that may shortly be parted." The solemn act of love and reverence for the one who had delivered them from the delusion of the green witch was appropriately followed by acts of reconciliation and forgiveness.

In our times, the word *icon* has re-entered the lexicon of Western society due to the advent of personal computers and other electronic devices. An icon, in this context, is a recognizable visual image through which we enter into a different world of sorts, known as an application.

When we double-click on our computer icon, we enter into

---

1 Archeological digs have uncovered a synagogue from the mid-third century BC in Dura-Europos that is covered wall-to-wall with Old Testament iconography.

something greater than what the eye initially encounters. These icons are "windows" through which we are taken into a virtual reality, a world designed to give us a particular experience.

Similarly, the sacred icons that are part of the Church's Holy Tradition are images designed to open to us the real world of God's Kingdom. They are often called "windows into heaven" inasmuch as they draw our hearts into the perspective of spiritual, or noetic, reality. The Kingdom of God, of course, is the ultimate "application" and reality we seek as Christians: "But seek first the kingdom of God and His righteousness, and all these things shall be added to you" (Matt. 6:33).

The Church's icons are designed to portray not the fallen and distorted world of sin that often becomes in our eyes "normal," but man and creation as made and redeemed by God in Christ through the Holy Spirit. Therefore, the holy icons purposely do not depict what we see with our fallen eyes, but present the purified and transfigured creation. They are *holy* icons, not worldly images.

Because the methodology of iconography developed by the inspiration of the Holy Spirit in God's Church, and because icons are made with prayer and fasting and in continuity with Church Tradition, they have been shown to be a means of His grace. In fact, traditional iconography has always been understood as a work of cooperation between God and the iconographer, with the guidance of the Holy Spirit and the intercessions of the one being depicted.

For this reason, in the experience of the Church, holy icons are not approached as one-dimensional depictions of the past but as participants in the eternal reality they depict, mystically making present the persons or events set forth. Not infrequently, through God's providence and power, they become agents of answered prayers or miracles.

Orthodox icons are not mere works of art, the creative expression of human thoughts and imagination to be admired and analyzed. They are prayerful renderings of spiritual truth, visual depictions of God's revelation to man as expressed in Holy Scripture and the whole of Church Tradition. As such, they are objects of devotion, veneration, and prayer. As Orthodox Christians bow before and kiss the Gospel Book, so do they reverence and kiss holy icons.

Historically, the attitude of Protestant Christians toward images, carved or painted, is for the most part negative. Today most Protestant Christians, and particularly evangelicals, reject the use and veneration of icons. Their churches are often bereft of any pictures or symbols, except perhaps the image of a barren cross. However, it is common to see depictions of Jesus or biblical figures in books, posters, and movies, particularly those intended for children. Yet most Protestants are taught that creating images of the divine is directly prohibited by the second of the Ten Commandments.

Before the Great Schism, the iconography of the Western Church was identical to that of the Christian East, as attested to, for example, by St. Mark's Cathedral in Venice (sixth century). However, a rather swift and definitive transformation of religious art took place in the West, solidified particularly due to the influences of the period called the Renaissance (fourteenth through seventeenth centuries).

The Renaissance, based in the philosophy of humanism, was

characterized by an enthusiastic rediscovery of ancient Greek culture, which was manifested in realms such as science and politics but also in architecture and art. It was during this period that the flat, nonrealistic, spiritualized, inverse perspective of the Christian icon was replaced by a fleshy, realistic depiction and the use of external perspective. The Lord was now depicted similarly to the Greek god, Zeus, muscular and burly, and the saints as the court of the gods. The modesty and restraint of traditional and biblical iconography were replaced by a celebration of the naked human body.

At the time of the Protestant Reformation, Lutherans took a more moderate view of images than did followers of Calvin or Zwingli. Luther allowed crucifixes and statues, as had become common among Rome's churches. Calvin was vehement in his rejection of the use of religious images, primarily arguing that one cannot depict the invisible and divine.

In general, the stance of classical Protestantism is to reject the *veneration* of icons as a form of idolatry. Even those denominations that allow for the existence of holy images have no practice of venerating them. In part this was a reaction against various abuses perceived within the Roman Catholicism of the time. However, today there is a revived interest in Orthodox iconography among Roman Catholics, Anglicans, and some other Protestants.

A Defense of Holy Icons

IDOLATRY OR HOLY IMAGE?

The Law of God given to Moses on Mount Sinai, the Ten Commandments, included a prohibition against images:

> You shall not make for yourself a carved image—any likeness *of anything* that *is* in heaven above, or that *is* in the earth beneath, or that *is* in the water under the earth; you shall not bow down to them nor serve them. For I, the LORD your God, *am* a jealous God. (Ex. 20:4–5)

But does the commandment actually refer to *all* images? If so, how do we make sense of the Lord's explicit instructions to make images of cherubim and other creatures—lions, oxen, palm trees, flowers—and adorn His own hallowed place of worship with them?

God ordered Moses to "make two cherubim of gold" and place them at either end of the mercy seat (Ex. 25:18) upon the ark of the covenant, the most holy object in the religious life of Israel. Ironically, this image-laden ark would contain the very commandment that is purported to have banned images!

It was precisely above the mercy seat, between the two carved images of cherubim, that, according to God's design, Moses would meet and speak with the Lord in the most intimate way (Ex. 25:22). In fact, according to the record of the Old Testament Scripture, the Lord of Hosts literally "dwells" between the images of these cherubim (1 Sam. 4:4; 2 Sam. 6:2). If the Lord had indiscriminately prohibited all images, He would be in contradiction to His own word.

It was not only on the ark and other furniture of the tabernacle but also in the sanctuary of the Jerusalem temple that God instructed images to be made. And these icons were not inconspicuous. For instance, there were two wooden cherubim, each ten cubits (15 feet) tall with a wingspan of the same length (1 Kin. 6:23–24). The walls of the temple, as well, both in the inner and outer sanctuaries, were covered with carved images.

Taking all of this into account, the only reasonable conclusion is that the purpose of the second commandment was a proscription against the idolatry that was so prevalent among the peoples that surrounded God's newly formed community of worshippers. For in the ancient Near East, the spiritual battle was not between the true God and *no* God (atheism), but between the true God and any number of false "gods." These idols, the result of either human imagination or demonic delusion, were represented in physical forms and then worshipped as deities.

The true God, however, had not been seen by anyone. As the Gospel testifies, "No one has seen God at any time. The only begotten Son, who is in the bosom of the Father, He has declared *Him*" (John 1:18). Even Moses was not allowed to see His face but only His "back" (Ex. 33:23). However, holy angels had appeared and been seen by human beings and thus could be represented as heralds of the heavenly realm. And the good things of creation, commanded by God to be represented artistically, are also reflections of God's creative power and divine glory.

"THE WORD BECAME FLESH"

It is clear then that a legitimate and divinely approved form of iconography existed in the Old Covenant, although it was by nature greatly limited. For God had not revealed Himself fully and visibly. This He did in the Incarnation of His Son and Word. Indeed, the entire New Covenant hinges on the reality that "the Word became flesh and dwelt among us, and we beheld His glory, the glory as of the only begotten of the Father, full of grace and truth" (John 1:14).

While God the Father is unseen, He is made visible through the Incarnation of His Son, who has joined our flesh, our humanity, to the divine nature. Christ has therefore truly become "the image [Greek, *icon*] of the invisible God" (Col. 1:15), and "in Him dwells all the fullness of the Godhead bodily" (Col. 2:9).

If the Word has not truly become flesh, then He has not overcome our sins in His own flesh, His death has not overcome the bondage of our death, and His Resurrection and Ascension have not glorified and raised up our humanity to the right hand of the Father. For this reason "every spirit that does not confess that Jesus Christ has come in the flesh is not of God" (1 John 4:3).

It is precisely the Incarnation that is the basis for the New Testament iconographic tradition that originated and flowered naturally within the bosom of the Church. The iconography of the Christian Church brings into vivid focus the shadowy picture preached by the prophets of the Old Testament. It has come into focus because the face of the eternal Son of God was revealed to the world. Thus Orthodox Christians confess that since Christ has truly come in the flesh, since the Person of the Son and Word of God has become Man with the same humanity as His creatures, He can be depicted visibly.

This is in no way idolatry, for He is the true and perfect revelation of the Father, true God of true God in human form, "the brightness of *His* glory and express image of His person" (Heb. 1:3). As the Lord proclaimed to His apostles, "He who has seen Me has seen the Father" (John 14:9). The holy icons of the Church testify to the reality of the Incarnation. As St. John of Damascus relates in his defense of the holy icons:

In former times God, who is without form or body, could never be depicted. But now when God is seen in the flesh conversing with men, I make an image of the God whom I see. I do not worship matter; I worship the Creator of matter who became matter for my sake.[2]

This divine Person depicted in the icon of Jesus Christ is the One whom the Apostle John witnesses "was from the beginning, which we have *heard*, which we have *seen* with our eyes, which we have looked upon, and our hands have *handled*, concerning the Word of life" (1 John 1:1, italics added). Unlike the Christ of the Gnostics and some other heretics, the Jesus of Orthodox Christianity is truly human, yet without any diminishment of His Godhead.

The iconoclasts (those who opposed the use of icons) from the eighth and ninth centuries mocked the Orthodox for depicting Christ since, they said, no one can depict the divine nature. Yet the icon does not seek to isolate and depict divine nature, but to depict the Person of Jesus Christ, who since the Incarnation is both God and Man. Every icon of Christ is an icon of the mystery of the Incarnation, "Immanuel [God with us]" (Is. 7:14).

But what of the icons of the saints? These are also icons of the Incarnation inasmuch as those pictured have incarnated Christ into their bodies, souls, and lives. It is Christ who lives in them; they have been sanctified by grace through the same Spirit that dwells in Christ by nature. Every saint, and to a lesser degree, every Orthodox Christian, is an extension and continuation of the Incarnation if for no other reason than that he carries within him the Flesh and Blood of the Lord in Holy Communion.

---

2   *On the Divine Images: Three Apologies Against Those Who Attack the Divine Images,* trans. David Anderson (New York: SVS Press, 1980), p. 23.

The Church herself has been described as the continuation of the Incarnation of the Lord, as more and more humanity is joined and added to the Body of Christ. This reality is what gives St. Paul the audacity to say, "I now rejoice in my sufferings for you, and fill up in my flesh what is lacking in the afflictions of Christ, for the sake of His body, which is the church" (Col. 1:24).

In the saints, the image of God (i.e., Christ) has been restored in its pristine beauty and clarity. In this sense, every true icon is an icon of Christ.

The Incarnation also provides the foundation for iconography in another way. Christ sanctified not only human nature in His Incarnation, but all creation. By uniting Himself physically with His own creation, He restored, redeemed, and sanctified it. The effects of Christ's Incarnation are cosmic, restoring the original purpose of His material world—to be a means of communion with God. Through His Incarnation the creation participates in the salvation and ultimate transfiguration of the whole cosmos.

In the context of the Church, where the mystery of the unity of heaven and earth in Christ is inaugurated, the material creation assists in communicating the life of God to her members. This is nothing less than a return to Paradise before the Fall, where all creation was a means of Adam's communion with the Lord. And now in the Church, water becomes the means of union with Christ in baptism, and oil the seal of the gift of the Holy Spirit. The apex of this sacramental grace of the Body of Christ is found in Holy Communion, where bread and wine become the very Body and Blood of Christ.

This redemptive potential of the material creation through Christ's Incarnation also applies to iconography, by which the gospel is expressed through wood and paint, natural elements of this earth. Through the prayer and creative work of the iconographer, in continuity with the Tradition of the Church, the physical creation again becomes a means of glorifying God and attaining communion with Him.

> The holy Apostles saw the Lord with their physical eyes. . . . But I too yearn to see them with my soul and body and to have them as a medicine against every ill. . . . Because I am a human being and have a body, I long to see and communicate with holy things in a physical manner too.[3]

For the Orthodox, the spiritual life is not limited to the soul as opposed to or in isolation from the physical world. Through the Incarnation, all of creation can participate and aid in the salvation of mankind in the Church. The Orthodox position is expressed eloquently by the great defender of the icons, St. John of Damascus:

> I do not worship matter; I worship the Creator of matter, who became matter for me, taking up His abode in matter, and accomplishing my salvation through matter. . . . I salute matter and I approach it with reverence. . . . I honor it, not as God, but because it is full of divine grace and strength.[4]

Yet true iconography is not a mere representation of this fallen and corrupt world, as it has been infiltrated and distorted by the prince of this world. It is not a picture of the "fleshly" or "old man," but of the man in Christ. It does not depict the physical world in its corrupt state. The canonical, traditional rule and methodology of icon painting ensures that what is depicted is

---

3   *Divine Liturgy*, p. 41.
4   *On the Divine Images*, pp. 61–62.

the redeemed and transfigured creation, where "Christ *is* all and in all" (Col. 3:11).

Through the agency of physical sight, Orthodox iconography opens "the eyes of [our] understanding" (Eph. 1:18) to see the spiritual reality of God's revealed truth. "While our physical eyes are looking at the icon, our intellect and the spiritual eyes of our heart are focused on the mystery of the economy of the Incarnation."[5]

And through the physical, the icon moves us beyond the physical to the spiritual, for "we are led by perceptible icons to the contemplation of the divine and spiritual."[6]

The holy iconography of the Orthodox Church is therefore scriptural. It expresses the theology and spirituality of the Church as witnessed in the Scriptures and the entire Tradition of the Church. Therefore, Christ is not depicted as *mere* man, but as the God-Man, divine and human, just as the Scriptures depict Him. "What Holy Scripture is to the literate, the icon is to the illiterate, and what the word is to our hearing, the icon is to our sight."[7]

St. John's sentiment is an echo of the teaching of another saint, Gregory the Great, Pope of Rome from AD 590–604.

> For what writing presents to readers, this a picture presents to the unlearned who behold, since in it even the ignorant see what they ought to follow; in it the illiterate read.[8]

Just as the Church sifted through and compiled the canonical books of New Testament Scripture over time with the guidance

---

5   *Divine Liturgy,* p. 41.
6   *In Defense of the Holy Icons,* 94:1261a.
7   St. John of Damascus, quoted in *Divine Liturgy,* p. 40.
8   Epistle to Bishop Serenus of Marseilles, in NPNF 2, Vol. 8, 53.

of the Holy Spirit, she also recognized, refined, and canonized an iconographic method and form that witness to the truth and repercussions of the Incarnation of the Son of God.

WORD AND IMAGE

"A picture paints a thousand words." This saying reveals a profound truth about the nature of and relationship between word and image. A word is a verbal image, and an image communicates something that may also be expressed in words.

Both words and images are modes of communication and expression. Both may be holy or profane, true or false, edifying or confusing. According to the Christian revelation, Jesus Christ is the Word of God, and He is also the Image of God. The written words that make up the Bible together form a verbal image of Christ, whereas the Church's painted images of Christ are scripture in picture.

If all of this is true, what prevents the gospel from being preached and taught and even encountered through images? Why should the message of salvation and grace be restricted to words, or to a particular language for that matter? Why can a word be holy but not an image?

The Orthodox response is, of course, that images are indeed capable of conveying the truth and holiness of God's revelation. Both the word of Scripture and the depiction of the icon can serve as means of encountering the message of the gospel.

Neither the sound nor the string of letters in a human word has a purely objective meaning. The English word "table" means nothing to a man who speaks only Chinese. Show the same man a picture of a table or place him in front of one, and he immediately understands the reality you are trying to convey. A word is a symbol, an image. It represents a reality.

Neither word nor image is an end in itself; both are means of conveying a reality. It is the reality—and ultimately an experience of the reality—that we are after. The word itself is not the reality; it is meant to lead us to experience the reality. That said, through their association with the reality they represent, both word and image in some sense are mingled with the reality. This is particularly true with the Scripture and iconography.

Yet only the eternal Word of God, Jesus Christ, expresses the reality of God perfectly. He is God's Word. God needs only one Word to fully and perfectly describe Himself. But this perfect Word cannot be exhausted or fully described with human words or images. Both canonical Scripture and canonical iconography have been given to the Church by the Holy Spirit to lead us to the one Word of God. As the disciple whom Jesus loved wrote:

> And there are also many other things that Jesus did, which if they were written one by one, I suppose that even the world itself could not contain the books that would be written. Amen. (John 21:25)

Thus the Seventh Ecumenical Council declared that the Lord Jesus Christ should be preached not only in words but through the image of the holy Cross, in holy icons, in churches, on liturgical vessels, embroidered into holy vestments, and so forth.

VENERATION AND WORSHIP

Since the Seventh Ecumenical Council officially sanctions not only the making of icons but their veneration, we should address the issue of the distinction between veneration (or honor) and worship. By those who lack an understanding of this historical and scriptural distinction, the veneration shown to the holy icons in the Orthodox Church is often misconstrued as the worship given to God.

The Church has always made a distinction between veneration (showing reverent honor or respect) and worship. It should be stated immediately and unambiguously that absolute worship is due only to God (Father, Son, and Holy Spirit) and in the Orthodox Church is never given to anyone or anything else. This is made clear by one of the heroes of the faith, St. Athanasius of Alexandria, the defender of Christ's divinity against the Arians:

> We the faithful do not worship images as gods, as did the heathen Greeks—God forbid!—but our only purpose and desire is to see in the image a reflection of the facial form of the beloved. . . . Just as when Jacob was about to die, he bowed down before the point of Joseph's staff, not honoring the staff but its owner, so also the faithful do not embrace images for their own sake, but kiss them as we often embrace our children or our parents, to show the affection in our hearts.[9]

Veneration of holy people and things has always existed among God's people. Even today,

> The Jews understand the difference between veneration and worship (adoration). A pious Jew kisses the Mezuza on his door post, he kisses his prayer shawl before putting it on, he kisses the tallenin, before he binds them to his forehead, and arm. He kisses the Torah before he reads it in the Synagogue. No doubt, Christ did likewise, when reading the Scriptures in the Synagogue.[10]

---

9   *Hundred Chapters to Antiochus the Prefect,* 38.
10   From Fr. John Whiteford, http://orthodoxinfo.com/general/icon_faq.aspx.

However, while the distinction between veneration and worship has always existed in the hearts and minds of people, distinct words did not exist, whether in Hebrew, Greek, or Latin. So in the Old and New Testament Scriptures the same word is used for the worship given to God and for the reverence shown to human beings, angels, or holy objects. The word often translated into English as *worship* simply means "to bow down before" or "to fall to the ground." It was used to describe both the worship of God and the veneration or honor shown to people and things.

For example, the word used for the Apostle Peter's worship of Jesus (Luke 5:8) is the same one used when the myrrh-bearing women bow their faces down to the ground before two angels at the empty Tomb of Christ (Luke 24:4–5). Abram fell on his face in worship before God (Gen. 17:3), and Abraham bowed down twice before the people of Heth (Gen. 23:7, 12). Moses bowed low to the earth when God passed by him (Ex. 34:8), and Joshua, his successor, fell down before the ark of the covenant, repenting to God (Josh. 7:6).

Various English translations (KJV, NKJV, NRSV, GNT, TLB, etc.) use the word "worship" for the act of Joshua before the Lord's Commander, the Archangel Michael (Josh. 5:14). The same is true in the Wycliffe Bible, except that this early English translation also includes a parenthetical translation that reads, "(And Joshua fell down onto the ground, and honoured *him*, and said, What saith my lord to his servant?)" Thus in one English translation the words "worshipped" and "honored" are used for the same act!

It should be clear from the few examples above that both worship and veneration or reverence are represented by the same action and the same word. How is one to tell the difference between the two? There is only one way: by the context and the intention of the one who bows down.

Therefore, when St. Paul commands Christians to "greet one another with a holy kiss" (Rom. 16:16; 1 Cor. 16:20), is he asking them to worship one another? When the wedding service in the old Anglican Book of Prayer asked the bride and groom to address one another with the words, "With my body I thee worship," was it inviting them to idolatry? Of course not! On both counts we have an expression of holy veneration quite distinct from the worship that should be extended only to God.

Yet when icons are venerated, or the Virgin Mary is venerated, blessed, shown honor, or praised in word or song by Orthodox Christians, many Protestants perceive these as acts of worship belonging to God alone. This is because the distinction between worship and veneration generally does not exist outside the Orthodox and Roman Catholic experience. Whatever forms of reverence for the holy once existed in Protestantism (for example, a reverent handling of the Bible and perhaps even kissing it)[11] are almost unknown today.

However, the idea of veneration is not completely lost In American culture. It is still common for people to place their hand on their heart in the presence of the nation's flag. It is still considered insulting to trample upon the same flag. And when someone returns to his country after being held captive in a for-

---

11 A video on YouTube (https://www.youtube.com/watch?v=XvV8TlGGqOQ) shows Chinese Christians (Protestant) receiving Bibles. In their great joy they immediately begin kissing the covers or respectfully placing them to their foreheads. This is a very natural expression of holy reverence and veneration.

eign land, he often bows down and kisses the ground to express his love for his country.

Two separate words for worship and veneration only began to be distinguished clearly after the iconoclastic controversy. In his defense of the icons, St. John of Damascus used the term *latreia* for the absolute worship given to God alone and the word *proskinesis* to refer to the reverence or veneration (also called "relative worship") shown to holy people and things. For the most part these same two words continue to be used to distinguish the worship of God from the veneration of icons.

THE HOLY SCRIPTURES ON HOLY IMAGES

Holy images used in places of worship

Ex. 25:18: "And you shall make two cherubim of gold; of hammered work you shall make them at the two ends of the mercy seat."

Ex. 25:22: "And there I will meet with you, and I will speak with you from above the mercy seat, from between the two cherubim which *are* on the ark of the Testimony, about everything which I will give you in commandment to the children of Israel."

Ex. 26:1: "Moreover you shall make the tabernacle *with* ten curtains *of* fine woven linen and blue, purple, and scarlet *thread*; with artistic designs of cherubim you shall weave them."

Ex. 26:31: "You shall make a veil woven of blue, purple, and scarlet *thread*, and fine woven linen. It shall be woven with an artistic design of cherubim."

1 Sam. 4:4: So the people sent to Shiloh, that they might bring from there the ark of the covenant of the LORD of hosts, who dwells *between* the cherubim.

2 Sam. 6:2: And David arose and went with all the people who *were* with him from Baale Judah to bring up from there the ark of God, whose name is called by the Name, the LORD of Hosts, who dwells *between* the cherubim.

1 Kin. 6:23–24: Inside the inner sanctuary he made two cherubim *of* olive wood, *each* ten cubits high. One wing of the cherub *was* five cubits, and the other wing of the cherub five cubits: ten cubits from the tip of one wing to the tip of the other.

1 Kin. 6:29: Then he carved all the walls of the temple all around, both the inner and outer *sanctuaries*, with carved figures of cherubim, palm trees, and open flowers.

1 Kin. 6:32: The two doors *were* of olive wood; and he carved on them figures of cherubim, palm trees, and open flowers, and overlaid *them* with gold; and he spread gold on the cherubim and on the palm trees.

1 Kin. 7:29, 36: On the panels that *were* between the frames *were* lions, oxen, and cherubim. And on the frames *was* a pedestal on top. Below the lions and oxen *were* wreaths of plaited work.... On the plates of its flanges and on its panels he engraved cherubim, lions, and palm trees, wherever there was a clear space on each, with wreaths all around.

Col. 1:15: He is the image [Greek, *icon*] of the invisible God.

Rom. 16:16; 1 Cor. 16:20; 2 Cor. 13:12: Greet one another with a holy kiss.

Veneration and reverence toward holy objects

Ex. 3:5: Then He said, "Do not draw near this place. Take your sandals off your feet, for the place where you stand *is* holy ground."

Josh. 7:6: Then Joshua tore his clothes, and fell to the earth on his face [or "worshipped"] before the ark of the LORD until evening, he and the elders of Israel; and they put dust on their heads.

1 Sam. 5:4: And when they arose early the next morning, there was [the idol] Dagon, fallen on its face to the ground before the ark of the LORD.

Consequences for lack of reverence toward holy objects

1 Sam. 6:19: Then He struck the men of Beth Shemesh, because they had looked into the ark of the LORD.

2 Sam. 6:6-7: And when they came to Nachon's threshing floor, Uzzah put out his hand to the ark of God and took hold of it, for the oxen stumbled. Then the anger of the LORD was aroused against Uzzah, and God struck him there for his error; and he died there by the ark of God.

THE CHURCH FATHERS
ON HOLY IMAGES

"The Martyrdom of Polycarp" (AD 69–155; author unknown)

Thus we, at last, took up his bones, more precious than precious stones, and finer than gold, and put them where it was meet. There the Lord will permit us to come together according to our power in gladness and joy, and celebrate the birthday of his martyrdom, both in memory of those who have already contested, and for the practice and training of those whose fate it shall be. (Kirsopp Lake translation; 18:2–3)

Eusebius of Ceasarea (c. AD 260/265–339/340)

Even now the inhabitants of those regions near where Abraham worshipped those who appeared to him honor it as a holy place. Indeed, the oak tree is still to be seen there, and there is a picture of those whom Abraham entertained reclining at table. (*Exposition on the Gospels*, Fifth Book)

St. Athanasius the Great of Alexandria (c. AD 296–373)

We the faithful do not worship images as gods, as did the heathen Greeks—God forbid!—but our only purpose and desire is to see in the image a reflection of the facial form of the beloved. Therefore if the image should be obliterated, we would throw it into the fire as so much scrap lumber. Just as when Jacob was about to die, he bowed down before the point of Joseph's staff, not honoring the staff but its owner, so also the faithful do not embrace images for their own sake, but kiss them as we often embrace our children or our parents, to show the affection in our hearts. (*Hundred Chapters to Antiochus the Prefect*, 38)

St. Basil the Great (c. AD 329/330–379)

Now arise, you renowned painters of the champions' [martyrs'] brave deeds, who by your exalted art make images of the General [Christ]. My praise for the crowned champion is dull compared with the wisdom which inspires your brush with its radiant colors. . . . As I look at the detail in your painting of his struggle, I see his hand among the flames; your image has made his victory even more brilliant for me. (*Sermon on the Blessed Martyr*, Barlaam)

The image of the emperor is also called the emperor, yet there are not two emperors . . . for the honor given to the image is transferred to the prototype. Therefore, the One [Christ] whom the image materially represents is He who is Son by nature. (*Thirty Chapters to Amphilochius on the Holy Spirit*, 18)

Both painters of words and painters of pictures illustrate valor in battle; the former by the art of rhetoric; the latter by clever use of the brush, and both encourage everyone to be brave. A spoken account edifies the ear, while a silent picture induces imitation. (*Sermon on the Martyr Gordius*)

St. Gregory of Nyssa (c. AD 335–c. 395)

Then the father [Abraham] proceeds to bind his son [Isaac]. I have often seen paintings of this touching scene, and could not refrain from shedding tears, so vivid was the scene reproduced by the artist. (*Sermon on the Divinity of the Son and the Spirit, and on Abraham*)

St. Ambrose of Milan (c. AD 340–397)

But I was caught up into ecstasy during which a face was revealed to me, which resembled the blessed apostle Paul, the same face which was painted on the icon which showed him teaching so wisely. (*Epistle to the Italians*)

St. John Chrysostom (c. AD 349–407)

And I love this image molded in wax, of him [David] who was full of righteousness. For I see the angel in the icon fighting the barbarian horde. . . . Not only do you long to call fervently upon his [Christ's] holy name; but also to look upon the image of his bodily form. What you do with his name you also accomplish with his image. For everyone rejoices to put his image everywhere, on rings, goblets, dishes, and on bedroom walls. (*Sermon concerning the single authorship of the Old and New Testament and on the garments of the priests*)

CHAPTER 10

The Intercessions of the Saints

Now when He had taken the scroll, the four living creatures and the twenty-four elders fell down before the Lamb, each having a harp, and golden bowls full of incense, which are the prayers of the saints. (Rev. 5:8)

Cornelius has died and been raised with Christ in baptism. He partakes of His resurrected Body and Blood in the Eucharist. As a member of the Body of Christ, he is united to the resurrected Lord and is a "partaker of the divine nature" (2 Pet. 1:4).

All of this has been made possible by the Resurrection of Jesus Christ, by His victory over death and the devil. This was the preaching of the Apostle Peter, the good news that the Son of God became man "that through death He might destroy him who had the power of death, that is, the devil" (Heb. 2:14).

Cornelius understands this to mean that, for those who are in Christ, death also no longer reigns, "no longer has dominion" (Rom. 6:9). "Isn't it true," he thinks to himself aloud, "that after the Lord's Resurrection the saints who had died were raised, coming out of their graves and appearing to the disciples in Jerusalem?" (See Matt. 27:52–53.) He pauses thoughtfully for a moment. "Surely, death cannot hold those who are united to

Jesus. Surely death itself cannot separate us from the love of Christ!" (See Rom. 8:35, 38.)

Cornelius also knows that God has united "all things in Christ, both which are in heaven and which are on earth" (Eph. 1:10). This communion of heaven and earth in Christ is particularly evident in the assembly of the Church, where not only Christ is present, but both angels and "the spirits of just men made perfect" (Heb. 12:23).

He understands that those who are "dead in Christ" (1 Thess. 4:16) and those "members of Christ" (1 Cor. 6:15) on earth cannot be separated by death, for both are living in Him. Did not Jesus say that the Father "is not the God of the dead, but of the living" (Matt. 22:32)? And did not Jesus speak to Moses on the mountain (Matt. 17:3) during his earthly ministry?

Reflecting on these things, Cornelius understands with more clarity why the Church calls upon the prayers of those saints who have departed this life, yet are "with Christ" (Phil. 1:23).

Introduction

With the Resurrection of Jesus Christ, a new and glorious reality dawned upon the whole creation, especially for those united to the resurrected Christ by faith in baptism. For the good news of the gospel, as summed up in the Orthodox Christian paschal hymn, is that "Christ is risen from the dead, trampling down death by [His own] death, *and upon those in the tombs bestowing life!*" As the first Adam sowed corruption and death into the fabric of the human race, the Resurrection of Jesus, the "New Adam," initiates a renewed, grace-filled humanity that is impervious to the tyranny and power of death.

This new "race" of man, of which Christ is the "father" (Is. 9:6) and the "firstborn" (Rev. 1:5), is birthed in the baptismal font and nourished by the incorruptible food and drink of Christ's own deathless Flesh and Blood received in the Eucharist. Baptism is described by the Apostle Paul as our participation in Christ's death, that "we also should walk in the newness of life" (Rom. 6:4), that is, the resurrected life. And the Lord Himself identifies the participation in His Body and Blood as the means by which we are raised unto "eternal life" (John 6:54). So central to the gospel is the preaching of Jesus' Resurrection and its implications for mankind that the Athenians imagined St. Paul preached *two* deities, Jesus and the Resurrection (Greek: *anastasios*; Acts 17:18).

The Christian faith is not primarily a set of doctrines or moral teachings, but a new way of life inspired and made possible by the reality of the Resurrection. In the Person of the resurrected Christ, humanity has been given the potential to participate in the divine life, to be shot through with the uncreated grace and energies of God Himself. This potential begins to be realized in each human person when he or she is joined by "water and the Spirit" (John 3:5) to the Church, which is itself the resurrected "body of Christ" (1 Cor. 12:27).

The Body of Christ, those who are united to Him, are no longer futilely bound by the limitations of corrupt nature, nor by the spiritual separation that has its source in sin and death. For Christ overcomes the division between heaven and earth, uncreated and created, invisible and visible, male and female, and finally, life and death.

All of this is to emphasize that the Resurrection of Jesus is not merely an abstract doctrine to believe in, not merely an isolated past event to assent to intellectually, but an organic reality to enter into and assimilate into one's being in Christ's Body, the Church. The Resurrection is the very life and atmosphere of God's Church, made present by the Holy Spirit, and breathed into our souls by means of the divine worship of the Church through the union of heaven and earth in Christ.

The natural implication of this unity of heaven and earth in the Church, as attested to by the Scriptures and the saints, is the union and communion shared by those who are "in Christ." This union transcends death. Death has no more power for those joined to Christ. Because of the Resurrection of Christ, death can no longer separate man from God nor man from his brother in Christ, whether from the living or among the departed.

Therefore, the ancient Christian practice of calling upon the intercessions of the departed saints was and is born from a living faith in the radical consequences of the Resurrection of Jesus. For "God is not the God of the dead, but of the living" (Matt. 22:32). If indeed the departed in Christ are alive in Him, then the earthly Church will naturally keep the memory of, relate to, and call upon as intercessors with Him those members of the heavenly Church who are sharers in the eternal fruits of His Resurrection.

As the first generation of Christians, and most especially the apostles, began to depart to eternal life, the Church naturally remembered them and sought their prayers before the throne of God, especially when they gathered together for the Eucharist. Inasmuch as the Eucharist is the "remembrance" (Luke 22:19; 1 Cor. 11:24; in Greek *anamnesis*, re-calling, re-presenting) of the Lord's death and Resurrection and a participation in the eternal heavenly liturgy, it supplies the most fitting experience of the communion between the living and departed. In the Epistle to the Hebrews, the Apostle Paul clearly acknowledges the presence of "the spirits of just men made perfect" (i.e. departed saints) along with "an innumerable company of angels" in the midst of the eucharistic assembly (Heb. 12:23).

As evidenced by the earliest surviving liturgical texts from throughout the world, the Church consistently and universally entreated the martyrs—often recent martyrs from the local region—for their intercessions on behalf of those Christians still racing toward the finish. In particular, the memory of the martyrs was kept on the date of their martyrdom, when the Church gathered to celebrate their birth into eternal life. We have direct testimony of this practice from the middle of the second century in an eyewitness account of the martyrdom of St. Polycarp, Bishop of Smyrna, an eighty-six-year-old disciple of the Apostle John. After his remains were burned by the centurion, we hear the following from the account:

> Accordingly, we later took up his bones, more precious than costly stones and finer than gold, and deposited them in a suitable place. And there, in so far as it is possible, the Lord will grant that we come together with joy and gladness and celebrate the birthday of his martyrdom both in memory of those who have contended [for the faith in martyrdom] in former times and for the exercise and training of those who will do so in the future.[1]

In the Revelation of St. John, we are given a glimpse of the active concern shown in heaven by the martyrs for their persecuted brethren below, for they cry to the Lord for His swift intervention,

---

1   *Apostolic Fathers,* p. 148.

saying, "How long, O Lord?" (Rev. 6:10). It is not an accident that, in this same passage, the souls of these interceding martyrs are found "under the altar." Here we see testimony of the Church's ancient practice of placing the bone of a martyr inside the altar on which the Eucharist will be offered. It also reveals the continuity of heavenly and earthly worship in the Church.

The practice of requesting the intercessions of departed Christians is also attested to by the inscriptions on tombs in the catacombs, both those of martyrs and those of other departed Christians, including children and even baptized infants. The fact that the intercessions of the departed existed in the eucharistic prayers of local churches in every region of the Roman Empire suggests that the source of this practice is the oral instruction passed down by the apostles themselves.

St. Augustine provides a theological explanation of the Church's liturgical practice.

> Neither are the souls of the pious dead separated from the Church which even now is the kingdom of Christ. Otherwise there would be no remembrance of them at the altar of God in the communication of the Body of Christ.[2]

In another place he specifically mentions the practice of asking for the intercessions of the martyrs:

> At the Lord's table we do not commemorate martyrs in the same way that we do others who rest in peace so as to pray for them, but rather that they may pray for us that we may follow in their footsteps.[3]

---

2   *The City of God* 20:9:2 [AD 419].
3   *Homilies on John* 84 [AD 416].

THE PROTESTANT POSITION

The Protestant Reformers, who disagreed among themselves on other issues, universally rejected the invocation of the saints, at least as it was practiced in the Church of Rome.[4] Martin Luther called it "one of the abuses of the Antichrist" and simply "idolatry."[5]

Much of this rejection came about in reaction against the abuses associated with indulgences, which, in Luther's words, "are granted to the living and the dead (for money) and by which the pope sells the merits of Christ together with the superabundant merits of all the saints and the entire Church."[6] The current Catholic Catechism defines an indulgence as:

> a remission before God of the temporal punishment due to sins whose guilt has already been forgiven, which the faithful Christian who is duly disposed gains under certain prescribed conditions through the action of the Church which, as the minister of redemption, dispenses and applies with authority the treasury of the satisfactions of Christ and the saints.[7]

The doctrine of indulgences was in fact the major catalyst for the Protestant Reformation and had become intertwined with Rome's teaching and practice with regard to the departed saints. This is because the treasury of satisfactions (or "merits")

---

4   Ironically, earlier in his life as a Roman Catholic, Luther attributed his being saved from death during a storm to his prayers to St. Anna, the mother of the Virgin Mary. It was as a result of this event and an oath he made to her in his prayer of desperation that he became a Roman Catholic monk. (V. Rev. Josiah Trenham, *Rock and Sand: An Orthodox Appraisal of the Protestant Reformers and Their Teachings*, Columbia, MO: Newrome Press, 2015, p. 11.)

5   Denis R. Janz, ed., *A Reformation Reader: Primary Texts with Introductions* (Minneapolis, MN: Fortress Press, 1999), p. 125.

6   *Ibid.*

7   *Catechism of the Catholic Church*, p. 370.

included both the infinite merits resulting from the work of Christ *and* the merits acquired by the saints through their prayers and good works. Since, it was taught, the saints had accumulated "merit" over and above what was necessary for their own salvation, these extra merits could be transferred to Christians in the form of indulgences for the benefit of their souls and for a reduction of time in purgatory after death.

The Roman Church makes a distinction between the guilt of sin and the temporal punishment that, it maintains, always accompanies sin. The guilt of sin committed after baptism is forgiven in Christ through the Sacrament of Confession, but the temporal effects of sin remain and require purification. This purification can be accomplished by various good (meritorious) works, often prescribed as penances, or by indulgences that may lessen or completely alleviate the punishment. In Roman Catholic theology, penances are prescribed to make satisfaction for the temporal punishment for sin and thus to reduce or eliminate the need for time spent in purgatory (purifying fire) after death.

For the Reformers, Christ had satisfied the debt of sin, and there were no works man could do to contribute to his salvation. For those who believe in Christ, there was no longer any debt to be paid or punishment to be had. As the Reformers sought to condemn and root out the innovative doctrine of indulgences, they also eliminated belief in the role of the saints in the salvation of the faithful. They rejected the Roman teaching of the treasury of merits and considered the merits of the saints unnecessary and irrelevant to salvation. Viewing the issue through the same Roman perspective, and concerned to avoid any appearance of salvation being achieved through works, they could see no value in Christians invoking the prayers of what Luther called "angels and dead saints."

Luther's rejection of the intercessions of the saints was part and parcel with his rejection of the Roman Mass in general,[8] along with the masses in honor of the saints, various fasts and feast days for them, and other liturgical practices. His main concern was that Christians might "trust in" the saints for their salvation. He did believe that the angels in heaven pray for Christians, and even allowed the possibility that the saints in heaven pray for those on earth, but he adamantly rejected the idea of Christians "praying to" the saints in heaven.

Certainly, the fact that the Reformers embraced sola scriptura also influenced their rejection of the intercessions of saints. As Luther interpreted, "There is not a single word from God demanding us to call upon either saints or angels to intercede for us, and that there is no example of such in the Scriptures."[9] With the Scriptures as the sole source for discerning authentic Christian doctrine and life, the Church Tradition would not stand. The many abuses of the time—indulgences, false relics, and an assortment of excessive and superstitious attitudes and practices related to the saints—simply reinforced the view of the veneration of saints as an obstacle to pure Christian life.

Today, in some mainline Protestant denominations, there remains a certain distant appreciation for the example of the early Christian saints and martyrs as sources of inspiration.

---

8   Luther abhorred Rome's teaching that every Mass was a "re-sacrifice" of Christ. (See Admonition Concerning the Sacrament, Luther's Works, vol. 38, *Word and Sacrament*, pp. 117–118).

9   *An Open Letter on Translating*, Martin Luther (AD 1530), http://www.bible-researcher.com/luther01.html

However, the notion that the saints may be active in the lives of believers as intercessors and agents or conduits of God's grace and power is missing. For all practical purposes, the lives of the saints have no role or value in the ecclesial or personal lives of Protestant Christians. The one exception would be the stories of the righteous in the Old Testament, and to a lesser degree, those in the New Testament.

CLARIFICATIONS

Orthodox Christians do not *pray to* the saints as Protestants understand this phrase. Rather, we ask the saints in heaven to pray for us to our Lord and Savior Jesus Christ. In Old English the word *pray* can mean to "ask imploringly," to "request," or in general to communicate. For example, "Pray tell me, where you are going?" Praying to saints does not imply worship or the kind of prayer that is offered to God. Prayer in this sense means asking those departed in Christ to pray for us before God.

For most evangelicals, even the term "saints," as it is usually used in Orthodoxy, is objectionable. This is because Protestants seek to emphasize that all Christians are called to be holy (the word *saint* means "holy"), and the term is generally used for all Christians in the New Testament. Again as a reaction against certain practices among Roman Catholics, evangelicals reject what they see as creating a separate class of believers by calling them saints.

In the Orthodox Church, we affirm the truth that all those who believe and are united to Christ in holy baptism are indeed holy. But we simultaneously embrace what became the practice in the early centuries of the Church, to refer to those who excelled in holiness among the saints as "saints" in a more particular sense. Note that in the Divine Liturgy the priest invites the faithful to Holy Communion with the words, "Holy things are for the holy" (i.e., the saints, referring to all Christians who have not disqualified themselves from Holy Communion through sin).

THE HOLY SCRIPTURES ON THE INTERCESSIONS OF THE SAINTS

It is true that there is very little explicit evidence for prayer to the departed in the Holy Scriptures. However, the whole context of the Scriptures shows us that through His redemptive work, His Cross and Resurrection, Christ has broken down the barrier between heaven and earth, and therefore between those who are in Christ, whether in heaven or on earth. Most Protestant Christians have not considered deeply these implications of Christ's Resurrection.

The following biblical quotes reveal how reality itself has changed due to the Lord's destruction of death and His Resurrection. By the death of Christ, the limitations and barriers between heaven and earth, departed and living, church in heaven and church on earth, have been abolished.

Separation between heaven and earth abolished

Matt. 27:51 (Mark 15:38; Luke 23:45): Then, behold, the veil of the temple was torn in two from top to bottom. [Note: The veil or curtain of the temple separated the holy place from the Holy of

Holies, where only the High Priest was allowed to enter once per year. The curtain of the temple not only symbolizes the barrier between God and man, but also between heaven and earth. "From top to bottom" indicates that the heavenly and earthly realms are no longer separated.]

Righteous dead are raised and appear to those on earth

Matt. 27:52–53: And the graves were opened; and many bodies of the saints who had fallen asleep were raised; and coming out of the graves after His resurrection, they went into the holy city and appeared to many.

Heaven and earth united in Christ

Eph. 1:10: that in the dispensation of the fullness of the times He might gather together in one all things in Christ, both which are in heaven and which are on earth—in Him.

The dead in Christ are alive

Matt. 22:32: "God is not the God of the dead, but of the living."

Rom. 14:8–9: For if we live, we live to the Lord; and if we die, we die to the Lord. Therefore, whether we live or die, we are the Lord's. For to this end Christ died and rose and lived again, that He might be Lord of both the dead and the living.

Jesus, the Incarnate Christ, talks with Moses and Elijah

Matt. 17:1–3: Now after six days Jesus took Peter, James, and John his brother, led them up on a high mountain by themselves; and He was transfigured before them. His face shone like the sun, and His clothes became as white as the light. And behold, Moses and Elijah appeared to them, talking with Him.

Angels and saints in heaven intercede for the saints on earth

Rev. 5:8: Now when He had taken the scroll, the four living creatures [angels] and the twenty-four elders fell down before the Lamb, each having a harp, and golden bowls full of incense, which are the prayers of the saints [on earth].

Angel offers prayers of the saints on earth

Rev. 8:3-4: Then another angel, having a golden censer, came and stood at the altar. He was given much incense, that he should offer *it* with the prayers of all the saints upon the golden altar which was before the throne. And the smoke of the incense, with the prayers of the saints, ascended before God from the angel's hand.

Angels and departed saints present at Christian worship

Heb. 12:22-23: But you have come to Mount Zion and to the city of the living God, the heavenly Jerusalem, to an innumerable company of angels, to the general assembly and church of the firstborn *who are* registered in heaven, to God the Judge of all, to the spirits of just men made perfect.

THE CHURCH FATHERS ON THE INTERCESSIONS OF SAINTS & ANGELS

Clement of Alexandria (c. AD 150–c. 215)

In this way is he [the true Christian] always pure for prayer. He also prays in the society of angels, as being already of angelic rank, and he is never out of their holy keeping; and though he pray alone, he has the choir of the saints standing with him [in prayer]. (*Miscellanies* 7:12 [AD 208])

Origen (AD 184/185–253/254)

But not the high priest [Christ] alone prays for those who pray sincerely, but also the angels . . . as also the souls of the saints who have already fallen asleep. (*Prayer* 11 [AD 233])

St. Cyprian of Carthage (c. AD 200–258)

Let us remember one another in concord and unanimity. Let us on both sides [of death] always pray for one another. Let us relieve burdens and afflictions by mutual love, that if one of us, by the swiftness of divine condescension, shall go hence first, our love may continue in the presence of the Lord, and our prayers for our brethren and sisters not cease in the presence of the Father's mercy. (*Letters* 56[60]:5 [AD 253])

St. Methodius of Olympus (died c. AD 311)

Therefore, we pray [ask] you, the most excellent among women, who glories in the confidence of your maternal honors, that you would unceasingly keep us in remembrance. O holy Mother of God, remember us. (*Oration on Simeon and Anna* 14 [AD 305])

And you also, O honored and venerable Simeon, you earliest host of our holy faith, and teacher of the resurrection of the faithful, do be our patron and advocate with that Savior God, whom you were deemed worthy to receive into your arms. (*Ibid.*)

St. Cyril of Jerusalem (c. AD 313–386)

Then [during the Eucharistic prayer] we make mention also of those who have already fallen asleep: first, the patriarchs, prophets, apostles, and martyrs, that through their prayers and supplications God would receive our petition. (*Catechetical Lectures* 23:9 [AD 350])

Hilary of Poitiers (c. AD 310–c. 367)

To those who wish to stand [in God's grace], neither the guardianship of saints nor the defenses of angels are wanting. (*Commentary on the Psalms* 124:5:6 [AD 365])

St. Ephrem the Syrian (c. AD 306–373)

You victorious martyrs who endured torments gladly for the sake of the God and Savior, you who have boldness of speech toward the Lord himself, you saints, intercede for us who are timid and sinful men, full of sloth, that the grace of Christ may come upon us, and enlighten the hearts of all of us so that we may love him. (*Commentary on Mark* [AD 370])

Remember me, you heirs of God, you brethren of Christ; supplicate the Savior earnestly for me, that I may be freed through Christ from him that fights against me day by day. (*The Fear at the End of Life* [AD 370])

Early Prayer to the Virgin Mary (prior to AD 250)

Under your compassion we take refuge, Theotokos; do not overlook our prayers in the midst of tribulation, but deliver us from danger, O only pure, only blessed one.[10]

Anonymous Catacomb Inscriptions (AD 300–350)

Atticus, sleep in peace, secure in your safety, and pray anxiously for our sins. (*Funerary inscription near St. Sabina's in Rome [AD 300]*)

Pray for your parents, Matronata Matrona. She lived one year, fifty-two days. (*Ibid.*)

---

10   A description of the discovery and dating of an ancient fragment with this prayer is found in Frederica Mathewes-Green, *The Lost Gospel of Mary* (Brewster, MA: Paraclete Press, 2007), pp. 83–88.

St. Basil the Great, Bishop of Caesarea (c. AD 329/330–379)

By the command of your only-begotten Son we communicate with the memory of your saints . . . by whose prayers and supplications have mercy upon us all, and deliver us for the sake of your holy name. (*Liturgy of St. Basil* [AD 373])

St. Jerome (c. AD 347–420)

But if the apostles and martyrs while still in the body can pray for others, at a time when they ought still be solicitous about themselves, how much more will they do so after their crowns, victories, and triumphs? (*Against Vigilantius* 6 [AD 406])

Blessed Augustine of Hippo (AD 354–430)

At the Lord's table we do not commemorate martyrs in the same way that we do others who rest in peace so as to pray for them, but rather that they may pray for us that we may follow in their footsteps. (*Homilies on John* 84 [AD 416])

OBJECTIONS AND RESPONSES

Since the topic of the intercession of the saints is usually met with many objections and misunderstandings, along with Bible passages that seemingly contradict or forbid it, we have provided a series of common objections (O) with responses (R) in order to provide more insight into this normative Christian practice.

O: But in the parable of Lazarus and the Rich Man (Luke 16:19–31) it is said that there is a "great chasm" between heaven and earth.

R: The "great chasm" spoken of (v. 26) is between heaven ("the bosom of Abraham") and the torment of Hades, not between heaven and earth. When the rich man requests that the Lord send Lazarus to his seven brothers on earth, the Lord refuses, not because this is not possible, but because his brothers would not believe even if it occurred.

O: But why waste time praying to the saints when we can pray to the Lord?

R: We could say the same thing in regard to asking for the prayers of Christians still living on this earth—something we do all the time, and something we all know we need. We also ask those Christians who have departed, who are with Christ and in an even greater spiritual condition, to pray for us. We are not lone rangers in the spiritual life; we need the prayers and help of others. Unlike those still living in this world, the saints do not get tired or distracted or forget to pray for us. They have a boldness before Christ that most on earth do not. As the Scriptures say, "The effective, fervent prayer of a righteous man avails much" (James 5:16).

There is no competition between the Lord and His saints, since the saints, like the angels, are the ministers of His will and glory. It is Christ who is glorified in and through the saints. As He Himself says, "I am glorified in them" (John 17:10). Christ loves His saints, the lives they led, and even their death, for "Precious in the sight of the LORD / is the death of His saints" (Ps. 116/115:15). They are saints because they share in His glory and the glory of His Father by the grace of the Holy Spirit. His saints have become vessels of His divine grace, which He freely shares with those who have faith in Him. As such they testify to Him and His holiness, and all they do is for His glory and directed by His will. As Christ is the icon (image) of God by nature, so the saints are also by grace.

By God's grace, the Orthodox Church does not have a history of excessive or abusive practices with regard to the saints' intercessory prayers, nor has the Church ever discouraged the faithful from praying directly to God, whether the Father, the Son, or the Holy Spirit, as is attested to by the services and prayers of the Church.

O: In the Old Testament God forbids conjuring up the spirits of the dead (Deut. 18:11).

R: First we have to understand that the practices warned about and forbidden in the Old Testament were pagan in origin and purpose, and they relied not upon faith in the true God but in demonic sorcery, witchcraft, and the like. They were practiced for sinful and evil purposes. God's primary intention in these warnings was to protect the spiritually immature people of the Old Covenant from adopting the pagan religion of their neighbors.

Next, we must remember that Christ's death and Resurrection have changed everything—the nature of death has been transformed and essentially made powerless. Through Christ the righteous dead have been raised with Him and are alive in Him. Through the Holy Spirit, members of Christ's Church ask these living and resurrected saints to pray to the Lord on their behalf.

O: We should not ask for the intercessions of the saints since, as the Scriptures say, "For *there is* one God and one mediator between God and men, *the* man Christ Jesus" (1 Tim. 2:5).

R: It is true that Christ alone is the Mediator between God and man, since He alone is both God and Man. Christ alone can save man from sin and death. He alone broke down the barrier that separated man from God and restored our union with God the Father. The saints are not mediators in this sense, nor do we imagine that they accomplish the redemption that Christ does. Rather, through their prayers they beseech the Savior to save us. They pray to the Lord that He extend to us the salvation that only He could and did accomplish. They are able to intercede with Christ for our needs and well-being. They are not separated from Christ the Mediator but are "members of Christ" (1 Cor. 6:15), yet no longer hampered by the limitations of this world. They are God's faithful servants and "members of the household of God" (Eph. 2:19). The servants work for their Master. Servants run errands for and carry messages to the Master, yet they are not the Master. Finally, if we believe the saints in heaven cannot be mediators in the sense of praying to Christ for us, then we must cease asking the prayers of those living on this earth, since, using the same logic, this would transgress the Scriptures regarding Christ as the only Mediator.

O: How do you know the saints can hear you?

R: How do you know they cannot? The Lord said, "The hour is coming, and now is, when the dead will hear the voice of the Son of God" (John 5:25). While this refers to Christ's descent into Hades after His Crucifixion, the Church has never taught that the dead are cut off from the goings-on of this world. According to the Revelation of St. John, the souls of the martyrs were well aware of the turmoil and persecutions on earth (Rev. 6:9). The saints can hear us because they are united to Christ and share in His attributes by grace. They share in His divine glory and virtue, through which they are the agents of miracles, both during their earthly lives and after. They hear inasmuch as Christ hears and according to His will and their freedom in Christ.

CHAPTER 11

Veneration of the Virgin Mary

For behold, henceforth all generations will call me blessed.
(Luke 1:48)

Through the teaching of the apostle, Cornelius and his family learned that Jesus, the Son of Mary the Virgin, was the Christ, the Son of God. The apostle had referenced the prophecy of Isaiah, "Therefore the Lord Himself will give you a sign: Behold, the virgin shall conceive and bear a Son, and shall call His name Immanuel [God is with us]" (Is. 7:14).

Cornelius and his family were overwhelmed by a sense of awe about this Virgin Mother, still living in Jerusalem at that time. "This woman cannot be like any other in the history of Israel," thought Cornelius to himself. "What must she be like?—The one who was chosen by God out of all generations to nourish God's own Son! She must be an angel in the flesh."

Of course he could not immediately comprehend all the implications of her unique place as the mother of the Lord. "What a special place of honor she must hold in God's Church!"

His heart swelled with desire to meet her, to see her sweet face and bow before her in honor as he would before the greatest of all queens. His wife marveled that the mystery of salvation was effected through a woman and that it was her flesh, and hers alone, that gave flesh to the Savior of the world. The first woman, Eve, had brought pain and travail to the whole human race, but this woman, through her love and obedience, brought salvation and grace.

The apostle had preached to them of Jesus Christ—His perfect fulfillment of the Law and the Prophets, His victory over sin and death, the promise of forgiveness through faith and repentance and of eternal life through His Resurrection. For this is the *kerygma,* the word of salvation that is preached to the unbaptized, those yet outside the family of believers.

But upon entering into the life of the Church, they are becoming acquainted with the "apostles' doctrine" (Acts 2:42) or dogma ("decrees" in Acts 16:4), whereby they are being initiated more deeply into the whole mystery of faith, "to comprehend with all the saints what *is* the width and length and depth and height—to know the love of Christ which passes knowledge; that you may be filled with all the fullness of God" (Eph. 3:18–19).

In contrast to the public preaching of the gospel, as they were now learning, the Church's dogma is carefully guarded and not shared with those outside, lest the holy things be misconstrued, mocked, or degraded through familiarity. The Lord had likened this to throwing pearls to swine (Matt. 7:6). For this reason many of the Church's practices, teachings, sacramental rites, and prayers are purposely left undocumented and passed down only by word of mouth.[1] The dogma reflects the inner life and teaching of the Church, the more intimate and experiential knowledge accessible to those within the Christian fold and family.

Having now come into the Church's family life, the newly illu-

---

1   St. Basil the Great (AD 330-379): "We have unwritten tradition so that the knowledge of dogma might not become neglected and scorned through familiarity" (*On the Holy Spirit,* p. 66).

mined Cornelius is coming to an even greater appreciation for the unpretentious matriarch of the Church, Mary. As he meets Christians from Jerusalem, he is beginning to hear the unwritten stories of her exemplary devotion to the will of God from childhood, the grace she experienced with the announcement of her conception and the overshadowing of the Holy Spirit, her tender and sacrificial love for her Child and the mysteries she pondered in her heart, the suffering at the foot of the Cross prophesied by the elder, Simeon (Luke 2:34–35), the exultation of the Resurrection, and her relationship with the Apostle John and with all the apostles as they fulfilled their ministry of reconciliation.

But mostly, he hears and sees the great reverence the whole Church has for her and the specific ways and words by which they honor and bless her. And if he were blessed to meet her, surely he would beg for her prayers to her Son and God, believing in both her intimacy with the Lord and her Son's special love for her who nurtured Him.

Why Mary?

Having addressed in the previous chapter the context for the Church's practice of entreating the departed saints, we can now more aptly discuss the place of the one who has been venerated by all generations as the saint of saints: the Holy Virgin Mary.

Who was this woman, and why is all this fuss made over her? The Scriptures and the Tradition of the Church make it clear, if we have eyes to see. She was the "highly favored ["graced"] one" (Luke 1:28), chosen out of all generations to become the "mother of [her] Lord" (Luke 1:43), the one who said *yes* to God on behalf of all mankind, the first to receive Jesus the Christ personally and intimately into the fabric of her being and become a temple of the Holy Spirit, the one without whom there would be no "Body of Christ" (1 Cor. 12:27). She was given the distinct honor among all mankind to be called "blessed" by "all generations" (Luke 1:48).

Only a young teen at the time of the angel's visitation, she had a spiritual maturity, faithfulness, and humility that exceeded that of other righteous men and women of much greater age and social status. While the apostles cowered in fear both before and after the Crucifixion of the Lord, Mary risked being put to death for being found with child outside marriage, calmly and courageously responding to God's calling: "Let it be to me according to your word" (Luke 1:38).

THE NEW EVE

The impact of the Virgin's life and ministry cannot be overemphasized, for by her acceptance of God's will she literally reversed the consequences of the decision of the first woman, Eve. St. Irenaeus, Bishop of Lyons, wrote just this in about the year AD 180:

> For in no other way can that which is tied be untied unless the very windings of the knot are gone through in reverse: so that the first joints are loosed through the second, and the second in turn free the first. . . . Thus, then, the knot of the disobedience of Eve was untied through the obedience of Mary.[2]

This sentiment from the greatest theologian of the second century was not a mere isolated thought. For an earlier saint, apologist, and martyr of the Christian faith, Justin the Philosopher (born AD 100), had previously taken up the same theme. Con-

---

2 *Against Heresies*, 3:22.

trasting Eve's disobedience with Mary's obedience to God, he writes:

> For Eve . . . conceiving the word from the serpent, brought forth disobedience and death. But Mary . . . when the angel announced to her that the Spirit of the Lord would come upon her . . . answered: Be it done to me according to your word.[3]

St. Irenaeus also sees the Mother of the Lord as the pivotal point in God's work of redemption, emphasizing her role as "a cause of salvation" for the world.

> Just as she [Eve] . . . being disobedient, became a cause of death for herself and the whole human race: so Mary . . . being obedient, became a cause of salvation for herself and the whole human race.

As the Apostle Paul envisioned Jesus Christ as the New Adam (1 Cor. 15:22, 45), the early Church recognized Mary's role in the drama of salvation as that of the "New Eve." For as through a woman sin and death came into the world, through the New Eve, the Virgin Mary, life is restored to Adam. Tertullian (c. AD 155–240) explains:

> God, by a rival method, restored His image and likeness. . . . For into Eve when she was yet a virgin had crept the word that established death, likewise, into a Virgin was to be brought the Word of God that produced life: so that what had gone to ruin by the one sex might be restored to salvation by the same sex.[4]

---

3   *Dialogue with Trypho,* 100.
4   Tertullian, *On the Flesh of Christ,* 17.

THE ARK OF THE COVENANT

In the dispensation of the Old Covenant, God had prepared, with particularly great care, a dwelling place for His divine words[5] written in tablets of stone. The ark that held the Ten Commandments was constructed according to God's own specific instructions, using the most precious of materials (Ex. 25:10–22). First, it was made with acacia,[6] an extremely dense and strong wood resistant to decay. God then commanded Moses that it be lined with pure gold both inside and out. On top of the cover or mercy seat of the ark, God instructed that two large images of cherubim be made of pure gold and placed on either side with wings outstretched. It was there, at the mercy seat, where the wings of the cherubim met, that God promised to meet and speak with Moses.

If God took such an active role in the construction of a box that would hold His written word, with how much greater care did He choose and prepare the earthly vessel that would contain His Incarnate Word? If he specified with precision and loving care every measurement and detail of the resting place of those tablets of stone, would He not also prepare a fit and holy dwelling place for the measureless "Son of His love" (Col. 1:13)? If He constructed the lifeless ark of testimony out of precious and pure materials, surely He would adorn the living ark of the New Covenant, the Virgin Mary, with virtues and purity of soul and body. And if He treasured the tablets themselves upon which His Law was written, how much more did He cherish the holy

---

5   The term for "Ten Commandments" in Hebrew more literally means "Ten Words."

6   Ex. 25:10. The Greek version of the Old Testament used by the apostles, the Septuagint, translates acacia wood as "incorruptible wood" (OSB).

vessel who carried the Law-Giver Himself, and who became the living Book of the Word of God?

The Old Testament ark was the point of union between God and His people and their most treasured object of faith. Carried in procession by the priests, the ark took the first and most prominent place among the people as the instrument of God's presence and leading (Num. 10:33; Josh. 3:13–17) as well as of His power and protection (Num. 10:35). The very sight and presence of the ark was a cause for rejoicing (1 Sam. 6:13) and blessing (2 Sam. 6:12). And when the ark of the Lord was brought into the newly built Temple of Solomon, the glory of the Lord filled the temple to such a degree that the priests could not even remain there (1 Kin. 8:10–11).

Similarly in the Christian Church, the Virgin, the ark of our salvation, is rightly given the most honored place and is a great a cause of rejoicing, for through her we have seen the Face[7] of God, Jesus Christ. As one of the Church's hymns explains it:

> God took flesh of thy pure blood; wherefore, all generations do hymn thee, O Lady, and throngs of heavenly minds glorify thee, for through thee they have clearly seen Him Who ruleth all things endued with human nature.[8]

As the tangible vessel for the Incarnation, the Virgin Mary has become the new Mercy Seat, "more honorable than the

---

7   When Christ says, "Take heed that you do not despise one of these little ones, for I say to you that in heaven their angels always see the face of My Father who is in heaven" (Matt. 18:10), is He not speaking of Himself, the pre-eternal Son and Word of God? The Scriptures tell us, "No one has seen God [i.e., the Father] at any time. The only begotten Son, who is in the bosom of the Father, He has declared Him" (John 1:18). It is the Son who is the "Face" of God.

8   Prayer Book, Fourth Edition—Revised (Jordanville, NY: Holy Trinity Monastery, 1986).

cherubim," by whom God is encountered in the Person of Jesus Christ.

The Church's Tradition, its living and apostolic memory, portrays the Virgin Mary as precisely this beautiful and holy ark of God's presence and virtue. St. Athanasius the Great (c. AD 296–373), the champion of Christ's divinity at the Council of Nicaea, attests to her way of life even before the Annunciation:

> Mary was a pure virgin, serene in her state of soul, doubly enriched. In fact she liked good works while fulfilling her duties, and upholding right thoughts on faith and purity. She did not like to be seen by men but prayed to God to be her Judge. She was in no haste to leave her home, had no acquaintance with public places, preferred to remain constantly indoors living a withdrawn life, like the honey bee. She gave generously to the poor whatever in her household was left over. . . . Her words were discreet and her voice measured; she did not shout and was watchful in her heart to speak no wrong of another, not to even willingly listen to wrongs spoken of.[9]

In his *Letter to the Virgins* he sums up concisely, "You have the conduct of Mary, who is the example and image of the heavenly life."[10]

St. Ambrose of Milan (c. AD 340–397) offers a similar and somewhat more detailed description:

> She was a virgin not only in body, but also in mind, who never stained the genuine disposition of her virginity with guile. She was always humble in heart, grave in speech, prudent in mind, sparing of words, studious in reading, resting her hope not on

---

9   Quoted in *The Life of the Virgin Mary, the Theotokos* (Buena Vista, CO: Holy Apostles Convent, 1997), p. 79.
10 *Ibid.*

uncertain riches, but on requests of the poor, intent on work, and modest in discourse. She sought God as the judge of her thoughts and not men (1 Cor. 4:4). She never sought to injure anyone but to have goodwill towards all. She never thought to rise up before her elders nor to envy her equals. She avoided boasting, loved virtue and to follow reason. Never a word passed her lips that was not with grace. She never disagreed with her neighbors nor despised the lowly. She never avoided those in need and never despised anyone though they were poor. She never laughed at anyone but covered all that she saw with her love.[11]

Venerating the Virgin

According to the Church Fathers, the ark was a type or prefiguring of that which was to come. This type was realized in the person of Mary, who contained the uncontainable God in her womb.

The Church has also recognized many other prophetic types that point to the mystery fulfilled in Mary in the Old Testament Scriptures. Some of these are listed here:

» The bush that burned but was not consumed (Ex. 3:2)
» Jacob's ladder (Gen. 28:10–17)
» The house that Wisdom built (Prov. 9:1–11)
» The rod of Aaron that budded (Num. 17:8)
» The jar of manna (Ex. 16:33)
» The tongs that held the burning coal (Is. 6:6)
» The dewy fleece (Judg. 6:38)
» The tabernacle (Ex. 40:1–5, 9–10, 14–35).
» The temple and the holy of holies (1 Kin. 7:51—8:11)

---

11 *Op. cit.*, p. 78.

Considering all this, it is not difficult to understand why the Church has always honored and reverenced the Virgin as the holy of holies among mere men and women, while worshipping her Son as God and Lord.

Even the Reformers extended great reverence to the Lord's mother. In a Christmas sermon, Martin Luther confesses Mary as the "highest woman and the noblest gem in Christianity after Christ. . . . She is nobility, wisdom, and holiness personified." He adds, "We can never honor her enough."[12] John Calvin also grants her the supreme place among Christians: "It cannot be denied that God in choosing and destining Mary to be the Mother of his Son, granted her the highest honor."[13] Even the more radical Reformer, Ulrich Zwingli, acknowledges that "God esteemed Mary above all creatures, including the saints and angels—it was her purity, innocence and invincible faith that mankind must follow."[14]

This esteem for the Virgin is not an academic interest for theologians but a real devotion to be shared and held dear among all who love the Incarnate Lord. A Christian's reverence for Mary is in proportion to his devotion to Christ. The Orthodox agree with Zwingli on this point: "The more the honor and love of Christ increases among men, so much the esteem and honor given to Mary should grow."[15] For Luther, she is the mother of everyone who belongs to Christ:

> Mary is the Mother of Jesus and the Mother of all of us even though it was Christ alone who reposed on her knees. If he is

---

12 Sermon, Christmas, 1531.

13 John Calvin, *Calvini Opera* [Berlin: Braunschweig-Berlin, 1863–1900], 45:348.

14 G. R. Potter, *Zwingli* (Cambridge: Cambridge University Press, 1976), p. 89.

15 Ulrich Zwingli, *Zwingli Opera, Corpus Reformatorum*, vol. 1, pp. 427–428.

ours, we ought to be in his situation; there where he is, we ought also to be and all that he has ought to be ours, and his mother is also our mother.[16]

All of this is a matter of the heart, for "The veneration of Mary is inscribed in the very depths of the human heart.[17]

THE PROTESTANT PROBLEM WITH MARY

Despite the clear views of the original Reformers, the Church's devotion of honor and love for the Holy Virgin Mary is one of the greatest stumbling blocks for today's Protestants to overcome. As on many points of Orthodox doctrine and practice, the Protestant view has devolved radically since the time of the Reformation. For evangelicals in particular, the traditional veneration offered to the Theotokos through praise and prayers evokes not merely theological objections, but often highly charged negative emotional reactions.

The traditional devotion and liturgical prayers of the Church are literally frightening to many evangelical Christians. When speaking to them, Orthodox Christians must bear this in mind, as we are not only dealing with doctrinal disagreements but also with fear. The source of that reaction is the concern that any veneration and prayer offered to the Mother of God amounts to worship and ultimately places the Virgin on par with the Lord Jesus Christ Himself.[18] This of course would be tantamount to denying the unique role of Christ as God and Savior.

---

16   Sermon, Christmas, 1529.
17   Sermon, September 1, 1522.
18   The recent Roman Catholic movement to pronounce the Virgin as "co-redeemer" with Christ is not only unorthodox but part and parcel of the Protestant reticence to extend the proper honor to her.

Some of the alarm stems from real or imagined corruptions of piety found in the Roman Church, either at the time of the Reformation[19] or as currently practiced. For this reason contemporary Protestantism has been purged of any genuine reverence toward the Virgin Mary. However, these concerns have also been enflamed by the doctrine of the immaculate conception.

THE IMMACULATE CONCEPTION OF MARY?

The doctrine of the immaculate conception of the Virgin Mary, promoted and finally officially adopted by Rome in 1854, has helped to fuel the fears we mention. Today, many people (even Roman Catholics) erroneously believe it refers to the conception of Christ by the Virgin Mary through the Holy Spirit. In actuality, the immaculate conception refers to the conception of Mary herself by her parents Joachim and Anna; the doctrine asserts that Mary was miraculously born without original sin. The official pronouncement by Pope Pius IX reads as follows:

> The most Blessed Virgin Mary was, from the first moment of her conception, by a singular grace and privilege of almighty God and by virtue of the merits of Jesus Christ, Savior of the human race, preserved immune from all stain of original sin.[20]

---

19 Martin Luther believed the Roman Catholic practices of his time had gotten out of hand: "Furthermore, how will you endure [the Romanists'] terrible idolatries? It was not enough that they venerated the saints and praised God in them, but they actually made them into gods. They put that noble child, the mother Mary, right into the place of Christ. They fashioned Christ into a judge and thus devised a tyrant for anguished consciences, so that all comfort and confidence was transferred from Christ to Mary, and then everyone turned from Christ to his particular saint. Can anyone deny this? Is it not true?" (Luther's Works, vol. 47, *Christian in Society IV*, p. 45).
20 *Apostolic Constitution: Ineffabilis Deus* (1854): DS 2803. See *Catechism of the Catholic Church*, p. 124.

The Orthodox Church has always rejected the doctrine of the immaculate conception as both unnecessary and untrue. It is unnecessary because the Orthodox East never embraced St. Augustine's distinctive opinion that original sin consists of the *guilt* of Adam, passed down to all who are born of him. In the medieval Latin Church, this became the normative teaching and understanding. Around the twelfth and thirteenth centuries, Augustine's interpretation led to a popular belief that eventually became enshrined in Roman Catholic dogma as the immaculate conception. Using the innovative idea of original guilt as the theological premise, the logic flows as follows:

» The guilt of sin justly deserves a sentence of condemnation and separation from God.

» Therefore, unless the stain of original guilt is removed, the justice of God requires that all who came before Christ must be in a condition of gracelessness and damnation.

» However, the Mother of God also came before Christ.

» This is problematic because, as St. Augustine also taught, the Church had always deemed that she was exceptionally holy and blameless before God.

» Therefore, logic requires that the Virgin must have been conceived *without* original sin (i.e., guilt) so that she could be the pure vessel for the Incarnate Son of God.

According to the Western view, the stain of guilt intrinsically came with God's vengeful wrath and the judgment of hell.[21] So how could the humanity of the most holy Mother of God be tainted with such an indelible sentence of condemnation for

---

21   It was precisely for this reason that the Roman Church taught for centuries that infants who died without baptism were condemned to hell, or at least to Limbo.

sin? And how could she provide a worthy human nature to the sinless Christ and Lord if her own humanity bore the guilt of Adam? In the face of this dilemma, it became increasingly popular to suggest that the Virgin was conceived without the original sin otherwise universally shared by all mere mortals.

Despite what seems to be a logical necessity, St. Augustine himself never taught that the Theotokos was somehow exempt from original sin. In fact, he teaches the opposite, declaring, "There is no one born of Adam who is not subject to condemnation."[22] The most likely explanation for this is that such a thing had never been part of the Church's teaching. It was a speculation that even the great Bishop of Hippo dared not make, as he indeed had great reverence for Church Tradition. He also may have realized—as Orthodox Christians do—that if the Virgin was outside the stream of our fallen humanity, she could not have offered it to her Son, who would then also have a human nature different from that of those He desired to save.

A miraculous conception of Mary was certainly not conceived by the numerous Fathers of the East.[23] It would not have been, since in Orthodox thought, original sin does not transmit the guilt for Adam's sin but only the consequences and the condition. It is essential to understand that according to the Orthodox Church, these consequences do *not* include the personal guilt of Adam, or even guilt by association.[24] Original sin is a human condition caused by the entrance of a foreign

---

22 George S. Gabriel, *Mary: The Untrodden Portal of God* (Glen Rock, NJ: Zephyr Publishing, 2000), p. 66.

23 Many Fathers wrote about Mary's sinlessness (i.e., her lack of personal sins), but not of an exemption from original sin.

24 St. Augustine wrote that all yet to be born personally sinned in/with Adam, as we all were in his loins at the time of the Fall.

element (sin); it is not a pronouncement of guilt. The Church Fathers consistently describe this state of fallenness in terms of spiritual illness that requires curing and restoration to health (Matt. 9:12), not a condition of guilt requiring a just retribution of wrath. The fallen condition is an existential problem, not a juridical one.

While the sin of Adam and Eve created a change in the human condition[25] and a disordering of the human energies (resulting in both blameless and blameworthy desires),[26] along with an unnatural compulsion toward sin, human nature itself is not the problem; the problem is the disease of sin. Fallen man does not inherit guilt at his conception, nor does he inherit a human nature that is inherently sinful. Instead he receives a nature that is death-bound due to the sin of his ancestor and ill with the sickness of corruption and death.

We acquire guilt only by our own personal sins and choices when we follow the prompting of our disordered desires. We remain free to choose good or evil, although after the Fall this requires some level of ascetical effort and even "force" (see Matt 11:12). In spite of her fallen condition, the Mother of God chose God's will, and yet she, like all mere mortals, was in need of a Savior, as she could not overcome death. As the Apostle Paul writes, "Nevertheless death reigned from Adam to Moses, even over those who had not sinned according to the likeness of the

---

25   The Church Fathers universally teach that, due to sin, even the physical body of Adam changed. Before the Fall it was in a state of incorruption, lighter and less sensual, did not need clothing or shelter, was clothed with the light of God, and did not experience pangs of hunger or any compulsive physical desires.

26   Blameless desires or passions include fatigue and hunger; the blameworthy include sloth, gluttony, etc.

transgression of Adam, who is a type of Him who was to come" (Rom. 5:14).

The doctrine of the immaculate conception is not only unnecessary but also untrue, inasmuch as neither the Scriptures nor the Fathers of the Church make an exemption for anyone from the consequences of Adam's sin and fallen human nature.

At a time when the doctrine was gaining ground, the discussion alarmed such notable Western saints and theologians as Bernard of Clairvaux and Thomas Aquinas, who rejected the idea outright as innovative and discordant with Church Tradition.

Bernard considered it "unapproved by reason, unjustified by ancient tradition" and called it "a novelty invented in spite of the teaching of the Church, a novelty which is the mother of imprudence, the sister of unbelief, and the daughter of lightmindedness."[27] He reasoned that, if Mary were conceived without original sin, her parents and ancestors would need to have been so as well. This is echoed by St. John Maximovitch in his treatise on the Theotokos.

> The teaching that the Mother of God was purified before Her birth, so that from Her might be born the Pure Christ, is meaningless; because if the Pure Christ could be born only if the Virgin might be born pure, it would be necessary that Her parents also should be pure of original sin, and they again would have to be born of purified parents, and going further in this way, one would have to come to the conclusion that Christ could not have become incarnate unless all His ancestors in the flesh, right up to Adam inclusive, had been purified beforehand of original sin. But then there would not have been any need

---

27   Epistle, 174.

for the very Incarnation of Christ, since Christ came down to earth in order to annihilate sin.[28]

Despite the objections of even the two notable Latin saints mentioned, the first liturgical feast of the Immaculate Conception of Mary was held regionally in the West in the fifteenth century and spread elsewhere from there. Taken in the most positive light, the motivation for the teaching and accompanying feast was viewed by those who adopted it as a way of honoring and praising the Virgin more fully. For surely extending to her the privilege of exemption from original sin and a fallen nature—a status beyond that of any other creature—was the greatest compliment one could give to her and an assurance of her special grace.

However, from Orthodoxy's point of view, far from exalting the Theotokos, the teaching actually denigrates and demeans her true greatness. Is there any praise in being conceived in a condition that would preclude the possibility of sin? Is not the true glory and praise of Mary the fact that she willingly embraced virtue at every juncture of her life for the sake of faithfulness to God? As St. John Maximovitch asserts, "It is not an exaltation and greater glory, but a *belittlement* of her, this 'gift' which was given Her by Pope Pius IX."[29] He elaborates further on this position:

This teaching, which seemingly has the aim of exalting the Mother of God, in reality completely *denies all Her virtues*. After all, if Mary, even in the womb of Her mother, when She could not even desire anything either good or evil, was preserved by

28   St. John Maximovitch, *The Orthodox Veneration of Mary the Birthgiver of God*, trans. Fr. Seraphim Rose (Platina, CA: St. Herman of Alaska Press, 1994), pp. 58–59.
29   *Op. cit.*, p. 60.

331

God's grace from every impurity, and then by that grace was preserved from sin even after Her birth, then in what does Her merit consist? If She could have been placed in the state of being unable to sin, and did not sin, then for what did God glorify Her? If She, without any effort, and without having any kind of impulses to sin, remained pure, then why is She crowned more than everyone else? There is no victory without an adversary.[30]

THE "CHAMPION LEADER"

And so the Orthodox Church believes the immaculate conception does not glorify but demeans the Virgin, as it strips her of free will and her spiritual courage and effort in choosing the way of righteousness. It "denies Her victory over temptations; from a victor who is worthy to be crowned with crowns of glory, this makes Her into a blind instrument of God's Providence."[31] Instead of a passive instrument, the Orthodox sing of her as the "Champion Leader,"[32] like a military general who leads Christians into battle. She was indeed special and set apart, but not without her own cooperation with God.

The righteousness and holiness of the Virgin Mary were precisely manifest in the fact that She, being "a human being just like us," so loved God and gave Herself to Him, that by Her purity She far surpassed the rest of mankind.[33]

---

30   *Op. cit.,* p. 59. In the same work, St. John also argues that this doctrine "makes God unmerciful and unjust; because if God could preserve Mary from sin and purify Her before Her birth, why does He not purify other men before their birth, but rather leaves them in sin? It follows likewise that God saves men apart from their will, predetermining certain ones before their birth to salvation" (p. 59).

31   *Op cit.,* p. 60.

32   Kontakion of the season of Great Lent.

33   *Orthodox Veneration of Mary,* p. 59.

Only the God-Man, Jesus, who was conceived of the Holy Spirit, is sanctified from the moment of conception.[34] As a mere mortal, Mary remains a daughter of Adam, in need of purification after conception, bearing the fallen nature that can only be renewed in Christ, and subject to the death that only Christ can overcome. And if her nature were different from our own, Christ would also receive and save a different humanity, not ours.

Therefore, the Church venerates the Virgin Mary, not as the great exception from the condition of fallen man, but as one among and with all mankind. Yet while tempted to sin and to break fidelity with God, she continually overcame the frailty of the fallen condition, struggling to overcome any sinful inclination in cooperation with the Holy Spirit. This is her glory: that she gave herself completely to God's will through her own ascetical effort to reject the desires of her fallen nature out of love for God. It was in this way that her heart was purified to "hear the word of God and keep it" (Luke 11:28).

She was certainly set apart (i.e., consecrated, holy) both by her exceptional virtue and through her role as the Mother of the Lord, but she is not set apart in the sense of being ontologically different from the rest of humanity. It is true that God, in His divine foreknowledge and providence, prepared her, this most pure and godly young woman, to be the Mother of Life. In fact it was His plan from all eternity to create this most worthy vessel to bear the Savior.

And so she was not, as some say in ignorance, "just any Jewish girl." She was not ordinary in terms of virtue. Nor was she

---

34 Again, the Roman Catholic St. Bernard of Clairvaux writes, "No one is given the right to be conceived in sanctity; only the Lord Christ was conceived of the Holy Spirit, and He alone is holy from His very conception" (Epistle, 174).

a temporary and expendable convenience to be discarded once she had served God's purpose. Rather, she who would give birth to the Lord of Glory was the fruit of God's patient, loving, and arduous cultivation. Once Adam and Eve were expelled from Paradise, His activity began for the express purpose of producing this living paradise, where the Tree of Life, Jesus, would spring up and become the source of the heavenly and eternal Food for all who come to Him. From the time the first Eve fell into sin in the Garden of Eden, God began tilling the soil to grow this most beautiful plant, Mary, who would bud forth the Unfading Flower. It can be said that this was the very purpose of all God's activity recorded in the Old Testament Scriptures.

The Church sees the pinnacle of this progression of ancestral holiness in her righteous and elderly parents, Joachim and Anna, who with God's intervention conceived her, as much as is possible, without sinful, selfish passion. Instead of the immaculate conception, the Orthodox Church simply celebrates the Feast of the Conception of Mary.[35] While her conception was the fruit of her parents' prayer, exceptional purity of heart, and faithfulness to God, Mary was not miraculously exempt from the fallen condition.

Her holiness did not come from the removal of original sin but from God's favor, resulting from her humility and purity of heart, her unrelenting love of God and desire to do His will. She bore fallen nature, was subject to death, and was in need of the Savior, yet she chose to live in purity and righteousness while awaiting His coming.

Because of her extreme humility, she could never have imag-

---

35   This feast has been celebrated since about the sixth to seventh century on December 9 each year.

ined she would be asked to give birth to her Savior.[36] For this reason God chose her, since by her exceptional purity she had become "highly favored." St. Gregory Palamas tells us that when the Holy Spirit overshadowed her and Christ was conceived in her (at the Annunciation), she was further graced by God and was perfected in Him. This was her personal "pentecost" before Pentecost. Like the apostles on the Day of Pentecost, she was wholly filled with God's grace.

This does not mean she was incapable of faults and mistakes, but that she had an uninterrupted prayer and communion with God. As St. Ephrem, the great fourth-century ascetic and hymnographer, puts it, "I do not say that Mary became immortal, but that being illuminated by grace, She was not disturbed by sinful desires. . . . The Light abode in Her, cleansed Her mind, made Her thoughts pure, made chaste Her concerns, sanctified Her virginity."[37]

THE HOLY SCRIPTURES ON THE VENERATION OF THE VIRGIN MARY

Veneration of the Virgin Mary

In the Scriptures, the Theotokos receives veneration from both angels (Luke 1:28) and men (Luke 1:42) and herself prophesies that "all generations shall call me blessed" (Luke 1:48). It is therefore the will of God that she should be honored. The Lord,

---

36 This is why she was "troubled" at the angel's greeting, "'Rejoice, highly favored one, the Lord is with you; blessed are you among women!'" (Luke 1:28). Note that she was not troubled by the presence of the angel; rather "she was troubled at his saying, and considered what manner of greeting this was."

37 *Homily Against Heretics*, 41.

who gave the command to "Honor your father and your mother" (Ex. 20:12), also honors her both by obeying her at the wedding in Galilee (John 2:3–10) and by ensuring her well-being, giving her over to the Apostle John, even as He suffered, hanging on the Cross (John 19:26–27).

Luke 1:26–28: Now in the sixth month the angel Gabriel was sent by God to a city of Galilee named Nazareth, to a virgin betrothed to a man whose name was Joseph, of the house of David. The virgin's name *was* Mary. And having come in, the angel said to her, "Rejoice, highly favored *one*, the Lord *is* with you; blessed *are* you among women!"

Luke 1:39–45 (summarized): In the first chapter of Luke, St. Elizabeth, mother of St. John the Baptist, also venerated her, praising her with the words of the angel, "Blessed are you among women" (1:42). She places herself below the Virgin and considers herself unworthy to receive "the Mother of my Lord" (1:43). These praises are accentuated by the fact that Semitic culture would normally require the younger woman to show honor to the elder. Here the usual order is reversed. According to the Scriptures, these words of Elizabeth are not mere personal sentiment but are inspired by the Holy Spirit (1:41). Elizabeth also praised Mary's faith, saying, "Blessed is she who believed" (1:45).

Luke 1:48: [And Mary said:] "For behold, henceforth all generations will call me blessed."

Mary in the Old Testament

Ex. 25:10–11: "Thus you shall make the ark of testimony from incorruptible wood. . . . You shall overlay it with pure gold; inside and out you shall overlay it" (OSB).

(As the Lord Himself directed that the ark should be made with great care out of incorruptible wood and pure gold, He also prepared a holy Virgin out of all generations and adorned her with purity to become His dwelling place.)

Ex. 25:17–22: "You shall make a mercy seat of pure gold. . . . And there I will meet with you, and I will speak with you from above the mercy seat."

(The "mercy seat," the place where God is made known, has now become the holy Virgin through whom He took flesh, through whom we have seen and know the Lord and His salvation. She is the mercy seat of the world, since it is due to her that Jesus Christ speaks to us.)

Num. 10:33: So they departed from the mountain of the Lord on a journey of three days; and the ark of the covenant of the LORD went before them for the three days' journey, to search out a resting place for them.

(Of old the people of Israel processed with the ark in the first and foremost place. In the Church the personal ark of God, Mary, is also given the first place among the people of God.)

1 Kin. 8:10–11: And it came to pass, when the priests came out of the holy place, that the cloud filled the house of the LORD, so that the priests could not continue ministering because of the cloud; for the glory of the LORD filled the house of the LORD.

(The same glory of God, but even more directly in the Person of the Word of God, filled the Virgin Mary.)

1 Sam. 6:13: Now *the people of* Beth Shemesh *were* reaping their wheat harvest in the valley; and they lifted their eyes and saw the ark, and rejoiced to see *it*.

(The Virgin is and should be a cause of rejoicing to the faithful inasmuch as it was through her that the Lord was made manifest to us.)

2 Samuel 6:12: Now it was told King David, saying, "The LORD has blessed the house of Obed-Edom and all that *belongs* to him, because of the ark of God."

(The Mother of God is a source of blessing to those who receive and honor her.)

THE CHURCH FATHERS ON THE VENERATION OF THE VIRGIN MARY

St. Irenaeus, Bishop of Lyons (c. early second century–AD 202)

As Eve was seduced by the speech of an angel . . . so also Mary received the good tidings by means of the angel's speech . . . being obedient to this word . . . that of the virgin Eve, the virgin Mary might become the advocate and as by a virgin the human race had been bound to death, by a virgin it is saved. (*Against Heresies* 3, 19 [AD 130])

St. Gregory Thaumaturgus (c. AD 213–270)

Mary, you are the vessel and tabernacle containing all Mysteries. You know what the patriarchs did not know; you experienced what was not revealed to the Angels; you heard what the prophets did not hear. In short, everything that was hidden from preceding generations was made known to you; even more, most of these wonders depended on you. (*The Greatest Marian Prayers: Their History, Meaning, and Usage*, Anthony M. Buono, New York: Alba House, 1999, BX2160.2 .B86,1999, p. 110)

St. Ephrem the Syrian (c. AD 306–373)

Blessed Virgin . . . you are holy and inviolate, the hope of the hopeless and sinful, I sing your praises. I praise you as full of every grace, for you bore the God-Man. I venerate you; I invoke you and implore your aid. Holy and Immaculate Virgin, help me in every need that presses upon me and free me from all the temptations of the devil. Be my intercessor and advocate at the hour of death and judgment . . . for you are holy in the sight of God, to whom be honor and glory, majesty and power forever. Amen. (http://www.stmarouncathedral.org.au/#!blessed-virgin-mary/c1ke0)

St. Athanasius the Great, Bishop of Alexandria (c. AD 296–373)

It is becoming for you, O Mary, to be mindful of us, as you stand near Him who bestowed upon you all graces, for you are the Mother of God and our Queen. Come to our aid for the sake of the King, the Lord God and Master Who was born of you. For this reason you are called "full of grace." (*The Greatest Marian Prayers,* p. 111)

Blessed Augustine, Bishop of Hippo (AD 354–430)

Blessed Virgin Mary, who can worthily repay you with praise and thanksgiving for having rescued a fallen world by your generous consent? . . . Accept then such poor thanks as we have to offer, unequal though they be to your merits. Receive our gratitude and obtain by your prayers the pardon of our sins. Take our prayers into the sanctuary of heaven and enable them to bring about our peace with God. . . . Holy Mary, help the miserable, strengthen the discouraged, comfort the sorrowful, pray for your people, plead for the clergy, intercede for all women consecrated to God. May all who venerate you, feel now your help and protection. . . . Make it your continual care to pray for the people of God, for you were blessed by God and were made worthy to bear the Redeemer of the world, who lives and reigns for ever. (*The Greatest Marian Prayers*, p. 112)

THE PROTESTANT REFORMERS ON MARY

The Church's appropriate practice of the veneration and honor of Mary was not lost on the Protestant Reformers. Most Protestants, and certainly evangelical Christians, do not hold the position of their fathers in the faith.

Martin Luther (1483–1546)

The veneration of Mary is inscribed in the very depths of the human heart. (Sermon, September 1, 1522)

[She is the] highest woman and the noblest gem in Christianity after Christ. . . . She is nobility, wisdom, and holiness personified. We can never honor her enough. Still honor and praise must be given to her in such a way as to injure neither Christ nor the Scriptures. (Sermon, Christmas, 1531)

No woman is like you. You are more than Eve or Sarah, blessed above all nobility, wisdom, and sanctity. (Sermon, Feast of the Visitation, 1537)

Is Christ only to be adored? Or is the holy Mother of God rather not to be honoured? This is the woman who crushed the Serpent's head. Hear us. For your Son denies you nothing. (Sermon, Wittenberg, 1546: Weimar edition of Martin Luther's

Works, English translation edited by J. Pelikan [Concordia: St. Louis], Vol. 51, pp. 128–129)

Mary is the Mother of Jesus and the Mother of all of us even though it was Christ alone who reposed on her knees. If he is ours, we ought to be in his situation; there where he is, we ought also to be and all that he has ought to be ours, and his mother is also our mother. (Sermon, Christmas, 1529)

She is full of grace, proclaimed to be entirely without sin— something exceedingly great. For God's grace fills her with everything good and makes her devoid of all evil. (Personal ["Little"] Prayer Book, 1522)

John Calvin (1509–1564)

To this day we cannot enjoy the blessing brought to us in Christ without thinking at the same time of that which God gave as adornment and honour to Mary, in willing her to be the mother of his only-begotten Son. (*A Harmony of Matthew, Mark and Luke*, Edinburgh: St. Andrew's Press, 1972, p. 32)

It cannot be denied that God in choosing and destining Mary to be the Mother of his Son, granted her the highest honor. (*Calvini Opera*, vol. 45, p. 348)

Ulrich Zwingli (1484–1531)

God esteemed Mary above all creatures, including the saints and angels—it was her purity, innocence and invincible faith that mankind must follow. (G. R. Potter, Zwingli, London: Cambridge Univ. Press, 1976, pp. 88–89)

The more the honor and love of Christ increases among men, so much the esteem and honor given to Mary should grow. (*Zwingli Opera, Corpus Reformatorum*, vol. 1, pp. 427–428)

It was given to her what belongs to no creature, that in the flesh she should bring forth the Son of God. (In *Evang. Luc., Opera Completa* (Zurich, 1828–42), vol. 6, 1:639)

I esteem immensely the Mother of God, the ever chaste, immaculate Virgin Mary. (E. Stakemeier, *De Mariologia et Oecumenismo*, ed. K. Balic, Rome: Pontificia Academia Mariana Internationalis, 1962, p. 456)

It was fitting that such a holy Son should have a holy Mother. (*De Mariologia*, 456)

OBJECTIONS AND RESPONSES

O: If it is important, why doesn't the Bible teach about the veneration of the Virgin Mary?

R: The Bible does touch on the veneration of Mary, as shown in the Scriptures listed above. The Virgin Mary is mentioned more and given greater honor than any other woman in the Bible. Early Church Tradition says that, out of humility, Mary did not want much written about her. However, it is also true that the books of the Bible were not written to proclaim Mary or to discuss the veneration she received within the Body of Christ. The Gospels were written primarily to proclaim the kerygma or preaching of Christ's death and Resurrection. The epistles were written largely to deal with theological and pastoral problems confronting the churches.

We might also note that there are many things held by Protestants that are not explicitly recorded in the Scriptures. For example, the New Testament never refers to "a personal relationship with Jesus" or "accepting Jesus into your heart." Neither does Scripture instruct Christians to worship on Sundays nor provide instructions for how to worship. The Scriptures do, however, explicitly state that "all generations shall call [Mary] blessed" (Luke 1:48).

O: If Mary is worthy of veneration, why did the Lord seem to disrespect her on several occasions?

When it was told to Him that His mother and brothers were asking to see him, He turned to His disciples and said, "Here are my mother and my brothers" (Matt. 12:49). This seems to indicate that His mother was of less importance than His disciples.

When His mother prodded Him to do something at the wedding in Cana, He said, "Woman, what does your concern have to do with Me?" (John 2:4).

On another occasion, a woman called out to Him, praising the womb that bore Him and the breasts that nursed Him. He responded, "More than that, blessed *are* those who hear the word of God and keep it!" (Luke 11:28).

All of these passages give the impression that Jesus played down any honor that might be given to His mother.

R: Let's take each passage of Scripture individually.

Matt. 12:47–50: In the case of His mother and brothers asking to see Him, there is no disparagement. Yet He did have to show that His physical kinship and family ties could not take priority over His spiritual mission and the spiritual relationship that was the purpose of His ministry. In this way He taught—both His family and His disciples—that it is more blessed to be in spiritual relationship with Him rather than merely physical. And so He adds, "For whoever does the will of my Father in heaven is My brother and sister and mother" (Matt. 12:50). Ironically but fittingly, Mary, His mother, is precisely the premier example of one who did the will of the Father. Responding to God's invitation to do His will, she said, "Let it be done to me according to your word" (Luke 1:38).

John 2:1–10: At the wedding in Cana of Galilee, the Lord honored and obeyed His mother by hearing her request and acting upon it. She had great influence with Him and interceded with Him for the sake of the wedding party. Most English Bibles mistranslate His response, "Woman, what does your concern have to do with Me?" which more accurately is translated, "Woman, what concern is that to you or to Me?" In the Hebrew culture, the term "woman" is not a disparaging one, nor would the One who commands us to honor father and mother dishonor His own mother. On the contrary, the Lord's reference to his mother as "woman" reflects the dignity and goodness of that which He created in the beginning (see Gen. 2:21–25).

Luke 11:27–28: In the last passage, again the Lord does not disparage the role of His mother but redirects the enthusiasm of the woman in the crowd to the more important virtue of His mother: that she heard the word of God *and kept it*. This passage is also sometimes mistranslated so that it sounds as if the Lord is contradicting and rejecting the woman's praise of His mother. However, in reality Jesus agrees with her assessment but adds something to it. It can be translated, "Yes indeed, but more . . ." Or as the NKJV translates it, "More than that, blessed *are* those who hear the word of God and keep it!"

O: The ark was held in honor because it contained the commandments. Why does the Church continue to reverence Mary long after the Lord came forth from her?

R: If we truly understand the nature of God and the impact of His holiness and grace, we will also have the answer to this question. For we see throughout the Scriptures that whatever God touches or uses for His purpose is forever consecrated, never again to be considered ordinary or commonplace.

We have examples in two other holy objects that also came to be housed in the Old Testament ark—Aaron's staff that budded and the jar of manna. Who would be so spiritually unfeeling as to use this miraculous staff as a walking stick? Or who would use the manna, the remnant of the food from heaven that God sent to the people of Israel, as an afternoon snack? The people of God recognized and honored these items as holy relics still carrying the fragrance of God's handiwork, as a bottle of perfume retains its scent long after it is emptied.

The same reverence is seen for the vessels used in the service of God in the tabernacle (Ex. 40:9; Lev. 8:10). God Himself commanded that they be consecrated with oil and thereafter never used for ordinary purposes. (Even the specially prepared oil itself is called "holy" [Ex. 30:25].) These inanimate objects were set apart and became holy because they participated in the holy worship of the holy God.

God's grace and activity are not ineffectual commodities that are here today and gone tomorrow. They are the substantial, enduring presence of the uncreated and eternal; His divine life and energies transform and penetrate whatever they touch.

If the inanimate utensils of the worship of God were holy and consecrated and transformed by God's presence, the Virgin Mary, in whom the eternal Son of God was animated in the flesh, is the holiest vessel of all. Because of her faithfulness, even after the Lord's birth, she is worthy of the greatest veneration.

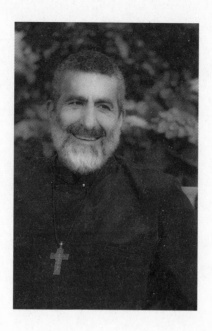

About the Author

The Rev. Fr. Michael Shanbour is a lifelong Orthodox Christian and pastor of Three Hierarchs Orthodox Mission in Wenatchee, Washington. He received his M.Div. at St. Vladimir's Orthodox Theological Seminary in 1989. He has been active in youth, camp, music, and Christian education ministries. Fr. Michael was ordained to the holy priesthood in 2001 and pastored mission parishes in Topeka, Kansas, and Spokane, Washington, before being assigned to Three Hierarchs. He is blessed to live in Wenatchee with his wife, Makrina, and son, Simeon.

Also from
Ancient Faith Publishing

An Introduction to God
Encountering the Divine in Orthodox Christianity
by Fr. Andrew Stephen Damick
Speaking to non-believers and believers alike, Fr. Andrew Damick attempts to create a sacred space in which we can encounter God. In this compact volume, he distills the essence of the traditional Christian faith, addressing the fundamental mysteries of where God is, who God is, why we go to church, and why Christian morality matters. If you've only heard about the Protestant or Roman Catholic version of Christianity, what he has to say may surprise you—and make you long to encounter God in Jesus Christ.

Ask for the Ancient Paths
Discovering What Church Is Meant to Be
by Fr. James Guirguis
At a time when so many disaffected Christians are trying to recreate the Church from scratch, Fr. James offers a clear and accessible apology for simply returning to what Christ's Church was always meant to be.

Becoming Orthodox
A Journey to the Ancient Christian Faith

by Fr. Peter Gillquist

After a long and difficult journey, 2000 weary evangelical Protestants finally found their way home. This is the story of a handful of courageous men and their congregations who risked stable occupations, security, and the approval of lifelong friends to be obedient to God's call. It is also the story of every believer who is searching for the Church. Where Christ is Lord. Where holiness, human responsibility, and the Sovereignty of God are preached. Where fellowship is more than a covered-dish supper in the church basement. And where fads and fashion take a back seat to apostolic worship and doctrine.

Orthodoxy & Heterodoxy
Exploring Belief Systems through the Lens of the Ancient Christian Faith

by Fr. Andrew Stephen Damick

Are you an Orthodox Christian who wonders how to explain to your Baptist grandmother, your Buddhist neighbor, or the Jehovah's Witness at your door how your faith differs from theirs? Or are you a member of another faith who is curious what Orthodoxy is all about? Look no further. In *Orthodoxy & Heterodoxy*, Fr. Andrew Stephen Damick covers the gamut of ancient heresies, modern Christian denominations, fringe groups, and major world religions, highlighting the main points of each faith. This book is an invaluable reference for anyone who wants to understand the faiths of those they come in contact with—as well as their own.

Thirsting for God in a Land of Shallow Wells

by Matthew Gallatin

This outstanding book will help Orthodox readers more deeply appreciate their faith and will give Protestant readers a more thorough understanding of the Church. Beginning in the street ministry days of the Jesus Movement, Matthew Gallatin devoted more than 20 years to evangelical Christian ministry. He was a singer/songwriter, worship leader, youth leader, and Calvary Chapel pastor. Nevertheless, he eventually accepted a painful reality: no matter how hard he tried, he was never able to experience the God whom he longed to know. In encountering Orthodox Christianity, he finally found the fullness of the Faith. In *Thirsting for God,* Gallatin expresses many of the struggles a Protestant will encounter in coming face to face with Orthodoxy: such things as Protestant relativism, rationalism versus the Orthodox sacramental path to God, and the unity of Scripture and Tradition. He also discusses praying with icons, praying formal prayers, and many other Orthodox traditions.

All titles available from store.ancientfaith.com

Ancient Faith Publishing hopes you have enjoyed and benefited from this book. The proceeds from the sales of our books only partially cover the costs of operating our nonprofit ministry—which includes both the work of **Ancient Faith Publishing** and the work of **Ancient Faith Radio**. Your financial support makes it possible to continue this ministry both in print and online. Donations are tax-deductible and can be made at www.ancient-faith.com.

To request a catalog of other publications,

please call us at (800) 967-7377 or (219) 728-2216

or log onto our website: **store.ancientfaith.com**

ANCIENT FAITH RADIO

Bringing you Orthodox Christian music, readings,

prayers, teaching, and podcasts 24 hours a day since 2004 at

www.ancientfaith.com